The Ugandan
Morality Crusade

I0025234

The Ugandan Morality Crusade

*The Brutal Campaign Against
Homosexuality and Pornography
Under Yoweri Museveni*

DEBORAH KINTU

McFarland & Company, Inc., Publishers
Jefferson, North Carolina

Library of Congress Cataloguing-in-Publication Data

Names: Kintu, Deborah, 1962– author.
Title: The Ugandan morality crusade : the brutal campaign against
    homosexuality and pornography under Yoweri Museveni /
    Deborah Kintu.
Description: Jefferson, North Carolina : McFarland & Company, Inc.,
    Publishers, 2018. | Includes bibliographical references and index.
Identifiers: LCCN 2017048600 | ISBN 9781476670683 (softcover :
    acid free paper) ∞
Subjects: LCSH: Homosexuality—Law and legislation—Uganda. |
    Gays—Legal status, laws, etc.—Uganda. | Human rights—Uganda.
    | Pornography—Law and legislation—Uganda. | Uganda—Social
    conditions—1979– | Uganda—Politics and government—1979– |
    Museveni, Yoweri, 1944–
Classification: LCC KTW420.6 .K56 2018 | DDC 345.6761027—dc23
LC record available at https://lccn.loc.gov/2017048600

British Library cataloguing data are available

ISBN (print) 978-1-4766-7068-3
ISBN (ebook) 978-1-4766-2953-7

© 2018 Deborah Kintu. All rights reserved

No part of this book may be reproduced or transmitted in any form
or by any means, electronic or mechanical, including photocopying
or recording, or by any information storage and retrieval system,
without permission in writing from the publisher.

Front cover images © 2018 iStock

Printed in the United States of America

McFarland & Company, Inc., Publishers
  Box 611, Jefferson, North Carolina 28640
  www.mcfarlandpub.com

To the memory of David Kato,
a Ugandan gay rights activist
who was brutally murdered
on January 26, 2011

Table of Contents

Preface

I was born and raised in Uganda where I lived through dictator Idi Amin's eight-and-one-half years' reign of terror. As a third grader in 1972, I witnessed Amin's brutal crackdown on Ugandans of Asian descent. Most were of Indian or Pakistani origin and their families had lived in the country for more than a century. Ugandan Asians, among them several classmates and family friends, were summarily expelled from the country they called home. Even at that tender age, it was glaringly evident to me that the mass expulsion of my fellow Ugandans was unjustified and inhumane. It is that singular incident, more than anything else, that led me to care deeply about the plight of persecuted minorities. Idi Amin claimed that economic considerations informed his decision to expel the minority Asian population. In reality, Idi Amin's actions were an overt display of racism best expressed in his assertion "to see that the whole Kampala street is not full of Indians. It must be proper black and administration in those shops is run by the Ugandans." This reprehensible act of "othering" Ugandan minorities—sadly, celebrated by some Ugandans—was a harbinger of more egregious times that awaited Ugandans.

After the expulsion of the minority Asian population, Amin turned to victimizing other Ugandan groups based on their ethnicity, tribe, education, and religion. Women were a particularly vulnerable group, bearing a disproportionate share of the Amin regime abuses. Morality laws curtailed women's freedoms and banned them from wearing trousers, wigs, and miniskirts. Women violating the morality laws were harshly penalized. Amin presided over a government that tortured and murdered its people with abandon. Idi Amin's excesses are detailed in numerous books, newspapers and magazines. *Newsweek* magazine featured him on the cover of its March 7, 1977, issue with the title "Idi Amin's Reign of Terror." He also made the *Time* magazine cover of March 7, 1977, which referred to him as the "Wild Man of Africa." Amin was overthrown in April 1979. Unfortunately, the post–Amin governments were no better. Democracy and the rule of law continued to elude the Ugandan people. When General Museveni's guerrilla forces toppled an unpopular regime in January 1986, there was euphoria. The new president, Yoweri K. Museveni, was pragmatic, intelligent and appeared honest in his stated goal of steering Uganda to a democratic path where every citizen would enjoy fundamental human and civil rights.

I was among the young people that greeted General Museveni's ascendancy to power with jubilation. Images of past repressions and flagrant abuse of human rights by an autocratic state gave way to abundant optimism for a democratic Uganda where all would be treated equally under the law. But like many leaders in Africa who emerge on the political scene driven by a strong current of public optimism and goodwill, General Museveni wasted little time in eroding public trust. This was a disappointing turnaround, a betrayal of the implied compact that the general had with Ugandans at the start of his presidency. Civil liberties were severely curtailed, and General Museveni and his lieutenants wielded extraordinary political, military and economic influence, to the detriment of the common good. Intractable corruption and capricious nepotism were the order of the day. General Museveni's military was embroiled in brutal internal and external wars, which left tens of thousands dead. Many more were displaced from their homes and villages. And the government increasingly resorted to force to crush political dissent.

It was against a backdrop of the public's increasing disillusionment and demands for regime change that a coalition of ruling party functionaries and the Christian clergy, especially those professing a profound and conservative evangelism, embarked on a crusade against LGBT Ugandans and urban women. In 1999, General Museveni ordered the police to arrest homosexuals. What followed was a coordinated hateful campaign against LGBT Ugandans. Ten years after the order for arrests, in 2009, David Bahati, a Ugandan legislator, introduced the anti-homosexuality bill in Uganda's Parliament. The proposed law was dubbed the "Kill the Gays" bill because of a clause that called for executing gays caught engaging in "aggravated homosexuality."

Proponents of the "Kill the Gays" bill argued that homosexuality was "un–African" and against Christian teaching. But homosexuality is not a "foreign" import and actually predates the arrival of the British colonial administrators, who first introduced "sodomy" laws. I have LGBT relatives and friends, and prior to General Museveni's and the religious clerics' campaign against sexual minorities in the late 1990s, there are no records of harassment, intimidation or imprisonment of Ugandans because of their sexual orientation or gender identity. A dear friend, believing that the many years I had spent in the West (I left Uganda in the 1990s) shielded me from biases against LGBT people, confided in me about his sexuality. He was a gay Christian man who struggled with a difficult and lonely journey of fear and internal conflict. He lamented the increase in anti–LGBT rhetoric that followed General Museveni's orders to the police to arrest homosexuals. The harsh pronouncements and threats against LGBT people had left him feeling isolated, stigmatized and unwelcome by the church. I embraced and reassured him I loved and cared about him just the way he was—homosexual and Ugandan. I had previously written letters to major Ugandan newspapers in which I decried the injustice and hypocrisy of General Museveni's morality laws. My friend feared that the Western media, with its cynicism and general disinterest in African affairs, would fail to bring the widespread abuses of Uganda's sexual minorities to the attention of the international community, which had the political and economic clout to force General Museveni to respect the rights of all Ugandans irrespective of sexual orientation or gender identity.

The conversation with my gay friend coupled with my deep aversion to the politics of "othering," hitherto best exemplified by Idi Amin's disenfranchisement and expulsion of Ugandan Asians, stirred in me profound feelings of empathy and solidarity with LGBT Ugandans, propelling me to start work on this book. But very quickly it became apparent to me that I needed to broaden the book's scope to encompass the anti-pornography laws which largely targeted urban women and were championed by the same political and religious coalition fighting against LGBT Ugandans. I therefore documented the evolution of the anti-pornography law, examined its relationship to the anti-homosexuality law and its impact on urban woman. Both laws were integral to a political strategy to win legitimacy through legislating and policing morality, policies likely to curry favor with a patriarchal and conservative rural population. After all, most Ugandans live in rural areas. Over the course of several years, I followed the national conversation on morality as it unfolded in Uganda's newspapers and the international media. I had the good fortune of visiting Uganda multiple times. During those trips, I held honest and lively conversations with LGBT Ugandans. Those conversations, some of which continued by email, provided unique insight into how the community organized itself to defend fundamental human rights in an increasingly intolerant and hostile environment. For further insight, I interviewed some of Uganda's leading and courageous human rights activists engaged in fighting for the human rights of sexual minorities. I held conversations with straight Ugandans about the rights of LGBT people, their fellow citizens. Some were supportive and others were outright hostile. Importantly, I could not have written this book without the insight of countless people, mostly in Uganda, who willingly engaged with me in conversation and shared their thoughts on General Museveni's morality laws. To them I owe a profound debt of gratitude.

These interviews and conversations did not necessarily represent the totality of Ugandans and their thinking about the morality laws but they nonetheless offered a prism through which to better contextualize the nature of the politico-religious alliance that provided impetus to legislating morality through two odious laws—the anti-homosexuality and the anti-pornography legislation. Whereas the anti-homosexuality law criminalized LGBT people, the anti-pornography legislation largely affected urban women, limiting their rights and liberties in public spaces. The anti-pornography law was a throwback to the Amin era and, among other things, banned women from wearing dresses deemed immodest.

General Museveni systematically sought to appropriate the morality laws as the most single important tenet of his political legacy. Where Idi Amin dreamed of filling the streets of Kampala with "proper" black Ugandans, General Museveni sought to banish LGBT people from Uganda's streets in order to create a preserve with an exclusively heterosexual population. This book argues that General Museveni's disdain for women's rights set the stage for the passing of the anti-pornography bill, which provided a legal basis for government to control women's bodies by prescribing what they must wear—just like Idi Amin had decreed decades before. And in a deliberate plan to dial back the tremendous progress women in Uganda had made in their struggle for equal rights over the years, General Museveni formed an alliance with Christian churches, many of which reveled in anti-women rhetoric. General Museveni's morality laws, built on a mythic ideal of an African moral purity far superior to Western values, are a stark reminder of the flagrant disregard of civil rights, widespread abuse of human rights, and the general disdain for fundamental freedoms that have plagued and continue to define post-independence Uganda.

I

The Rise of the Anti–LGBT Crusaders

"When I was in America some time ago, I saw a rally of 300,000 homosexuals! If you have a rally of 20 homosexuals here, I would disperse it."[1]—Yoweri Kaguta Museveni, President of the Republic of Uganda

Twenty-first century Africa has made modest, albeit slow, progress towards the establishment of democratic governance, rule of law and respect for human rights. The harsh autocratic African strongman ruling for decades and presiding over a repressive regime is increasingly a rarity. Uganda, a landlocked East African country ranked among the poorest in the world, has the unfortunate distinction of being in the bracket of countries without a stellar democratic record. Political dissent is routinely muzzled. The country is tightly controlled by its autocratic ruler, General Yoweri Kaguta Museveni. General Museveni is one of Africa's longest serving presidents. The general has ruled Uganda since 1986 when his guerrilla force overthrew a vicious and undemocratic government. At the time, the general scoffed at African leaders who did not relinquish power. He promised to be different from these autocratic leaders and not overstay his welcome. After his first swearing-in ceremony as president of Uganda in January 1986, an eloquent General Museveni, riding on the coattails of popular goodwill, declared: "The problem of Africa in general and Uganda in particular is not the people, but leaders who want to overstay in power."[2]

General Museveni promised the people he would step aside after serving five years. He would pass the presidential baton on to a democratically elected successor. But more than three decades later, the general is still the president of Uganda and is showing no signs of loosening his ironclad grip on power. When he appeared on the British Broadcasting

Corporation's *HardTalk* program in 2012, General Museveni was reminded of his 1986 disdain of the old-school African autocrat who clung to power. He insisted his statement had been misconstrued and taken out of context. He claimed he was referring to African dictators that hold on to power for decades without being democratically elected.[3] This blatant insincerity added yet another layer of cynicism to a Uganda public disillusioned with the general's numerous unfulfilled promises.

Although a parliamentary democracy on paper, Uganda is a de facto dictatorship. General Museveni's government goes through the routine of conducting elections to largely please and silence the West. Museveni's ruling party, the National Resistance Movement (NRM), has made the intimidation and harassment of the political opposition a routine staple. Parliamentarians, particularly the majority belonging to the ruling NRM party, are in hock to General Museveni. Significant public policy cannot be made without the general's nod and blessing. In Uganda, just like in several sub–Saharan African countries, the president's whims often set the tone for subordinates. In order to pass and implement legislation, especially laws that are contentious and unpopular, General Museveni relies on loyal cadres in his orbit of close confidantes. The general's grand design for the country appears to hinge on a singular purpose—a desire to rule for life and possibly establish a dynasty.[4] For a long time, General Museveni justified his hold on power by arguing he was the only visionary in the country capable of transforming a largely agrarian economy into an African industrial behemoth. He promised to lead the country from its dismal Third World status to an enviable place in the First World with prosperity guaranteed for all. But the longer he held on to power the more it became obvious that the promise of better times for the citizenry would not be fulfilled. He had little to offer beyond a corrupt and inept autocratic regime that excelled at patronage, cronyism and stifling dissent. Political opponents were routinely beaten and arrested on bogus charges. Meetings organized by the political opposition or civil society groups were anathema to General Museveni. He ordered police and paramilitary squads to forcibly break up the gatherings. Government-sponsored rabble gangs and paramilitary groups like the "Black Mamba Hit Squad" and the "Kiboko Squad" unleashed unmitigated violence against civilians. Uganda's military was increasingly mired in the affairs of neighboring countries, where they fought senseless wars that claimed the lives of hundreds of thousands.

By 1995, General Museveni had been in power for nine years, during which period he had become increasingly repressive. To calm the masses who demanded delivery on his democratic promise, General Museveni introduced a new constitution. The new constitution limited the president to serve a maximum of two five-year terms. When elections were organized in 1996, the government argued that the president's prior decade-long rule did not count since he had governed the country under an older constitution that did not specify presidential term limits. It therefore meant that General Museveni could run for his "first" term in 1996 and be eligible for a "second" five-year term in the 2001 presidential election. In the 1996 election, General Museveni was said to have won with over 75 percent of the vote. However, it was a sham election. The political opposition candidates for president could appear on the ballot but were explicitly barred from campaigning. General Museveni claimed then that democracy was bad for Uganda as it fostered religious and ethnic sectarianism. Ugandans were skeptical about this assertion, especially coming from a regime that had stepped up repression and stifled the political opposition.

The Ugandan president is a wily man, and a master political tactician. In the build-up to the 2001 election, when the president would ostensibly be running for his last constitutionally allowed five-year term, it became apparent that General Museveni would amend the constitution and throw out presidential term limits. But how was he going to award himself a life presidency without alienating Ugandans even further? It is argued here that General Museveni, among others, rebranded his image as a tough African nationalist with the fortitude to resist the immoral West's imperialist hegemony. To this end, he courted and cultivated a close relationship with Christian conservatives, in both government and civil society. He unashamedly rode on the religious conservative's narrow morality-based agenda that had the potential of rallying the rural masses. Most Ugandans live in the rural countryside. General Museveni's morality laws, chiefly the anti-homosexuality and anti-pornography laws, were borne of cynical political opportunism. General Museveni aligned himself with Christian conservative forces and recruited legislators and government officials to plant homophobia into the popular imagination.

In April of 1998, as Anglican Communion bishops were preparing to attend the every-tenth-year Lambeth Conference in Canterbury, Bishop Nicodemus Engwalas Okille of the Anglican Church of Uganda (commonly called the Church of Uganda—COU) accused Western church leaders of lobbying him to support homosexuality.[5] Human sexuality, and homosexuality in particular, was a divisive issue in the Anglican Communion. It was one of the themes included for consideration at Lambeth

1998. It is therefore unsurprising that in the run-up to Lambeth 1998 some liberal and conservative Global North bishops aggressively courted support among fellow bishops, particularly those in the so-called Global South, to rally around their position on homosexuality. Bishop Okille was a hardcore conservative known for railing against urban youth culture. He scoffed at young men wearing chains, earrings and braided hair, a hairstyle he believed ought to be exclusively reserved for women. He alleged these aesthetic accessories were an external manifestation of homosexuality. Bishop Okille claimed homosexuality was not a human right but an "uncultured norm."[6] Unwittingly, Bishop Okille became the first high-ranking member of the Ugandan Christian clergy to disassociate homosexuality from issues of human rights and advance the argument that sexual minorities could not enjoy equal protection of the law. Bishop Okille's claims of being recruited to support homosexuality were taken up by an editorial in the *New Vision*, a state-controlled newspaper under the management of William Pike, a British journalist.[7] The editorial was a contemptuously trenchant assault on homosexuality. It claimed: "In many African societies, Ugandan communities inclusive, homosexuality is so abominable that many call for acts of cleansing for those found to have this unnatural sexual orientation." The editorial further alleged that "Africa finds homosexuality as abominable as bestiality ..., incest ... and sex with corpses.... The Church retains a very important role in fighting these deeds, and cannot afford to compromise, otherwise its position in society and before God will be untenable." It did not take long before General Museveni joined the chorus of religious clerics condemning homosexuality during the run-up to Lambeth 1998.

On July 21, 1998, General Museveni called a press conference at the presidential lodge in Nakasero, a leafy Kampala suburb. He wanted to express his disgust at the aggressive way in which Ugandan journalists questioned visiting foreign dignitaries. The general was incensed at the feistiness of journalists when they asked Blaise Compaoré, the then president of Burkina Faso, during a May 1994 visit to Uganda, to explain his alleged role in the assassination of Capt. Thomas Sankara, the country's former president.[8] General Museveni claimed such questioning was an embarrassment and counter to the African values of hospitality. It is then that he lectured the assembled journalists on the differences between African and Western values. He cited homosexuality as a glaring example of the difference in the two value systems. Adopting a stern tone, Museveni said: "When I was in America, some time ago, I saw a rally of 300,000 homosexuals! If you have a rally of 20 homosexuals here, I would disperse it."[9] This was the first time a sitting Ugandan president had publicly pronounced himself on homosexuality. This chilling statement would shape subsequent debate on homosexuality and morality in the country for years to come. It is important to note that General Museveni's opening salvo against homosexuality came a few days before the opening of Lambeth 1998. Bishop Okille's remarks resonated within the COU. Archbishop Nkoyooyo (also spelled as Nkoyoyo), the Church of Uganda's prelate, corralled fellow bishops from Uganda, Rwanda, Burundi and the Democratic Republic of the Congo into opposing homosexuality at Lambeth 1998.[10] At the conference, Ugandan bishops declared themselves opposed to homosexuality and voted with the conservative bloc that staunchly held that homosexuality was immoral and an evil against God's laws. General Museveni lauded the Ugandan bishops for their anti-gay position, casting homosexuality as a cultural hotspot between Africans and Western society: "The bishops went to the Lambeth conference and the European bishops were agitating that the Church should accept homosexuality, *that homosexuals are also people created by God* and he had a reason for creating them. But the Africans stood their ground and said 'go to hell.'"[11]

In September 1999, General Museveni made a startling announcement. He had ordered police to find and arrest homosexuals.[12] The COU applauded General Museveni's draconian edict. Addressing a press conference at Entebbe International Airport on his return from a visit to the U.S., Archbishop Nkoyooyo gleefully told journalists he supported General Museveni's criminalization of homosexuality because it is "against the biblical teaching and African culture."[13] The United States condemned General Museveni for threatening "the arrest of homosexuals based on Ugandan legislation barring homosexual activity."[14] The U.S. further warned it would "view the arrest and imprisonment of persons based on their sexual orientation as a serious human rights violation, regardless of whether such arrests are sanctioned by Ugandan legislation." In spite of the U.S. reminding Uganda of its obligations under numerous international conventions, including the Universal Declaration of Human Rights, which bound the country to respect rights of individuals in general, defiant ruling party functionaries sprung to General Museveni's defense.[15] It is probable that General Museveni wanted the West to condemn him since this would likely be interpreted by Ugandans as interference by a Western power into the internal affairs of a sovereign African country and hence rally the country behind him.

Ugandan legislators, government functionaries, and the religious clergy created a misleading narrative about homosexuality. For example, they claimed homosexuals engaged in sexual defilement and were pedophiles. They canvassed the country, warning about an imminent moral and spiritual assault from rich Western forces that worked in cahoots with Uganda's lesbian, gay, bisexual, and transgender (LGBT) people with the sole purpose of spreading homosexuality.[16] In November 1999 an anti–LGBT lobby consisting of conservative Christian groups and legislators begun taking shape. Around this period, the Evangelical Fellowship of Uganda and the National Fellowship of Born-Again Churches invited legislators to attend a debate titled "The Homosexual Challenge in Uganda: Some Biblical and Secular Perspectives."[17] The debate was held at Kampala's upscale Sheraton Hotel. In a sense, it was the formalizing of the union between two groups of anti-gay activists—the born-again Pentecostals and self-identified born-again Christian legislators willing to implement General Museveni's policies. The Uganda Pentecostal movement, with its close ties to state power, would wrest control of the anti-gay agenda from the COU, playing a significant role in worsening conditions for LGBT Ugandans.

Born-again Ugandan legislators had their own parliamentary caucus—the Parliamentary Fellowship or the Uganda Parliamentary Prayer Fellowship. The Uganda Parliamentary Fellowship aligns its ideology to the U.S. Fellowship, a powerful and secretive organization in Washington, D.C. The born-again Ugandan legislators vocalized at every opportunity the urgency of fighting immorality and promoting righteous Christian living. Immorality was defined in broad and expansive terms. It encompassed participation in reality television shows, uploading YouTube videos, sex education pamphlets for schoolchildren, pornographic materials, homosexuality, miniskirts, and drinking. By the late 1990s, while General Museveni was said to be planning to change the constitution and lift the presidential term limits, morality issues had become both an obsession and fascination in the Ugandan social and political psyche. Conservative legislators and religious clerics kept up a tenacious anti-homosexuality commentary that drowned the voices opposed to changing the constitution to grant General Museveni a life presidency. The anti-homosexuality camp played to the anxiety and ignorance of the people, especially in rural areas. Their blistering condemnation of homosexuality left many convinced the country was descending into a fearful climate of total moral and spiritual degeneration. One government official claimed the country was under a "moral attack."[18] And Ms. Miria Matembe, the ethics and integrity minister (1998–2003) and a born-again Christian, warned of "too much immorality all around us. Homosexuality, lesbianism, name it."[19] Basoga Nsadhu, another government minister, lamented that most people in Kampala were spending too much time watching sex videos. He accused local FM radio stations of promoting immorality, claiming that they "get people playing sex, connect them to a microphone via a phone and relay it to the people. They do this repeatedly at a certain hour of the night. I have been recording them."[20] Meanwhile, not to be outdone on morality matters, Pastor Martin Ssempa, perhaps the most politically-connected and angriest Pentecostal minister at the forefront of a pugnacious anti–LGBT crusade, blamed the mushrooming internet cafes around the country for promoting homosexuality and lesbianism. The pastor alleged that Ugandan youth did not visit internet cafes to "search for knowledge but instead watch what homos and lesbians do on the internet."[21] This was a rather puzzling allegation, which suggested a paucity of heterosexual pornography on the internet. Surely, the pastor, a dual Ugandan and U.S. citizen, was internet savvy and he possibly would have been personally offended if a suggestion was made that a desire to "watch what homos and lesbians do" motivated his internet use. Pastor Ssempa fulminated against LGBT people, urging governments around the world to fight homosexuality with the same urgency of purpose the West had demonstrated in fighting terrorism in the wake of the 9/11 terrorist attacks in the U.S.

The COU clergy displayed a morbid preoccupation with homosexuality. They armed themselves with scripture, using biblical verses to legitimize gay harassment and condemnation. And they exploited every available avenue to portray homosexuality as against God's design, and most importantly, un–African. Liberal Western mores were viewed with profound disdain and utter contempt. It is ironic that a church that had often disparaged indigenous African traditions and customary practices as incompatible with Christianity now invoked those same values to justify its disapproval of homosexuality. Many COU clerics preached that the church did not welcome homosexuals.[22] The clergy even took their fight against immorality to the popular traditional king of Buganda (the kabaka), Ronald Mutebi. At a thanksgiving church service to commemorate the king's ninth coronation anniversary, COU bishops told the kabaka that some of his subjects were engaged in immorality. They recited to the kabaka a litany of immoral activities—indecent dressing, sexual defilement, lesbianism and homosexuality. Kabaka Mutebi's response was not an outright condemnation of LGBT people. He nonetheless suggested Kampala, Uganda's capital, had sunk into the abyss of immorality. The kabaka told the bishops about an incident at Kampala's Sheraton Hotel where he was accosted by aggressive sex workers: "The whores jumped into my car and I was shocked to see young girls fit to be my grandchildren going berserk over an old man like me."[23]

Immorality, and homosexuality in particular, was portrayed like a wildfire out of control, poised to engulf and destroy all in its fiery path. At Makerere University, the chancellor, Apolo Nsibambi, hardly known as a hard-nosed social conservative, lamented that homosexuality had finally penetrated the walls of the country's bastion of higher learning.[24] The Senate, the university's highest decision-making body, ratcheted up the paranoia, vowing to fight homosexuality. The Senate proposed to assemble a task force consisting of university staff and representatives of the student body with the express purpose of identifying homosexuals and undertaking appropriate punitive measures, possibly expelling them from the university.[25] The government mobilized university students to go out into the streets of Kampala to demonstrate against immorality and homosexuality. On at least one occasion the students baffled most ordinary Ugandans when they demonstrated against the promotion of condoms, a successful preventative strategy in Uganda's fight against the AIDS epidemic. It was evident some university students were either inspired by Christian conservative ideology or were eager supporters of General Museveni. As if the anti-homosexuality madness knew no bounds, a senior official in the education ministry threatened the expulsion of any student caught engaging in a homosexual act. He ominously warned that the ministry had "received reports that homosexuality is on the increase in our schools. It is up to head teachers to act swiftly and stop this evil from spreading further."[26] Stephen Langa of Family Life Network (FLN), who would play an influential role in the drafting of the country's morality laws and in the persecution of LGBT Ugandans, alleged that over 600 schools in the country were involved in homosexuality and lesbianism. He stepped up his efforts to have government enact stringent anti-gay legislation.[27]

Hardly did a day go by without a high-ranking government official warning of a homosexual crackdown or a religious leader condemning homosexuality and cautioning Christians to avoid recruitment into homosexuality. The Ugandan media was equally active, providing a constant stream of news stories depicting a country under siege from a West focused on enticing Ugandan youth into homosexuality. Homosexual acts were portrayed as particularly vile and violent. Horror stories of male "victims" of homosexuality with shredded and infected rectums that oozed pus were tabloid media staples. The anti–LGBT groups were masters at constructing layers of false narrative and deceptive propaganda. The Rev.

John Senyonyi, another stalwart of the Family Life Network, claimed that homosexuality decreased life expectancy by 25 to 35 years, and that homosexuals were prone to dying from chronic liver damage.[28] Newspapers carried sensational headlines that heightened the fear factor. For example, one paper proclaimed that "Homos Storm Schools."[29] Yet another fanned the flames of homophobia declaring "White Homos Beasts, Says Minister."[30] The anti–LGBT crusaders outcompeted each other in making consistently weird and ludicrous claims about homosexuality. This took on a particularly aggressive onslaught as General Museveni was midway through his last constitutionally permitted term in office. Barring a change in the constitution or a military coup d'état, Ugandans would bid farewell to General Museveni in 2006. He would have served an unprecedented twenty years as head of state, making him the longest serving Ugandan president. Prior to Museveni, that record was held by another military man, General Idi Amin. Idi Amin was in office for eight and one-half years.

The intense public condemnation and unrelenting harsh judgment of LGBT people created extreme fear and anxiety among ordinary people, who were led to believe homosexuality would destabilize traditional family values and threaten the predominance of a heterosexual patriarchal order. Ugandans began thinking that if their government chose not to fight homosexuality then the looming spiritual Armageddon would overwhelm their country. People dreaded the prospect that their children would become card-carrying LGBT members, sexual orientations and gender identities strongly disapproved of by the religious clergy and state agents. A *New Vision* editorial illustrates the drumming up of this fear, alleging that "the gay strategy is that as many people as possible adopt this lifestyle. There are many explanations for this but perhaps the comfort that 'we are many' is supreme. Scott Lively's book, *The Gay Movement: How to Recruit-Proof Your Child* exposes the methods used to recruit young children in the U.S. in the hope that the habit passes on to the next generation."[31] Scott Lively was also the author of *The Pink Swastika: Homosexuality in the Nazi Party*, which alleged homosexuals masterminded the Holocaust.

Unsurprisingly, appeals to the government to do something to save the country from an existential threat became louder by the day. With clerics and legislators keeping up a constant wave of anti-gay rhetoric which stripped homosexual Ugandans of their humanity, some in Uganda came to believe homosexuality was a danger to the public order. This was the case with Mr. James Wasula, who identified himself as a "law-abiding and concerned citizen of Uganda." Mr. Wasula's opinion piece in the state-controlled *New Vision* illustrates the state of paranoia that prevailed in the country and the desire of anxious citizens to see a muscular government response to stop homosexuality: "The press has more than once carried stories of the growing fraternity of lesbians and homosexuals and exposed their nooks. Unfortunately, much as the acts are criminal, the Police has not taken any step to apprehend the suspects.... The Police should visit the holes mentioned in the press, spy on the perverts, arrest and prosecute them. Relevant government departments must outlaw or restrict websites, magazines, newspapers and television channels promoting immorality—including homosexuality, lesbianism, pornography, etc."[32]

Going by the reports on homosexuality in the Ugandan media, which captured the utterings of legislators, religious clergy, and ordinary citizens, anti-gay hysteria had hit an all-time high by 2009. It was in this environment of deep anxiety where a siege mentality prevailed and the nation was plagued by false narratives of homosexuality that Mr. David Bahati, a hitherto obscure and lightweight Ugandan legislator of the ruling NRM party, made his grand entry. Uganda's anti-homosexuality bill emerged as a lynchpin of public policy following years of close relationships between an alliance of local and international Christian fundamentalists who subscribed to a theocracy on one hand, and on the other the arrogance and hubris of the ruling political party, personified by the president, General Museveni. The general sought to maintain a stranglehold over power in Uganda at any cost, including drumming up anti–LGBT sentiments if it served his grand political agenda. Historically and culturally, LGBT people have existed in Uganda without fear of persecution. Yet some ordinary Ugandans seized upon the incendiary anti-gay proclamations of the religious clergy and opportunistic politicians with a troubling zeal. The bill was cleverly promulgated under the guise of protecting impressionable Ugandans from the dangers of Western culture and indeed formed part of zealous efforts by legislators to further curtail freedoms in the name of fighting immorality.

In October 2009, Bahati introduced the Anti-Homosexuality Bill of 2009.[33] Because of a clause in the bill that called for executing gays caught engaging in "aggravated homosexuality," Bahati's bill is often referred to as the "Kill the Gays" bill. Bahati stated that the bill's overarching objective was to protect the "traditional" family by prohibiting and criminalizing same-sex relationships. It also supposedly aimed at "strengthening the nation's capacity to deal with emerging internal and external threats to the traditional heterosexual family." The bill broadened the definition of the offense of homosexuality to include "the intention of committing the act of homosexuality" and introduced what it referred to as "aggravated" homosexuality. According to the bill, a person commits the offense of aggravated homosexuality where the:

(a) Person against whom the offense is committed is below the age of 18 years;

(b) Offender is a person living with HIV;

(c) Offender is a parent or guardian of the person against whom the offense is committed;

(d) Offender is a person of authority over the person against whom the offense is committed;

(e) Victim of the offense is a person with disability;

(f) Offender is a serial offender; or

(g) Offender applies, administers or causes to be used by any man or woman any drug, matter or thing with intent to stupefy or overpower him or her so as to thereby enable any person to have unlawful carnal connection with any person of the same sex.

Bahati's bill was easily the most egregious piece of legislation to emerge out of post-independence Uganda. The bill proposed a mandatory life sentence for those found guilty of homosexuality and proposed the death penalty for "aggravated" homosexuality. A second conviction for engaging in the offense of homosexuality qualified as "aggravated" and therefore carried the ultimate sentence—death at the gallows. Aiding and abetting homosexuality or conspiracy to engage in homosexuality would be penalized with a minimum sentence of seven years. Ordinary Ugandans would be required to report any suspected acts of homosexuality to the police within 24 hours of knowing about the act or else risk a considerable fine and imprisonment for up to three years. People could go to jail for just knowing a gay person. Ugandans living abroad and engaging in homosexuality were not immune to the jurisdiction of Uganda's courts—they would be extradited back to Uganda where they would either be imprisoned for life or put to death. Challenged by progressives that saw his bill as draconian and unnecessary, Bahati presented the logic behind his bill in *The Independent*, a Uganda newspaper:

> This battle is about our children who are being lured into this vile and our moral stand as a country. Indeed, it is true that this bill was driven by our deep fear of God and the zeal to act according to his will but also the need to defend the age old traditional heterosexual family which is rooted in our culture as Ugandans. The vile evil is spreading in schools, churches and NGOs and if we don't take action now we shall reach a stage whereby it is the homosexuals who shall be tabling bills to criminalize all morals and legalize all manners of perversion.[34]

Overnight, Bahati's "Kill the Gays" bill propelled him from the obscurity of the backbenches of Uganda's Parliament to worldwide notoriety. And in parallel with Bahati's infamy, Uganda became the butt of jokes. Bahati, the lodestar and poster boy of the anti–LGBT movement in Uganda, was unapologetic about singling out a minority group and proposing severe punishment. He held a deep belief homosexuality was inconsistent with Ugandan culture and Christian teaching. Never mind that about 16 percent of Uganda's estimated 38 million people are non–Christians. Nonetheless Bahati was obsessed with imposing his interpretation of Christianity on every Ugandan. Bahati was not delusional or acting on his own personal conviction. He was merely the public face of an agenda bigger than his self-confessed interest of protecting Ugandan families and preserving the hegemony of a patriarchal, phallocentric, and heterosexual culture. If Christian conservatives had not displayed an interest in persecuting homosexuals, it is doubtful that General Museveni would have elevated the anti-gay agenda as a key strategy in a populist campaign that ultimately was always intended to bolster his fading popularity and usher him on a path to a life presidency.

Mr. Bahati presented his anti-gay stance as a simple matter of defending Christian morality. He claimed gays were not his bêtes noires and in fact he dearly loved them. But he had a duty, which verged on a divine calling, to protect Ugandan children from the evil and avarice of Westerners who he alleged were waging a protracted and sophisticated campaign to recruit children into homosexuality. In his crusade to establish a moral society whose sexuality is regulated through high-handed legislation, Bahati portrayed Ugandan children, and indeed all people, as easily manipulated and corrupted, and therefore easy fodder for Western gay recruiters. There was an urgency, he variously claimed, to enact and pass anti-gay legislation to protect Ugandan children. There was something eerily familiar about his crusade to demonize gays as child-recruiting social misfits deserving of execution. In pushing through General Museveni's political agenda of hate towards LGBT people, Mr. Bahati conveniently borrowed from a playbook of Christian conservatives in the U.S., groups with which he had established close ties.

One of the leading architects of the myth that gays had an agenda to recruit children was Anita Bryant, a bigoted self-styled defender of Christian morality. In 1977 Miami-Dade County passed legislation protecting homosexuals. Ms. Bryant, a former Miss Oklahoma and orange juice salesperson, would not take any of this. She argued that the law would grant homosexuals—at one point referring to gays as "human garbage" leading a "demon lifestyle"—a right to molest, recruit and morally pervert innocent children. She launched a hateful anti-gay "save our children" campaign, built on fallacies and tapping into the anxieties and ignorance of the general population. She proclaimed her message, which at its core was about the inability of homosexuals to reproduce; hence their resort to recruiting children to increase their ranks. This fallacy, which had no shred of facts to back it up, resonated in Miami-Dade neighborhoods. With a margin of more than two to one, voters overwhelmingly endorsed the repeal of the ordinance.[35] At about the same time that Ms. Bryant was in the throes of celebrating the victory of her anti-gay campaign, an organization calling itself the "National American Party for Manhood" reared its head in the suburbs of Los Angeles, distributing pamphlets that called for capital punishment of homosexuals.[36] Fast forward to over three decades later, a lowly legislator in Uganda became the unlikely champion of religious conservatives. Bahati's talking points were borrowed from Ms. Bryant's playbook and the hate-filled pamphlets of the National American Party for Manhood. U.S. religious conservatives provided the backbone of his philosophical foundation and moral compass. It is also worth noting that this imagery of homosexuals harming innocent children has its counterpart in Hitler's repulsive ranting against Jews whom he accused of systematically defiling young blonde girls.

On December 10, 2010, Bahati appeared on MSNBC's *The Rachel Maddow Show*.[37] During the interview Bahati labored to explain the inspiration behind his draft anti-homosexuality legislation—a steadfast obedience to his Christian God. He argued that his proposed legislation to kill gays should not lead people to equate him with Hitler, Saddam Hussein or General Idi Amin. The latter was the notorious Ugandan dictator who reportedly killed upwards of 500,000 people.[38] However, some accounts have challenged that high number, and have revised it downward to 1,200 people.[39] What Bahati did not tell Ms. Maddow was that although Amin's standards were generally depraved, the dictator did not persecute gay people. In the course of the MSNBC interview, Bahati presented himself as a good Christian and a "simple young man." Unfortunately, the image he attempted to construct of a compassionate and logical legislator trying to be reasonable was in stark contrast to his deep conviction, conveyed with a chilling earnestness, to execute gay Ugandans. It was evident Mr. Bahati was conflicted in his obligations as a legislator and his responsibilities of a self-described devout born-again Christian. Should he cave in to the notion of human rights as articulated by the West—and which rights must not be extended to gays in Uganda—or stand up in defense of the values of his God and Ugandan culture? Bahati was an evangelical Christian, a God-fearing person, so he affirmed during the one-on-one interview with Maddow. It was because of that that he drew upon his Christian faith to justify his bill's severe punishment for gay Ugandans. To be gay was to live in sin, and in the world inhabited by Bahati, the wages of sin is death. Bahati and the Uganda anti-gay lobby saw in homosexuality an incompatibility with "nature" and maintained it was a matter of common sense to judge same-sex relationships as incontrovertibly reprehensible and in violation of "God's law." Peter Lloyd has commented about this danger of moral certainty thus[40]:

> History overflows with misery inflicted by well-intentioned people who were convinced that they had seen the only true moral values, and who sought to convert or destroy those who would not agree. The Inquisition was premised on the moral certainty of the Roman Church. Its officers were wholly convinced that the Christian scriptures as interpreted by the Pope were true, and that they revealed an objective system of morality. On those grounds, any individuals who did not share those values were inescapably found to be a threat to the realization of Christian values in this world. Therefore, they were persecuted and ferociously tortured to make them recant their "heresies."

It is both remarkable and ludicrous that amidst many pressing issues confronting the country, Ugandan legislators dedicated an inordinate amount of time debating gender and sex over a period of many years. The discussions often descended into the theatrical and absurd. It was an interesting spectacle as day after day lawmakers outdid each other in proposing ways to establish a strict sexual moral code. In 2012, Stephen Fry, a British comedian and actor, conducted a television interview with the Reverend Father Simon Lokodo, a defrocked Roman Catholic priest and the Uganda minister for ethics and integrity at the time. Mr. Fry sought to understand from the minister why the Ugandan government prioritized gay persecution when there was a high incidence of men raping underage girls. Father Lokodo didn't seem to mind heterosexual rape and in fact appeared to encourage rapists: "Let them do it, and do it the right way ... at least it is the natural way of desiring sex."[41] As the top political appointee at the ministry of ethics and integrity and not just a rogue ruling party sidekick, Father Lokodo was an important member of General Museveni's government and the ruling party, the National Resistance Movement (NRM). Therefore, his stunning statement on rape cannot be shrugged off as the idiocy of an insensitive ex-priest or the ranting of a mindless political sycophant. Father Lokodo's permissive attitude towards heterosexual rape, abhorrent and reprehensible as it was, represented official government policy. Stephen Fry has described Father Lokodo as a "foaming, frothing homophobe of the worst kind."[42] Father Lokodo's ludicrous beliefs about the LGBT community were often in the shadow of Bahati's toxic views. Both men held warped and diabolical opinions. On one occasion Father Lokodo alleged that in his native Karamoja, a northeastern Uganda region, gays are rounded up and killed by firing squad because being homosexual is "a total perversity."[43] Obviously, this is a big lie from a minister of ethics and integrity.

There are not many countries around the globe that boast of national departments solely focusing on issues relating to ethics and integrity. But this should not come as a surprise in Uganda where corruption and nepotism in both the public and private sector is pervasive and widespread. When the directorate was formed in 1998 its principal mandate was to root out rampant corruption. It is generally accepted that the first minister to head this department, Ms. Miria Matembe, a salt-of-the-earth civil rights attorney and a hard-charging critic of General Museveni's decades of misrule, demonstrated resolve in stamping out corruption and fostering good constitutional governance. However, her vision of human rights failed to extend to homosexuals. She gloated over the fact that she was the first government official to physically harass homosexuals and deny them space to assemble and socialize.[44] But she was not the worst of the anti-gay ethics and integrity ministers. Despite her braggadocio at being the first to "*catch*" gays and disperse homosexuals from bars, she does not appear to have had interest in imprisoning gays. She was more nuisance than a threat to the LGBT community. Ms. Matembe fell afoul of General Museveni when she defied his orders to legislators to endorse changes to the constitution, changes which included dropping the two-term limit on the presidency and effectively crowning himself a life president. For her stance against the life-presidency project she was expeditiously given the sack. Throughout General Museveni's long authoritarian reign government officials were purged for any number of reasons, and these mostly had little to do with their performance but more because the president questioned their loyalty.

After Ms. Matembe's ouster in 2003 as minister of ethics and integrity, the department drastically changed course. Between 2003 and 2016, the ministry of ethics and integrity has been led by three different middle-aged men who displayed an astounding level of misogynist behavior and struggled to comprehend modern progress—Tim Lwanga (2003–2006), Nsaba Buturo (2006–2011) and Father Simon Lokodo (from 2011 and who still led the office in 2016). It is important to note that all these men were members of the Uganda Parliamentary Fellowship, a Christian conservative caucus of legislators. Acting on behalf of the Parliamentary Fellowship, and at times at their own initiative, they were intent on regulating all spheres of sexuality in the country, including female bodies and their dress. The ministers of ethics and integrity would pursue the passage and implementation of morality laws with a ferocity and zealousness that was both irrational and frightening. Many of their actions and utterances left most observers to conclude that these were men driven by a singular mission of stifling modernity and ushering the country back into the precolonial age. They eschewed the fight against graft and nepotism, which was the primary mandate of the ministry of ethics and integrity. Over the years, top government officials and their relatives were implicated in spectacular corruption scandals that galvanized the country. However, because of their proximity to the seat of power, these corrupt officials were deemed too powerful to investigate by the ministry of ethics and integrity. It therefore comes as no surprise that the ministry redefined its mission and placed emphasis on policing Ugandan morality. Suddenly, it was the ministry issuing orders on how Ugandans must dress and have sex, and what they should or should not read or view. The ministry of ethics and integrity transformed itself into a morality police of sorts whose primary concern was to establish a bureaucratic machinery to control the moral fabric of society. In this way, the ministry became a vehicle for implementing the agenda of Christian conservatives with powerful connections to state power while advancing General Museveni's political agenda of a life presidency.

Addressing journalists in Kampala in 2015, Father Lokodo announced the formation of a police squad with the express purpose of arresting prostitutes and their clients. The priest decried that many of the johns were folks holding high office (one cannot help think that he was referring to some of his fellow legislators and government ministers) or working in law enforcement. He also informed the journalists that he had written to local television stations that hosted two popular matchmaking programs "Be My Date" and *Abanoonya*—translated as "Those searching"—to halt the practice forthwith since, "matchmaking is not good; it is a form of prostitution."[45] More often than not, opposition to public policy in Uganda comes at a hefty price with dissenters routinely persecuted and imprisoned. But Father Lokodo's overbearing exuberance crossed the line for some people. Within four days of the *Daily Monitor*, a local daily, running the Lokodo matchmaking story, the online edition of the story sported vociferous comments that were mostly unflattering to Father Lokodo. He was roundly condemned as antiquated with views that were way out there.

Writing under the moniker TheAfricanThinker, one commentator observed: "The minister is an embarrassment to Uganda. He wants to micromanage the country as if it's his household. He is introducing Taliban-style religious laws on society." A particularly naughty comment came from Rambo who advised: "May be he [Father Lokodo] should let a prostitute pay him a private visit." At this, a comment from Ogwang-guji quipped: "No need for that visit. He may not even know what to do."

The year 2009 will stand out as one that Uganda's Parliament singularly focused on introducing bills designed to dictate public morality and private sexual conduct. Early in the year the government indicated it was drafting the anti-pornography bill, better known as the *miniskirt bill*.[46] The Christian religious clergy and some legislators alleged a direct link between pornography and homosexuality.[47] Apparently, Scott Lively, the American evangelical, had provided the evidence to the Ugandans, based on his own family story.[48] The Christian clergy therefore demanded government legislation against pornography as part of a broader strategy to fight homosexuality. The anti-pornography advocates broadly defined pornography to include "indecent" dresses worn by women—skinny jeans, bikinis, and mini-dresses.[49] Father Lokodo best summarized the intent of the anti-pornography law as a "campaign against vulgar and obscene way of exposing the human body for fun, or anyone who depicts unclothed or under clothed parts of the human body that are erotic."[50] These "vulgar and obscene" ways were conduits to homosexuality, an un–African behavior. Therefore, the Ugandan moralists viewed their fight against pornography within a larger context—combating homosexuality, which they believed was "un–African" and an import from a decadent and amoral Western society.

In December 2009, the Marriage and Divorce Bill was introduced for debate in Uganda's Parliament.[51] The bill sought to replace two colonial-era legislations—the Marriage Act and the Divorce Act. Both bedrocks of family law were anachronistic and decidedly disadvantaged women in matters of marriage, separation, divorce and inheritance rights. For example, the Divorce Act placed a huge hurdle for women seeking a divorce. It prescribed that for a woman to sue for divorce she had to prove her husband was guilty of the offence of "aggravated" adultery, defined as sodomy, bigamy, incest, bestiality, cruelty, rape or desertion. Husbands on the other hand were at liberty to divorce adulterous wives without the extra encumbrance of proving aggravation. In short, the law provided women little to no protection in a marriage or in its dissolution. Over a period of more than five decades, a coalition of feminist and progressive organizations and voices had led efforts to reform Uganda's family laws. These progressive reformers of Uganda's family laws also advocated for the abolition of certain customary practices deemed reactionary. These included the practice of paying "bride price" and "widow inheritance"— a practice of a man inheriting the widow of his deceased relative. The negative impact of bride price, which in Uganda's tribal societies validated a marriage, was best summarized by Professor Sylvia Tamale, a Harvard-educated lawyer and leading LGBT rights and human rights advocate in Uganda: "The customary payment of bride wealth now gives the husband proprietary rights over his wife, allowing him to treat her more or less like a chattel. This is especially so because it equates a woman's status in marriage with the amount of bride wealth exchanged and not her skills and abilities."[52]

The Marriage and Divorce Bill of 2009 therefore sought to "reform and consolidate the law relating to civil, Christian, Hindu, Baha'i and customary marriages; to provide for the types of recognized marriages, marital rights and duties; recognition of cohabitation in relation to property rights; separation and divorce, and the consequences of separation and divorce; and for related matters."[53] But the Marriage and Divorce Bill of 2009 is also relevant in the context of Bahati's "Kill the Gays" bill. It defined marriage as a union between a man and a woman, and it specifically prohibited marriage between persons of the same sex. Some in government, especially those championing a rigid conservative agenda, supported the bill as part of their grand design to legitimize the harassment of LGBT people in the event Bahati's "Kill the Gays" bill failed to garner enough support in Parliament. Once it became apparent Bahati's "Kill the Gays" bill enjoyed considerable backing from legislators, the government lost interest in reforming family law since it did not further General Museveni's populist agenda. The general said he opposed key provisions of the bill that related to divorce, bride-price, property sharing in event of divorce, cohabitation, and criminalizing marital rape.[54] On marital rape, General Museveni took issue with a clause that would grant a spouse a right to deny his or her partner sex where forceful sex results in civil and criminal liabilities. General Museveni, the guardian of patriarchal morality, suddenly accused proponents of the Marriage and Divorce Bill of receiving money from the West with the intent of undermining Ugandan culture.[55] He was contemptuous of a group of women's rights activists supporting the bill, accusing them of polluting "our women emancipation movement by introducing elements of *mercenarism* in marriages" and warning he would not permit the white man to distort African culture.[56] General

Museveni's allusion to "*mercenarism*" and rejection of the West's "cultural imperialism" as he pursued his morality agenda would become a recurring theme, be it as he frothed against the "disgusting" LGBT community or worked with his loyalists in Parliament and religious clerics to curtail women's rights and freedoms for political expediency. But the coup de grâce that effectively removed the bill from the legislative agenda was delivered in General Museveni's warning to lawmakers: "Instead of discussing development programmes that the NRM is trying to achieve, you are wasting time on this bill of yours that is causing confusion among the people."[57] The Marriage and Divorce Bill of 2009 had been killed, for there were weightier matters that General Museveni wanted addressed with urgency, such as putting a stranglehold on same-sex relationships and introducing legislation to limit women's freedom, a move that was made to further build the politico-religious coalition that had emerged as a nodal point of support in the general's life presidency scheme.

II

Myth of a Ugandan Sexuality and Gender Identity

"Not all males are men and neither are all females women."[1]—S. Nannyonga-Tamusuza, Ugandan academic

There is a whole body of literature that attempts to cast homosexuality as a foreign import and intrinsically inauthentic to sub–Saharan Africa. It argues that Africa is home to a single hegemonic sexuality and binary gender identity. This despite the continent's vast geographical, cultural and religious diversity. All black Africans, according to the purveyors of this myth, are genetically hardwired for straightness and therefore inherently heterosexual. In Africa, men love women and women love men. Non-normative sexual relationships, the argument goes, are an abomination and incidental to un–African cultural influences. Debauched Europeans and Arabs are often accused of introducing the practice to culturally gullible Africans. Father Lokodo claimed that the "whites brought this [homosexuality] culture to Africa."[2] Janet Museveni, the influential wife of General Museveni, and generally believed to be the behind-the-scenes force driving Bahati's "Kill the Gays" bill, made the invidious claim that homosexuality was a foreign import to Uganda, which the youth were engaging in as a form of experimenting with the "new sex fashions."[3] She would further argue homosexuality was not only un–African but unnatural. She had arrived at this stunning discovery, she proclaimed, by a studious observation of an absence of homosexuality among cows.[4] The Reverend Michael Esakan Okwi, a leading COU theologian, had equally not observed homosexuality in other members of the animal kingdom—there were no gay cockroaches, proof enough that homosexuality was unnatural.[5]

General Museveni, on the other hand, provided conflicting opinions

24

on homosexuality. At some point, he admitted to the presence of homosexuality in pre-colonial Uganda when he said, "We used to have very few homosexuals traditionally. They were not persecuted but were not encouraged either because it was clear that is not how God arranged things to be."[6] On another occasion he claimed homosexuals in his native region of Ankole in southwest Uganda were "either ignored or speared and killed by their parents. They wouldn't just go and wed another man publicly."[7] As for the few Ugandans practicing homosexuality, the general asserted they were motivated by "mercenary reasons," selling their bodies to Western visitors. It is these "mercenary homosexuals" that he sought to punish. Indeed, General Museveni further alleged that homosexuality was a learned behavior and not an inherited orientation: "Can somebody be homosexual purely by nature without nurture? The answer is: 'No.' No study has shown that. Since nurture is the main cause of homosexuality, then society can do something about it to discourage the trends."[8] He also suggested that women become lesbians because of "sexual starvation when they fail to get married."[9] General Museveni's allegations about lesbianism harks to Oskar Baumann's nineteenth-century hypothesis on the genesis of homosexuality on the island of Zanzibar, which he attributed to boredom with heterosexual intercourse.[10]

The principal face of persecution of LGBT people in Uganda concurred with the general. David Bahati cited the work of Ugandan scientists who "proved beyond reasonable doubt that it's [homosexuality] not inborn, it is not genetically linked, it is nurtured; it can be learned and unlearned."[11] However, both Bahati and General Museveni were bending the truth. The Ministerial Scientific Committee on Homosexuality which consisted of 11 reputable Ugandan scientists and doctors was appointed by General Museveni in January 2014 to advise the government on whether homosexuality was genetic or an acquired behavior that could be cured. The team performed a review of the scientific literature, and presented their final report and conclusions in February 2014. The Ugandan experts concluded that there is "no definitive gene responsible for homosexuality" and that homosexuality was neither an abnormality nor a disease. Critically, the report noted that the "evolution and emergence of one's self identity as a 'homosexual—be it gay or lesbian' must be governed by nature and nurture."[12] The scientists also reminded General Museveni of the existence of homosexuality in pre-colonial Africa and dispelled the myth that homosexuality was brought to Africa by white colonizers. Stephen Langa of Family Life Network (FLN), whose obsession with homosexuality and pornography was outright irrational, preached that homosexuality was by choice and could therefore be corrected. To prove that, FLN paraded eight young men before journalists at a press conference at Kampala's Grand Imperial Hotel. The men, said to be former homosexuals, described homosexuality as "abnormal" and "anti–Christian" and suggested it could be abandoned at the drop of a hat.[13] At least one of the men would later courageously reaffirm his sexual orientation, emphasizing that he had always been gay and it was not out of choice.[14] Powerful Pentecostal pastors at the forefront of the anti–LGBT crusade would subsequently parade some of these very men at various press conferences, and even before legislators, as they sought to highlight the dangers of homosexuality and demonstrate that they had successfully "cured" gay men. The young gay men at FLN's press conference were probably coerced into offering their testimonies and condemning homosexuality. Intimidation and bribery is commonplace in Uganda and religious leaders are not beyond engaging in such strategies if it promotes their cause. For example, in 2009, a gay rights activist alleged that Pastor Ssempa had promised him $2,000 to switch sides and support the pastor's anti–LGBT platform.[15] Pastor Ssempa was among the vocal clerics that maintained homosexuality was an acquired behavior. He famously said that "discrimination on the basis of the color of my skin, which I cannot change, is not equal to my sexual preference, which I can change."[16] Another Pentecostal minister and a fanatical anti–LGBT campaigner, Pastor Solomon Male (pronounced Mal-ay), claimed that homosexuality was a learned behavior and his teachings had "helped very many people, especially youths ... to quit homosexuality."[17]

There is a relatively large body of rigorous studies that seriously challenge and repudiate past constructs of a hegemonic African sexuality.[18] Professor Desiree Lewis of the University of the Western Cape in South Africa has eloquently challenged this: "The notion of a single 'African sexuality' indicates erroneous generalisation and essentialising about the wide-ranging behaviours, intimacies, practices and relationships associated with sexuality in different parts of the continent."[19] And Sylvia Tamale emphatically razed the fallacy of the much-touted absence of homoeroticism in pre-colonial Africa: "Trends both in the present and past reveal that it is time for Africans to bury the tired myth that homosexuality is 'unAfrican.' ... Ironically, it is the dominant Judaeo-Christian and Arabic religions upon which most African anti-homosexuality proponents rely, that are foreign imports."[20] L.G.B.T people were an integral part of pre-colonial Ugandan communities. Homosexuality was not an orientation that the pre-colonial Ugandan society perceived as immoral or "unclean."

It was not uncommon for young men to have sex with other young men, and mutual masturbation took place, and still does, without fear of condemnation. As Epprecht has noted, "Same-sex relationships existed in African societies with a wide variety of motives, practices and emotions involved, including affection and fertility control."[21]

Most Ugandan anti–LGBT proponents of the "un–African" theory could barely marshal empirical historical or socio-cultural evidence to lend credence to their assertion. Challenged to explain why he believed homosexuality was a foreign import to Africa, Bahati only managed a lame broad-brush statement that homosexuality was "un–African because it is inconsistent with African values of procreation, of a belief in continuity of family and clan."[22] Pastor Ssempa was equally unhelpful and could not provide empirical justification beyond insisting that homosexuality is "un–African; it is against nature, it is against the Bible."[23] Perhaps the most serious attempt at providing evidence to support the un–African nature of homosexuality was advanced by James Ikuya, a top consigliere in General Museveni's ruling party, who alleged that "homosexuality has, hitherto, not been known nor practiced in our communities. There is even no word for it."[24] But Mr. Ikuya's argument is seriously flawed and at odds with facts, particularly a vast body of ethnological literature.

The statement that Ugandan languages have no word for homosexuality is outright erroneous. It is an argument that was frequently advanced by anti–LGBT proponents to justify their belief that homosexuality or even other gender identities had a foreign genesis. Indeed, a people's culture and way of life is expressed in their language. Therefore, the absence of a word for homosexuality in Ugandan languages would be the undeniable proof of the non-existence of same-sex sexual liaisons in precolonial Uganda. The Dutch journalist Aernout Zevenbergen interviewed the Reverend Dr. Alison Barfoot, an important advisor to the Archbishop of the COU.[25] The Rev. Barfoot's credentials as a vicious critic of homosexuality within the Anglican Communion churches were impeccable if not outright frightening.[26] The Rev. Barfoot arrived in Uganda in 2004 after her Kansas parish defected from the U.S. Episcopal Church over the ordination of gay bishops. According to Political Research Associates, a research group that studies groups that undermine social justice, Barfoot wields considerable leverage in "steering the Uganda Anglican Church toward an oppositional stance on homosexuality."[27] In the course of the interview with Mr. Zevenbergen, Barfoot spoke about a COU meeting on homosexuality during which the clergy in attendance were each challenged to come up with a word for homosexuality in their native Ugandan languages.

The aim of this curious exercise was to provide evidence that none of the indigenous Ugandan languages had a term for homosexuality, hence supporting the notion that same-sex relationships were un–African. But as Barfoot revealed, this elementary exercise concluded that "homosexuality is not imported from the West or is just an aberration of present-day life. Homosexuality is also Ugandan, and it is also of the past."[28] It is therefore instructive that the Rev. Barfoot, one of the most conservative members of the Uganda clergy, dismissed the carefully crafted narrative claiming homosexuality was un–African. There was undoubtedly a sentiment of shame and embarrassment among many in the anti–LGBT movement to acknowledge the existence of homosexuality and alternate genders in the pre-colonial Uganda society. This was especially true in a country that takes pride in its conservative Christian mores.

The premise that homosexuality is foreign because Ugandan or African languages do not have a word for it has its equivalence in a widespread colonial-era misconception about color blindness. Some British colonialists believed Ugandans were inherently blind to certain colors of the visual spectrum. In 1905, Cunningham dispelled this myth and explained its origins:

> It has been said that the Baganda [the people of Buganda] are to a certain extent colour-blind. Emphatically this is not so. The reason is not that their eyes are incapable of seeing a difference between green and blue, or between violet and pink; it is that they have *no words* in their language to apply to all colours. Some of the principal colours have names, but with the others they give you the name of a flower of the colour required. That is sufficient for their purposes, but it leads the inexperienced to suppose that they do not recognise such colours as green, violet, pink, or blue."[29]

Incidentally, the Baganda and other Ugandan tribes have names for colors. Most significantly, as noted by the Rev. Barfoot, pre-colonial Ugandan societies had a long tradition of same-sex erotic relationships, and there were words for homosexuality and alternate gender identities.

Cultural traditions from across the Ugandan regional and tribal landscape provides evidence of same-sex intimate relationships in pre-colonial Uganda. Some of the male-male "intimate" relationships were nominal and entered into as part of a purification or cleansing ritual that protected the living. In such cases the male-woman could be ritually married to a man without engaging in anal penetrative sex. Ritual marriage did not have to be consummated. It is a classic example of love without sex. Ritual marriage as practiced in pre-colonial Uganda can be equated to the mystical betrothal of Catholic nuns and sisters to Jesus Christ. In 1920,

Driberg, a British anthropologist, documented the peaceful co-existence of transgender male-to-female people in the Lango region of northern Uganda where

> a small class of men known as *Jo Apele*, referred to also as *Jo Aboich*, or the impotents. These men ... are considered as the afflicted of god (*jok abalogi*, god ruins them). They acknowledge a mortal father, but believe that a divine agency operated at their fertilization (*jok manywala*, it was god who begat me). Being impotent they have all the instincts and nature of women, and as such are recognized by men and women alike. They accordingly become women (*dano mulokere, mudoko dano*, a man who has been transformed, who has become a woman). They wear the characteristic facial and bodily ornaments of a woman, ... they wear their hair long, dressing it in ringlets like women's hair, and take women's names; they do all women's work, weed, sweep the house and courtyard, cook the food, fetch fuel and water; they observe women's clan taboos, and like women, are debarred from owning property or from following men's pursuits such as hunting; they even simulate menstruation and wear the leaves prescribed for women in their courses.... Being women, therefore, in all except the physical characteristics, they are treated as such, and live with a man as his wife without offending against Lango law. Sometimes, but rarely, property passes on the "marriage," and their co-wives welcome him as a woman.[30]

It is unlikely the transgender women among the Lango were impotent; it is just how pre-colonial society attempted to explain alternate genders. Driberg also noted that transgender women were numerous in the Teso and Karamoja regions of Uganda. Father Lokodo, who reveled in denouncing LGBT people, was a Karamoja native. His ancestors might have found his persecution of sexual minorities at odds with time-honored cultural norms among his own people. Further, Jeremy Lawrance, an ethnographer and British colonial administration officer, noted that there were numerous "hermaphrodites" in Teso with the "the instincts of women and become women to all intents and purposes; their voices are feminine and their manner of walking and of speech is feminine. They shave their heads like a woman and wear women's ornaments and clothing. They do women's work and take women's names."[31] Jeremy Lawrance's fluency of the language of the Teso people placed him in a unique position to better understand and appreciate the Teso society and its culture more than his European peers.

Among the Baganda of southern and central Uganda, lesbianism is referred to as "*kasaawe*" and male homosexuality is known as "*bisiyaga*." The expression "*okulya e'bisiyaga*" refers to the act of male-to-male sexual intercourse.[32] *Ogung* is a term that the Acholi of northern Uganda have used for centuries to describe homosexual intercourse. In the pre-colonial Ankole kingdom, homosexuality was accepted and widely practiced. Professor Musa Mushanga, a respected academic, diplomat and adviser to

General Museveni, described the prevalence of male homosexuality among peoples of Mr. Museveni's ethnic group—the pastoral Bahima, a subgroup of the Ankole people of southwestern Uganda.[33] The Bahima are closely related to the Tutsi of Rwanda, and they share a number of customs and traditions. In the pre-colonial Tutsi society, young men who were away from home at warrior camps engaged in homosexuality, and some of these relationships lasted into adulthood.[34] It is perhaps with this in mind that General Museveni grudgingly conceded to CNN's Christiane Amanpour in a 2012 interview that before Uganda "came in touch with Europeans, we had some few homosexuals. I want to inform the world that those homosexuals were not killed as some people are claiming. They were not persecuted and they were not discriminated against."[35] General Museveni had also admitted as much in a BBC interview, emphasizing that homosexuality was not a new phenomenon in Africa, and that Africans "do not go around trying to promote it."[36] Importantly, General Museveni has admitted that his native Ankole language has a word for homosexuals—*ebitiingwa*.

There is no better place that demonstrates the flourishing of homosexuality in the pre-colonial Uganda society than the Buganda kingdom—one of the largest kingdoms in pre-colonial Uganda. The king of Buganda (kabaka) was undoubtedly the most powerful ruler in the Great Lakes region of East Africa. In April 1875, the British explorer Henry Stanley met Kabaka Mutesa I, the Buganda king. Stanley was effusive in his description of the kabaka, calling him the "foremost person of Equatorial Africa."[37] The kabaka was revered and feared in equal measure. He presided over an impressive court, which teemed with pageboys and slaves, nobles and chiefs, court officials and diviners. The king's subjects adhered to strict moral stipulations. For example, obscenity and the candid discussion of sexual matters in the public space were not permitted except under certain conditions, such as the ritual celebration of the birth of twins—"dancing the twins." "Dancing the twins" is a festive ritual characterized by frenzied dancing, invocation of mock sexual acts and a shockingly liberal usage of profanely obscene language. Men are at liberty to dance with other men and simulate male-male sexual intercourse. Elite and educated Ugandan Christians tend to deny the existence of rituals such as these or choose to cast them as heathen and immoral.[38]

Unlike their subjects, the kabaka and his aristocratic chiefs were not subjected to strict standards of moral conduct. They reserved the right to indulge in sexually explicit profanities and were at liberty to engage in freewheeling sexual licentiousness. When Kabaka Mutesa took a bath, a young male page was on hand to scrub and massage his back.[39] Women were prohibited in the presence of a bathing kabaka. This is a significant observation when framing the discussion about same-sex erotic relationships in Uganda. It was royal etiquette to segregate women from men. With the women absent in many of the palatial spaces, the men took the liberty to indulge in palace eroticism. And the institution of "palace pageboys" was central to the practice. The palace pageboys were sons of Buganda's aristocrats or young slaves captured in raids on neighboring tribes. It was a time-honored Buganda kingdom custom for important families to send a son to the king's palace, to serve the sovereign in the capacity of a "pageboy." In return, the families received generous favors from the king, and this could at times include the appointment of a pageboy, when he became of age, to an important chieftaincy. Most importantly Buganda kingdom royal etiquette required the lads to be virgins. There were hundreds of pageboys that roamed the king's palace in the hope the kabaka would recognize them and invite them into the intimacy of his inner circle. It is true the king did not get to know all the boys. However, there were some that he was attracted to, favoring and elevating them to an enviable station. These were the boys the king chose for sexual companionship.

Pederasty was common among men holding high office in the Buganda kingdom and was part of everyday life.[40] The practice was not viewed as dishonorable or something to be ashamed of. By apprenticing their sons to serve as pageboys to holders of high office, the families must have understood their sons would potentially have sex with their master. Same-sex sexual liaisons were an integral part of sexual articulation and expression. Indeed, *Quot hominess, tot sentententiate*—every culture has its beliefs. Pre-colonial Buganda kingdom had an uncanny parallel with contemporary Afghanistan where it is estimated that as many as 50 percent of the men in some ethnic regions engage in pederasty.[41] In April 2010 PBS's *Frontline* aired a documentary on Afghanistan's *bacha bazi* culture.[42] The *bacha bazi* (also known as *bacha bereesh*) are usually attractive boys who dress in women's clothing and wear female makeup and hairstyles. They perform dances for a mostly male audience and engage in sex with their older male patrons. Even powerful *mujahedeen* warlords have kept *bacha bazi* as their sex slaves. In the PBS documentary, a senior *mujahedeen* commander of the Northern Alliance confessed to having kept a boy lover because "every commander had one." It is surprising that pederasty would flourish in a religiously devout community. Understanding a people's traditions and their interpretation of the belief system frames the context within which such practices thrive. Chris Mondloch, writing in the *Foreign Policy* magazine, noted that "Pashtun social norms dictate that *bacha bazi* is not un–Islamic or homosexual at all—if the man does not love the boy, the sexual act is not reprehensible, and is far more ethical than defiling a woman."[43]

The king of Buganda's homoerotic relationships with his pageboys served an important cultural and political purpose. His subjects addressed him as "my husband—or our husband," or even more reverently as "My Lord and Husband." When males referred to the king as "husband" they in effect gave up their masculinity, acknowledging the king's dominance and control over their bodies and lives. In the traditional Buganda setting, women must fall upon their knees in supplication when greeting or talking to a man. However, when appearing before the king, all people, irrespective of gender, had to go on their knees in subordination to the sovereign's authority. Within the perimeter of the king's palace there was only "one man"—the king. All others were perceived and treated as the king's wives. Persons of peasant stock were either female-women or male-women irrespective of their gender or sexuality.[44] This was critical in projecting the masculine vitality and virility of the king to all his subjects who were conditioned by tradition to passively accept his dominance and subjugation, which in turn cultivated unquestioning obedience. This cultural emasculation of male subjects defined and strengthened the power relationship between the ruler and the ruled and constituted an essential ideological and political vehicle through which subjects could be controlled. Kabaka Mutesa I's harem boasted of 87 wives in addition to hundreds of concubines and pageboys.

When Kabaka Mutesa I died in 1884 he was succeeded by his 17-year-old son, Kabaka Mwanga. In keeping with royal Buganda tradition, Mwanga kept a harem of pageboys as well. He engaged in sexual intercourse with some of the boys. However, Mwanga's favorite among the pageboys was the "very pretty" Mwafu, the son of the kingdom's *katikkiro* or prime minister.[45] Some nineteenth century accounts of Mwanga's court describe it as a place of "revolting orgies."[46] Most contemporary Ugandans are uncomfortable discussing both Mwanga's or Mutesa's same-sex liaisons. They focus more on the events of 1886, when Mwanga committed 45 pageboys to a harrowing death. All the pageboys were recent converts to Christianity, which first arrived in Uganda about a decade earlier. Christian missionaries found many aspects of everyday life as "savage" and irreconcilable with Christian teaching and belief. It has been suggested Mwanga was forced to order the execution of the pageboys because of their refusal to submit to his sexual advances, citing the incompatibility of homosexuality with their new Christian faith. Even the king's favorite pageboy, Mwafu, rebuffed his advances.[47] Kenneth Hamilton noted that "Mwanga's rage is attributed to the fact that he saw the refusal of sex [by the pageboys] as associated with the 'anti-sodomy' teachings and power of the Christian missionaries. Christian missionaries, for their part, were 'alarmed by the well known images of sodomy' and had 'felt compelled' to sanction Mwanga."[48] Mwanga had the pageboys killed. Many of them were burned on the pyre at Namugongo, a neighborhood on the outskirts of Kampala. In executing the Christian converts, Mwanga was following in the footsteps of his father. Kabaka Mutesa I killed hundreds of Muslims for calling him a "kaffir" and challenging his authority. Over 70 converts to Islam were burned on the pyre in Namugongo—the very site where Kabaka Mwanga would execute the Christian pageboys.[49]

Undoubtedly, some of the pageboys' defiance of Kabaka Mwanga's sexual advances contributed to the king's rage. But it was unlikely to be the overriding consideration in ordering their execution. Muslim and Christian converts had displayed increasing intransigence, refusing to submit to and recognize their king's temporal and spiritual powers. Both Mutesa I and Mwanga could not sit idly by and watch the unraveling of deep-rooted customs that underpinned the power relationship between the sovereign and his subjects. Faced with an open challenge to the privileges of absolute authority the kings responded as they knew best—harsh punishment for the dissenters, including burning at the stake. Sadly, this display of ruthlessness to quell political dissent is still prevalent in contemporary Uganda, and has played out severally during General Museveni's decades long reign. Mutesa I and his son Mwanga did not invent the art of burning dissenters at the stake. The medieval Christian church excelled in the practice—heretics, Knights Templars, Joan of Arc, and countless others, were burned at the stake.

By 1844, Muslim traders had made their way from the East African coast to the king of Buganda's court. These traders not only bartered guns and clothes for slaves and ivory, but they also taught the tenets of Islam to the indigenous people, thus making Islam the first non-indigenous religion in Uganda. Indeed, Kabaka Mutesa I and his court embraced Islam. The kabaka built a large mosque in his capital and ordered his subjects to strictly observe Islamic rites. In 1875, Kabaka Mutesa I declared Islam as Buganda's state religion and he also served as the country's first Mufti.[50] A later successor, Kabaka Nuhu Kalema, who reigned from 1888 to 1889, would swear allegiance to the Islamic code of conduct. Nuhu Kalema also championed the establishment of a strict Islamic theocracy and introduced forced conversions to Islam.[51] The Islamic political and military bloc, which had propelled him to the kingship, preached jihad against non–Muslims.

When Henry Stanley, a zealous Christian, arrived at Kabaka Mutesa's court in 1875 for what became a 12-day visit, he saw the potential of Christianity to "undermine" Islam, a religion that had taken firm root across the kingdom of Buganda.[52] Stanley was also convinced that it was through Kabaka Mutesa I, who showed eagerness to abandon Islam and learn basic tenets of Christianity, that the Central African region could be Christianized and civilized. Accordingly, Stanley dispatched a letter that was published in London's *Daily Telegraph*, appealing to Christian missionaries of the "white race" to come and convert the people of Uganda, a land that distinguished itself in "all the pagan world" as a "promising field for a [Christian] mission" and where the "field and harvest" were "ripe for the sickle of civilization."[53] But Mutesa's interest in Christianity—or any other foreign religion for that matter—might have been motivated more by a desire to acquire arms and forge new alliances in his perpetual attempt to fight and subdue his enemies, particularly the neighboring powerful kingdom of Bunyoro. That Mutesa was using Christianity as the pretense to acquire military advantage over his political foes is evident in his 1876 correspondence to General Charles Gordon, better known as Pasha Gordon. General Gordon was an English military commander who had distinguished himself with valor during the Crimean War and had commanded a 3,500-man force of peasant Chinese that suppressed the Taiping Rebellion. After his successful expedition to China, Gordon was named Governor-General of the province of Equatoria in Sudan. Impatient that Stanley's Christian missionaries were yet to arrive in his kingdom, Mutesa I, a king whose pederasty was later to incense moralistic Western Christian missionaries, beseeched Pasha Gordon, a man generally believed to have struggled with unresolved homosexual inclinations, to help, telling him he wished to be a "friend of white men" and could he send "a priest who will show me the way of God" and also dispatch "excellent guns and good cannons."[54]

The first Christian missionaries to arrive in June 1877 were members of the Anglican Church Mission Society (CMS). They were followed in 1879 by Catholic missionaries. The Christian missionaries were coming to a kingdom with a significant Islamic footprint. There was bound to be hostility between the two camps. Thus, the late nineteenth century plunged Uganda in the middle of the rivalry between Christian and Muslim missionaries as they battled to win over Ugandan souls. Each camp tried to boost their religious credentials as the bona fide representatives of God/Allah through accusations, counter-accusations and scandalous innuendos directed at the other religion. In 1889 the intolerance and hatred between Muslims and Christians came to a head and a bloody religious war erupted. The Muslim forces thoroughly beat the Christians, expelling them out of Buganda kingdom. In 1890, the defeated force of Christians and traditionalists reorganized and launched a bold counter-attack. This time around the Muslim forces were routed. This effectively brought an end to Islamic dominance in Uganda. It is against this backdrop of religious rivalry and suspicion that Christian missionaries maligned and pilloried Islam, portraying Muslims as practitioners of immoral behavior, including homosexuality.

From the very beginning, Christian missionaries and colonial administrators embarked on a systematic campaign to dismantle the indigenous system of beliefs and customs that had been revered for centuries. Munyaradzi has noted that "missionaries had to castigate African thought and moral values in order for their Western values to gain acceptance and prominence over the local ones. Anything perceived African, from medicine to philosophical thought, religion to moral thought, ... were all castigated while everything perceived Western was embraced, cherished and preached as civilized and the best of all values."[55] The long-held custom of homosexuality as practiced within the king's palace and within the enclosures of many important chiefs of Buganda kingdom particularly incensed the Christian missionaries. It would be erroneous to suppose that homosexuality was limited to the centers of authority in Buganda—the king's palace and the royal enclosures of his chiefs. Homosexual activity occurred in rather ordinary public spaces. In a review of the early history of the Catholic Church in Uganda, Marinus Rooijackers noted that the pioneering priests, after three years of hard work winning African souls, decided to end their evangelizing mission and leave the country. The reason for this difficult decision was said to have centered around the fact that in the summer of 1882 the priests had noticed that some of the boys enrolled in catechism classes engaged in casual homosexual activity.[56] There is no evidence that these boys had been "initiated" into homosexuality by foreigners. In fact, homosexuality was commonplace in settings where young men came together for long periods of time as happens today in Uganda's single-sex boarding schools.[57]

The Christian missionaries demanded that the king and his people abandon age-old "heathen" customs. They promised the wrath of the gods would befall practitioners of what they saw as savage traditions, practices that were in conflict to the moral yardstick based on European Victorian values and Christian morality. The Muslim Arabs, on the other hand, "did not violently oppose Baganda customs and religious practices ... the customs the Christian missionaries found intolerable, such as polygamy, homosexuality ... were ... encouraged and practiced by the Arabs themselves."[58] Thus, it was convenient to create a narrative of King Mutesa I, who had been sympathetic to Islam, as a heathen king that engaged in the "evil" practice of homosexuality, which was introduced by Muslim Arabs. And when Mutesa I became ill with what the missionaries diagnosed as "chronic gonorrhea" purportedly acquired because of his homosexuality, the king's illness fit well into their proselytizing agenda. The missionaries expertly played to the people's fears and anxiety of gonorrhea, which had recently been introduced in the country because of increased trade with the outside world. Gonorrhea was used as a cudgel to discourage homosexuality and promote Christian morality. What the missionaries were saying came to this: you engage in homosexuality, you acquire gonorrhea and die a painful death like your king. As Megan Vaughan notes, the early English missionaries in Uganda saw a "connection between ... essential sinfulness [of Ugandans] and [venereal] disease."[59] Essential sinfulness in this context references sexual immorality—sexually transmitted diseases (syphilis was of particular concern), polygyny, and homosexuality. None lends more clarity to this belief of the liberating power of religion over sexually transmitted diseases than Albert Cook (1870–1951), an English medical missionary sent to Uganda by the CMS in 1897. Cook is credited for laying the foundation of western medicine practice in Uganda and his medical and social accomplishments are singularly phenomenal. In a 1908 correspondence to the prestigious British medical journal *The Lancet*, Cook laid out his case from a missionary perspective asserting that "Christianity from the beginning has acted as a deterring and restraining force, and is indeed, when intelligently accepted, the only true prophylaxis to this terrible scourge [of syphilis and other sexually transmitted diseases]."[60] Meanwhile, Bishop Albert Tucker of the Anglican Church in Uganda was convinced that sexually transmitted diseases threatened to wipe out an entire population of Ugandans and advocated the introduction of Christian morality to salvage Ugandans. The Rev. Henry Weatherhead of the CMS bemoaned the perceived pervasiveness of immorality as "the sin of Africa" and argued that before the advent of Christianity there "was practically no such thing as purity of thought or heart or life at all."[61] The Rev. Weatherhead was an important educator. He founded the prestigious

King's College, Budo, one of the first schools of higher learning in Uganda. His legacy in shaping Christian moral thought and value is still evident today in a succession of students that have passed through King's College, Budo, and gone on to hold positions of influence in both the public and private sector.

With the advent of Christianity and enacting of colonial laws that criminalized "sodomy" came the denial or even silence about homosexuality in Ugandan communities. Christian missionaries labeled homosexuality as evil and primitive, and evoked the image of God's wrath destroying Sodom and Gomorrah. The imagery of brimstone and fire raining upon a people because of immoral acts that offended a vengeful god was so powerful that many who heard it could not resist to repent, turn away from their traditional beliefs and customs, and embrace Christianity to gain favor before god and the European missionaries, and be saved. This was certainly the case with one of Uganda's famous early Christians and influential chief, Ham Mukasa. In his account of his conversion, Ham Mukasa credited a Salemani Kibanda for teaching him and other pageboys about the destruction of Sodom and Gomorrah. It is this particular teaching that appeared to put fear into his heart, leading him to desert the customary way of life and embrace the Anglican faith during the reign of Kabaka Mwanga II. Ham Mukasa is also an important figure in the Ugandan gay debate. He provided the first written account by a Ugandan alleging that Kabaka Mwanga was introduced to homosexuality by the Arabs at the king's court. Mukasa was an affable and eloquent man, trusted by the Christian missionaries and British colonial administrators. He was the exemplary loyal colonial student that the Europeans relied on to reach out to the people of Buganda to stamp out evil and primitive indigenous cultures, traditions perceived as incompatible with Christian and Victorian moral values. Homosexual relationships were characterized as "heathen" and dumped in the same category as cannibalism, sorcery, polygyny and other such practices that were inconsistent with not only Christian teachings but with the white world's definition and interpretation of civilization. On entering the service of the king as a page, Ham Mukasa claimed to have found "the king's court full of the *vilest customs*, introduced by Arabs and Turks (the people who came from Egypt). I was much afraid, for my parents had told me not to agree to such things; for they told me that if I did such things I should die at once. But in spite of this I was compelled to join with the rest."[62]

Ham Mukasa was by all accounts a candid man. He is the first Ugandan to openly admit engaging in same-sex eroticism. It would be almost a century later that David Kato, an LGBT activist who was brutally murdered in the wake of Bahati's "Kill the Gays" bill, would publicly identify himself as gay, and thus become the first openly gay Ugandan in the postcolonial era. It is remarkable that Ham Mukasa admitted to homosexuality. There are perhaps two main factors that gave him the courage to confess to engaging in the "vile custom" of his people. At the time of the publication of Ham Mukasa's account, Uganda was a place where century-old tribal traditions and customs still held sway. As previously noted, homosexuality was an acceptable practice among aristocratic chiefs. Therefore, an admission of homosexuality was unlikely to raise eyebrows or be condemned by the local Baganda. Christian missionaries and English administrators held Mukasa in high esteem, and in return he was loyal to them. To the Christian missionaries Mukasa's confession and repentance showcased the success of their evangelizing efforts. The natives were abandoning "amoral savage" practices, repenting their sins, and heeding the call to embrace Christian enlightenment.[63] What is certain about Mukasa's confession is that his parents were aware of homosexual practice at the king's court, further evidence that this was an accepted and expected behavior. As to homosexuality being introduced by "Arabs and Turks," that is a dishonest account, perhaps introduced to further malign Arabs and Islam. In fact, Ham Mukasa alluded to what appears to have been homosexuality in his father's household, which from all known historical accounts did not have "Arabs and Turks" to "teach" homosexuality to impressionable boys and men. Mukasa narrates that his father's home "had a large number of boys that were very evil lads" who got "drunk by smoking Indian hemp" and "persuaded me to smoke with them, and then they tried to teach me *other sins.* Had I not left the household I am sure I should have learnt the habits of those lads and I should have been just like them." It should be noted that Ham Mukasa used the terms "vilest customs" and "other sins" as euphemisms for male-male sex. This is understandable given that his narration comes to us through his collaboration with Anglican priests, notably Archdeacon Walker and the Reverend Joseph Mullins. These men, given their Victorian and Christian values, would refer to male-male sex in terms that did not offend their audience's moral sensibilities.

It is hardly credible that Islamic traders, strangers in the kingdom of Buganda, would teach the powerful king of Buganda about male-male sex as though it was a religion. And why is it that these same Arabs, who had traversed a large swath of land as they journeyed from the East African coast to the interior of Buganda, would not teach homosexuality to the chiefs and kings of the territories through which they traveled and traded? What was so peculiar about Kabaka Mutesa I or Kabaka Mwanga II that rendered them vulnerable to so-called Arab teachings of homosexuality? Both men were powerful autocrats, strong-willed, highly intelligent and fervent defenders of indigenous Buganda traditions and customs. They demanded and expected total subordination and submission to their will. Given this, it is improbable the Buganda kings would entertain receiving sex instructions from foreign visitors.

The repudiation of homosexuality in sub–Saharan Africa would set Africans apart from the rest of humanity. Indeed, this myth of a distinct and singular African sexual culture has over the years found favor among some, forming the basis of a repugnant and overtly racist stereotype of Africans and their sexuality. As Marc Epprecht, a Canadian academic and winner of the Desmond Tutu Award for Outstanding Contributions to the Study of Sexuality in Africa, has explained, "In colonial times, Africans' supposed stunted or brutish sexuality was thought to oppress and degrade women, engender laziness and stultify intellectual growth in men, threaten public health safety, and impoverish culture and the arts (no love or higher emotions, just lust and steely transactions)."[64] To some, that supposedly distinct biological make-up, including sexuality, explains many things about Africans as a people. Frankly, much of it is unflatteringly racist.

Murray and Roscoe trace the sexualization of "primitive" Africans to Edward Gibbon's 1781 *History of the Decline and Fall of the Roman Empire*, where in spite of Europeans having much knowledge about sub–Saharan Africa, he expressed his belief and hope that "negroes, in their own country" were exempt from homosexuality.[65] Further, Murray and Roscoe observed that the notion of absence of homosexuality was given credence by the nineteenth-century British Orientalist and explorer Sir Richard Burton. Burton is credited with introducing the dubious hypothesis of a "Sotadic Zone," which posited that homosexuality resulted from a confluence of climate, geography and race. Within the boundaries of the Sotadic Zone homosexuality was supposedly "popular" and "endemic." Sub-Saharan Africa was outside the limits of Burton's zone. He therefore concluded that the "negro race is mostly untainted by sodomy."[66] Burton is also famed for ridiculing Somali people for their belief that mosquitoes transmitted malaria.[67]

In more recent times the likes of Phillipe Rushton, a Canadian social science academic, analyzed the behavioral differences between his categorization of the world's three major racial groups—Orientals, Blacks and Whites. He asserted that there were "important race differences in brain size, hormone levels, even bone and tooth development, as well as sexual behavior, aggression, and crime," claiming that "the threeway pattern in which the races differ—Orientals at one end, Blacks at the other, and Whites in between—is true all around the world."[68] Rushton concluded by evoking the r-K Life History Theory explaining that "every species of plant or animal can be placed on the r-K scale. The r end of the scale means having more offspring, maturing earlier, having smaller brains and providing less parental care. The K end of the scale means having fewer offspring, maturing later, having larger brains, and providing more parental care. Humans are the most K species of all. Among humans, Orientals are the most K, Blacks the most r, and Whites fall in between."[69]

Most Africans would probably be appalled and offended by this simplistic and overtly racist theory that suggests Africans have an inherently distinct and problematic sexual culture. The dubious assertion, articulated by several Ugandan politicians and religious clerics, that Africans enjoy a biologically-determined single hegemonic sexuality is an extension of racist and misinformed theories on sexuality. At its core, the single hegemonic sexuality tenet aligns with those that have held that Africans are entirely hetero-normative because their behavior and ways of life are closer to primitive instincts. As Wayne Dynes noted, European conquerors of Africa "often held that 'sodomy' is a vice of advanced, even decadent civilizations. The Africans, being innocent 'children of nature' must be exempt from such corruption."[70] In fact, such theories are as dangerous as narratives that have been constructed over the centuries to portray black people as markedly different from the rest of humanity. Hence, in *An Universal History from the Earliest Account of Time to the Present (1736–1768)* Africans are said to be distinguished by being, "lazy, treacherous, thievish, hot, and addicted to all kinds of lusts, and most ready to promote them in others, as pimps, panders, incestuous, brutish, and savage.... It is hardly possible to find in any African any quality but what is of a bad kind: they are inhuman, drunkards, deceitful, extremely covetous, and perfidious to the highest degree."[71] Further, the *Universal History (1736–1768)* states that "St Austin [Augustine of Hippo], who was a native of that country [Africa], scruples not to confess, that it is as impossible to be an African and not lascivious, as it is to be born in Africa and not be an African." John Leo the African (Al-Hassan Ibn Mohammed Al-Wezaz, 1495–1552), a Moor of Andalusian descent and considered one of the leading experts on all matters African during his time, waxed lyrical about African sexual exceptionalism. He asserted that black people were more prone to "venerie" than any other race. William Smith, an eighteenth

century English traveler to West Africa, possibly projecting his sexual fan-
tasies about African women's purported lasciviousness and inherent sexual
aggressiveness, alleged that they

> miss no opportunity [for sex] and are continually contriving stratagems how to gain
> a Lover. If they meet with a Man they immediately strip his lower Parts, and throw
> themselves upon him, protesting that if he will not gratify their Desires, they will
> accuse him to their Husbands, as Joseph's Mistress did to Pharaoh.... If they can
> come to the Place the Man sleeps in, they lay themselves softly down by him, soon
> wake him, and use all their little Arts to move the darling Passion, and if he prove
> refractory they assure him, they will make such a Noise as shall occasion their being
> taken together; after which his Death will be inevitable."[72]

Bahati and his fellow anti–LGBT crusaders in Uganda cannot in good
conscience take exception to the racist notion of a problematic African
sexuality that has been championed by the likes of Rushton. The perception that Africans cannot be homosexuals or be of a gender other than
the binary male/female because of their inherent nature is at least as harm-
ful as the stereotypes around African sexualities peddled for centuries.

It is undeniable that Christianity in Uganda has a closely intertwined
and multilayered relationship with homosexuality, and the argument can
be made that homosexuality was the seed from which sprung the modern-
day Uganda Christian church. Kabaka Mutesa I, who engaged in same-
sex intercourse, had the presence of mind to appeal to both Stanley and
Pasha Gordon (who was probably gay) to send Christian missionaries to
Uganda. Ugandan Christian churches at the center of the anti-gay movement choose to be oblivious of the fact that some of the early devout
Christians, the pageboys at Mwanga II's court, probably had sex with the
king or with fellow pageboys. Today the 45 Christian pageboys (23 Protes-
tants and 22 Catholics) killed at Kabaka Mwanga's orders are best known
around the world as the Uganda Martyrs. They are commemorated every
third of June, and celebrated as the country's forefathers in the Christian
faith. Pope Paul VI canonized the 22 Catholic martyrs on October 18,
1964. Louis Massignon, a gay French priest in the Eastern Melkite Church,
was one of the leading voices that lobbied for the canonization of the forefathers of the Catholic faith in Uganda.[73] Among most Ugandans, there is
shame, embarrassment and a conscious effort to avoid questioning the
teachings of colonial missionaries that portrayed African tribal beliefs and
practices, including homosexuality, as savage, primitive and ungodly. Missionaries thus created and molded African sexuality to fit a Christian
norm. Equally, as Denis Altman has pointed out, the "strong hostility from
some African political and religious leaders towards homosexuality as a

'western import' is an example of psychoanalytic displacement, whereby anxieties about sexuality are redirected to continuing resentment against colonialism and the subordinate position of Africa within the global economy."[74] In a way, the denial of homosexuality in Uganda is a defensive response, to place as much distance between the contemporary Ugandan and his pre-colonial ancestors' expressions of sexuality and accommodation of diverse gender. Christianity and Western moral values created the environment for the prevailing climate of homophobia in General Museveni's Uganda.

III

Legislating and Policing Morality Over the Years

"I am totally against loose living by some women in Uganda.... I have already banned the mini-skirt and other sexy dresses. The next step will be to round up all town women and take them to camps in rural areas..."[1]—General Idi Amin, President of Uganda (1971–1979)

Uganda has never lacked a colorful array of self-styled arbiters of public morality, hell-bent on keeping the populace on a strict moral leash. There is no commonly accepted standard of public morality in Uganda. But that has not deterred the political leadership from defining behavior that constitutes immorality. Issues around regulating public morality have been a fixture in Uganda's political evolution, and in fact predate both General Idi Amin Dada and General Yoweri Museveni, two Ugandan military rulers who will no doubt be remembered in the annals of history for their unrelenting pursuit to legislate and police morality as a political strategy to deflect the populace from their domestic failures and administrative ineptitude.

The country has a history and pattern of elevating ordinary everyday activities and behaviors to a status of objectionable immorality and therefore requiring legislation. For example, Uganda's British colonial masters and Christian missionaries were intolerant of traditional forms of dancing that had for centuries entertained the kings of Buganda and their subjects. They found the combination of rapid gyrations of the waist and sensual thrusting of the hips as an objectionable display of crude salaciousness if not an outright manifestation of paganism. They promptly banned some traditional dances.[2] Decades later, in an ironic twist, the prime minister of Buganda (*katikkiro*), Paulo Neil Kavuma, outlawed "Western" dancing in bars and nightclubs. He alleged that "Western" dances promoted promiscuity. Men and women clinging tightly to each other in the name of "Western" dancing smacked of sexual lasciviousness, which offended the sensibilities of traditionalists. That was in the early 1950s when Kampala's nightlife was filled with youthful Ugandans dancing to the rumba and Afro-Cuban sounds. Responding to General Museveni's government ban of the miniskirt as part of the anti-pornography legislation, an exasperated reader writing in Uganda's *Daily Monitor* newspaper drew parallels with *katikkiro* Kavuma's 1952 ban of western music by observing[3]:

> In his 1955 book, Inside Africa, John Gunther narrates an account of the Katikkiro outlawing "Western" dancing in bars and nightclubs. He argued these venues had become haunts of vice, with husbands deserting their wives in droves in favour of prostitutes skilled in the intricacies of Western dancing. A firebrand editor called the Katikkiro a "fool" for this ridiculous law. The editor was arrested for slander, and sentenced to 18 months' imprisonment. A British judge let him out on bail but the Lukiko [Buganda kingdom's Parliament] endorsed the Katikkiro's view and the ban on Western dancing confirmed. The student journal at Budo called the law a fallacy of the greatest order, and observed of the Lukiko: "Instead of thinking of ways to develop the country, they engage themselves in political manoeuvres in order that they may be enabled to stay in office for a longer time. After throwing the editor of the Uganda Post [Jolly Joe Kiwanuka] into prison on political grounds, the.... Katikkiro introduced a Bill banning ballroom dancing. The Lukiko, in a state of frenzy coupled with fear to oppose the Bill on the part of the chiefs, lest they should lose their posts, passed the Bill. Incidentally, the Lukiko failed to say which was Western dancing. It seems we can still carry on with the samba, rumba and konga!" Over half a century later, the mini dress is banned. Some things in Uganda politics never change.

It is important here to observe a few things from the above letter, which draws attention to a 1950s episode to pass legislation aimed at curtailing and controlling the social space for political expediency. In the 1950s, urban dwellers, a sizeable segment of whom were beneficiaries of missionary education and also politically conscious, were agitating for Uganda's independence from Britain. It is this group that had assimilated Western tastes and patronized clubs like Kampala's Top Life Nightclub or Topaz. At the same time, the urban population was impatient and disillusioned with the political status quo, which was chiefly represented by the traditionalists in the Buganda kingdom. They agitated for independence from Britain and felt that the inept and corrupt *katikkiro's* government, supported by powerful traditional chiefs, could not be counted on to deliver on the promise of independence. Among those leading the charge against the Buganda prime minister was Joseph W. Kiwanuka, aka Jolly Joe. Jolly Joe, a mercurial and flamboyant figure, was the editor of the *Uganda Post*, an independent local newspaper that reveled in taking swipes at the prime minister's government, accusing it of gross incompetence and corruption. In the face of increasing adversity and criticism to his government, the *katikkiro* had to find ways to rally support for his government, particularly among the traditional chiefs, an important group that exerted disproportionate political authority and control over a large illiterate rural population. The *katikkiro*, just like General Museveni with his anti-gay or anti-pornography legislation six decades later, banned Western dancing for political expediency—to bring an independent-minded and restless urban population to heel through rallying the support of traditional chiefs and their rural constituencies, recasting the *katikkiro* as a powerful leader fighting against those forces that were eroding the moral fabric of society. Therefore, the ban was a convenient subterfuge to deflect general discontent with the government of the day and take the bite out of the political threat posed by an urban population clamoring for independence and a departure from the old way of life.

When the ban on Western dancing was announced, Jolly Joe's paper, *Uganda Post*, roundly condemned the prime minister. The prime minister interpreted the paper's criticism of his policy to ban Western dance as intransigence. He used the criticism to his advantage, accusing his nemesis, Jolly Joe, of being disloyal and disrespectful of the king of Buganda. The prime minister was supposed to act in the best interest of the king. Jolly Joe was promptly imprisoned. But not for long. Out of jail, he took the matter to the courts, which ruled the ban illegal. With the court's decision, the urban population had registered a rare victory over the old guard, the traditionalists epitomized by Paulo Kavuma, the prime minister of Buganda. There was an outburst of celebratory euphoria. Fred Masagazi, one of the country's top musicians of the 1950s and '60s, penned a song "*Kiwanuka ne dansi*—Kiwanuka and the dance." It was an accolade to Jolly Joe's victory over a zealously prudish *katikkiro* who had sought to use morality for political gain. Sadly, Jolly Joe Kiwanuka, a polemical politician and astute businessman, was murdered by Idi Amin's dreaded secret police in December 1973.

The singling out of groups or sub-groups as part of social engineering while striking a populist tone continued to be employed as a strategy in post-independence Uganda. General Idi Amin excelled at the practice. In January 1971, Idi Amin came to power after leading a successful military coup against the government of Dr. Milton Obote. By 1972, Idi Amin's repressive and authoritarian style of governance, including his foreign policy, was drawing much domestic and international criticism. After expelling Israelis, Ugandans of Asian descent, and the British from the country in 1972 following accusations ranging from economic sabotage to spying, Amin identified a new class that could be used as the whipping boy for his dysfunctional government. The urban woman was an easy prey for Idi Amin. His regime created an environment where terrorism against women flourished. Anti-women commentary ranged from the condescending to outright criminalization of women. Misogynist pronouncements were spiced with comedy, and the results were, more often than not, tragic. Idi Amin, who ruled Uganda by a combination of decree and deployment of terror and coercive tactics, went on to introduce several morality legislations that chiefly curtailed the rights of women.

About a year and a half into his presidency Idi Amin was the guest of honor at a graduation ceremony for police cadets. It was during that gathering that Amin surprised his audience—he was given to making major policy announcements in a chaotic and erratic manner. He declared that he wanted to inform the "people of Uganda that they should not be brainwashed by imperialists and be made to think that our women should wear mini-skirts."[4] Amin was making the point that miniskirts were immoral and incompatible with an African cultural authenticity that he was attempting to create. The populace braced for the possible banning of the miniskirt, which was popular especially among urban women. The country had not shielded itself from the buffeting winds of the 1960s counterculture, which changed the way women viewed and related with their bodies. The Single Girl phenomenon in the West, with its emphasis on women's economic, social and emotional self-sufficiency, had made ripples in Uganda. This in itself was a threat to the masculine power structure and traditional hierarchical order. To the urban Ugandan woman, covering the knees was so countryside and longer skirt lengths were passé. In fact, there existed a cultural and couture schism between the urban and progressive woman on one hand and the rural and traditional male on the other. The conservative male spoke of the allure of the countryside and its traditions of modest dressing. Often the battles between the two groups were fought in songs that received ample airtime on *Radio Uganda*. The 1960s "band" music era diva, Hadija Namale, composed *"Naiti."* The song was an ode to her self-designed and self-tailored mini-dress, a source of ongoing envy from passersby. The lyrics, which at their core celebrated the urban woman's independence from a patriarchal order, stitched a latticework of melodious seduction, twitching with caressing sultry tones. Countering her was Gerald Mukasa, a master of the folksy ostinato music played on a steel-stringed acoustic guitar, a style known as *kadongo kamu*. Mr. Mukasa's song was simply titled *"Miniskirt."* His forbidding and paternalistic lyrics ridiculed "indecent" miniskirt-wearing women for denigrating Uganda culture. He narrated that since the women had opted to half-dress they deserved being totally undressed, presumably by disapproving males.

The ban of the miniskirt finally came. It was codified in the Penal Code Act (Amendment) Decree of June 6, 1972, which briefly summarized its intent as "a decree to prohibit the wearing of certain dresses which outrage decency and are injurious to public morals and other purposes connected therewith." The decree further stipulated that a woman's dress could not be more than three inches above the knee-line. The same decree banned women from wearing hot pants and maxi skirts with frontal and or posterior slips extending above the knee. There was much confusion on how the police, who were supposed to enforce the law, would conduct measurements and what indeed was the reference point—mid-patella or from the lower part of the patella? The February 9, 1973, Penal Code Act (Amendment) Decree revised the length of a dress or skirt not to be shorter than 2 inches above the knee.

There were serious consequences for defying the miniskirt ban. On June 9, 1972, a beautiful 20-year-old woman, Harriet Nankumbi, was arrested while walking on Main Street in Jinja, Uganda's second largest city. Her crime? Dressing in a miniskirt. Appearing before Chief Magistrate T.S. Cotran, the government prosecutor accused Ms. Nankumbi of publicly conducting "herself in a manner likely to cause the breach of the peace."[5] She became the first official victim of Idi Amin's war on the miniskirt. She pleaded guilty to the charge of being "idle and disorderly" and was fined. The phrase "idle and disorderly" was later defined in another decree—The Penal Code Act (Amendment) (No.2) Decree, Decree 26 of 1974, and referenced the behavior of any person who:

(a) being a common prostitute, behaves in a disorderly or indecent manner in any public place;

(b) wanders or places himself in any public place to beg or gather alms or causes or procures or encourages any child or children so to do;

(c) plays at any game of chance for money or money's worth in any public place;

(d) publicly conducts himself in a manner likely to cause a breach of the peace;

(e) without lawful excuse, publicly does any indecent act;

(f) in any public place, solicits or loiters for immoral purposes;

(g) wanders about and endeavors by the exposure of wounds or deformation to obtain or gather alms

Most of the clauses defining "idle and disorderly" were applied mostly to women. Women accused of wearing mini-dresses or attire remotely construed as indecent endured insults, intimidation, beatings, and public humiliation at the hands of security personnel or self-styled local vigilantes.[6] Some women fought back. Of interest was the young miniskirt-wearing woman accosted by a group of men loitering in a Kampala street. The men made catcalls, threw insults and hurled rubbish at her. The mean-spirited among them advanced toward the girl, perhaps with intents of beating or undressing, or even raping her. Girls in miniskirts were often undressed when they ventured into public spaces. This was meant to humiliate and embarrass, and serve as a deterrent to future violation of Idi Amin's miniskirt decree. Instead of fleeing for dear life the young girl confronted her male persecutors. She opened her handbag and brandished a knife. She menacingly advanced towards her would-be molesters. She had turned the tables and the cowards fled in total disarray.[7]

In a further quest to define and create an image of the "authentic" Ugandan woman Idi Amin enacted more restrictive decrees and bylaws. Amin's fascination with women's dress extended beyond the miniskirt. Initially, there were suggestions that Idi Amin would ban women from wearing bell-bottom pants. However, Amin took this further and decided certain women should not wear trousers at all. Accordingly, Amin issued the Establishment Notice No. 1 of 1973—"The need for female public officers to dress decently while on official duty." The notice required female government employees to "dress neatly" and prohibited them from wearing "long trousers, tights and such like dresses."[8] The Notice further warned that any female government employee found in breach of the dress code "would be dealt with seriously."[9] Then in 1974 all women aged 14 and above were banned from wearing trousers. Also banned were long skirts with long slips because the government alleged that "after banning the minis, shameless women found another device to satisfy their appetites. They resorted to making very suggestive deep cuts in their long skirts…. Often the deep cut was made in the back."[10]

In addition, Idi Amin banned women from wearing wigs. It was reported the decision to ban wigs was one that Idi Amin was forced to make following receipt of "a heap of letters and innumerable oral demands from the people of Uganda of all walks of life to ban wigs."[11] But the final straw to break the camel's back came about when Amin "learnt from reliable sources that wigs craved by unsuspecting Uganda customers were made by the callous imperialists from human hair mainly collected from the unfortunate victims of the miserable Vietnam War, thus turning human tragedy into lucrative commercial enterprises."[12] Amin promised to disown any female family member who wore a wig. He went on to allege that subversive women concealed weapons under their wigs. Amin's secret police took these accusations seriously and meticulously studied female hairstyles as they evolved over the years, all the while trying to decipher if the hairstyles could be used to conceal weapons. A memo written by a certain Kejjo, an agent of Amin's much feared secret police, the State Research Bureau (SRB), illustrates this obsession: "When the wig was banned under government laws, women have changed over to other artificial hair which I think is the worst under the grounds that certain bad women elements can easily hide grenades in this round type of hair without suspicion."[13]

The foreign press christened Idi Amin "Big Daddy," which solidified his claim to being the "father of the nation" and appeared to grant him the legitimacy to oppress women even more. Idi Amin's erratic and brutal behavior ranked him alongside other vicious leaders of the 1970s such as Papa Doc in Haiti, Macias Nguema of Equatorial Guinea and self-proclaimed Emperor Jean-Bédel Bokasa of the Central African Republic. A critical commentary in *Transition* magazine referred to Amin as "not a man of the people; he is a man against the people, he is not so much human as anti-man."[14] Big Daddy also prohibited women from using perfumes and skin lightening creams such as the popular brands *Ambi, Clear Tone* and *Butone*, which were heavily promoted in widely read magazines such as *Drum*.[15] Idi Amin alleged that lightening creams made Ugandan women look like monkeys and gorillas or patients afflicted with leprosy, which caused their husbands to abandon them.

On learning that women in the Islamic world wore trousers without fear of reprisal, Idi Amin, who was Muslim, rescinded the trouser ban for Ugandan women.[16] I argue that by dispensing these favors, allowing women to wear trousers for example, Amin was positioning himself as the ultimate symbol of manhood and fatherhood, a status that was culturally and traditionally accorded to Ugandan kings. As the benevolent father figure—"Big Daddy"—he could extend favors to women, permitting them to wear trousers, and through that munificence, twisted as this is, he probably believed that in itself would win him the support of the women. Idi Amin situated the ban on miniskirts, women trousers, wigs and skin-lightening creams as part of an overall military and political strategy to demonstrate his true credentials as an African patriot fighting imperialism and Western cultural hegemony. Ali Mazrui, a notable scholar of Africa, referred to this posturing as "malignant sexism in the name of dignity of womanhood."[17] Amin wanted to be seen not only within Uganda but throughout the African continent as the single leader that could be counted on to reclaim the ascendancy of black power, and a man brave enough to fight imperialist and Zionist forces that were portrayed as destructive to the progress of black people worldwide. He could claim that he was not victimizing women but rather helping them reclaim their "Africanness," a heritage that celebrated virtuous living, unsullied by imperialist influences. Amin vowed that Ugandans would not follow standards and cultural norms of the imperialist West, but "African women must dress decently so that they can get the respect they deserve."[18] As has been noted by Desiree Lewis, black females are often "coerced into accepting discourses of tradition and authenticity, and ... are frequently figured (especially in male-centered nationalism) as those who must represent an original African essence untouched by westernisation."[19]

Idi Amin's officials ratcheted up the misogynist rhetoric and further aggravated an already toxic environment that degraded women. Amin variously accused women of engaging in subversive activities, like participating in armed robberies and hiding stolen cars.[20] A powerful and trusted Idi Amin lieutenant, Abdullah Nasur, the Governor of Central Province, railed against unmarried, unemployed urban women. He called them "prostitutes." Nasur threatened to round up and deport to the countryside all unemployed, beautiful women living in the capital, Kampala.[21] Mr. Nasur alleged that unemployed and beautiful women were responsible for the increased criminality in Kampala, especially if such women wore wigs, smelled good, and dressed in miniskirts or hot pants.[22] The decision to deport women to the countryside entranced some ordinary citizens. A Kampala lawyer, Mr. Wazarwahi Bwengye, represented this sentiment. Mr. Bwengye inveighed against divorced, urban women, whom he accused of orchestrating marriage break-ups by engaging in prostitution. He further claimed that urban women were recruiting their countryside kith and kin into prostitution. Bwengye urged Idi Amin to enact a decree that would put in place the mandatory screening of all unmarried women employed in bars, restaurants and even certain categories of offices. He suggested that "all unemployed girls and unmarried women who are not attending schools should be rounded up and be taken for rehabilitation on selected farms; any man or woman suspected of carrying VD [venereal disease] should be summoned by the health authorities or arrested by police and taken for medical examination; if found infected and infective he/she should be prosecuted, convicted and sentenced."[23] In the post–Amin era, this same Mr. Wazarwahi Bwengye would go on to a place of prominence in Ugandan politics, even contesting for the presidency in 2001. He garnered a paltry 0.31 percent of the vote.

It was probably out of a desire to demonstrate fairness as a paragon of morality and virtuous living that led Idi Amin's government to introduce morality legislation that would chiefly impact men. Ugandans were slapped with a decree that limited drinking hours. This led to a flourishing underground drinking scene, where the drinking fraternity gathered for a drink outside the official drinking hours. This phenomenon bred what came to be known as *"bitanda"* beer—crates of beer were squirreled away and hidden under beds (*bitanda*) in private homes doubling as underground bars. This was Uganda's equivalent of the U.S. prohibition-era speakeasies. Idi Amin broadened his morality war. He banned men's shabby hair and bushy beards. Adopting the benevolent "Big Daddy" image, Idi Amin claimed he had wanted Ugandans to self-police themselves and wear decent hair, but alas, the "Defense Council" had forced his hand into passing a decree to "curb the deteriorating standard of smartness especially among men."[24] The "Defense Council" alongside other positions like "Military Spokesman" and "Government Spokesman" really did not exist as distinct entities outside the person of Idi Amin. Wanume Kibedi, Idi Amin's foreign affairs minister from 1971 to 1973, alleged that Amin's constant reference to the "Defense Council" in the decision-making process was a way for the general to "create the impression that he worked with an advisory or consultative body."[25] The government reported that the Defense Council's effort to improve tidiness had received overwhelming support. The *Uganda Argus* newspaper quoted a Mr. Kyangwa claiming that he had yet to see an African man with long hair and added that he found it "funny for a man to have long hair like a woman."[26] Mr. Kyangwa was implying two things: (a) the "un–African" nature or "otherness" of male long hair, (b) the social unacceptability of men displaying traits or behaviors construed as feminine. Banning men from wearing bushy beards was said to be driven by Amin's sense of insecurity and low self-esteem. Idi Amin was a man obsessed with projecting an image of an African strongman, and he presided over a state that "reinforced a violent form of masculinity" where "real men" were "fierce, aggressive and loyal."[27] In Uganda, and much of the continent, there is a belief that a beard connotes masculinity, virility and wisdom. However, Idi Amin could not grow facial hair.[28] This deficiency was a personal affront to his position as the "chief" man and "Big Daddy," the very embodiment of masculinity and virility in the country. The hirsute men challenged that image.

Tragically, Idi Amin's morality decrees created and fostered a climate in which random acts of violence against women were committed. In March 1974 Idi Amin made a startling announcement on the government-controlled *Radio Uganda*. With immediate effect, he was divorcing three of his four official wives—Malyamu, Kay Adroa and Nora. On this news, *Voice of Uganda*, the government-controlled newspaper, carried a rapturous heading that proclaimed, "General Amin Has One Wife and Others Are Out!"[29] The reasons for the triple divorce were both hilarious and dubious. Amin claimed he was a cousin to Kay and therefore could not continue being married to her. Their marriage had lasted eight years. As for Malyamu and Nora, Amin accused them of engaging in illicit business activities. This was a crime that contravened Amin's "revolutionary" ethos. Amin's security operatives arrested Malyamu on April 10, 1974, at the Uganda-Kenya border. The government alleged she had been apprehended for attempting to smuggle bales of Ugandan textiles into neighboring Kenya. Malyamu was hauled in front of a magistrate who levied a fine of 800 Uganda shillings or the equivalent of $100 in 1974. Kay Adroa suffered a tragic fate. On May 20, 1974, she too was arrested, allegedly for being in possession of 15 rounds of ammunition. Of the arrest, the *Radio Uganda* announcer had this to say: "It is believed that the ammunition found with Miss Adroa is of the type used by highway robbers in Uganda." Shortly thereafter her dismembered body was discovered in a car trunk.

Another particularly disturbing and macabre death involved two women, both members of the Makerere University community. On February 13, 1976, security agents at Entebbe International Airport arrested Esther Chesire, a bubbly young twenty-something Kenyan student at Makerere University, as she prepared to board a flight to Nairobi. She was in the company of a fellow Kenyan college student, Sally Githere. Ms. Githere managed to escape from their captors, but Chesire, a niece of the then vice-president of Kenya, Daniel arap Moi, was not so lucky. She was never seen again, and it is presumed she was murdered. Following Chesire's abduction, the government of Kenya closed its borders with Uganda and a tense, hostile atmosphere erupted between the two countries. Open warfare looked increasingly likely. To mitigate further diplomatic fallout, Idi Amin appointed a Commission of Inquiry to investigate the circumstances of Chesire's death. When the Commission set about its work it called upon Mrs. Theresa Nanziri Mukasa-Bukenya to testify. She was the warden of Africa Hall, a women's residence hall at Makerere University. Esther Chesire was a resident of Africa Hall. Just before her meeting with the commission Mrs. Mukasa-Bukenya was visited by Amin's secret police—the State Research Bureau (SRB). The security men demanded that she provide testimony that would paint Chesire as an immoral woman, perhaps a prostitute. That way the regime could claim she was a victim of one of her jilted lovers. Mrs. Mukasa-Bukenya was an upright and incorruptible academic. She refused to be intimidated into providing false testimony. Men believed to be State Research Bureau operatives abducted her on June 23, 1976. The next day, her lifeless body was fished out of the Ssezibwa river.[30]

The case of Elizabeth Bagaya's short but dramatic stint in Idi Amin's cabinet is yet another illustration of the widespread public humiliation visited upon Ugandan women by their government in the name of enforcing morality. Bagaya was a beautiful, tall and regal woman of royal lineage. Her father was the King of Toro, a kingdom in western Uganda. She was Cambridge-educated and in 1965 made history as the first black African woman from East and Central Africa to be admitted to the English Bar. Under the nom de plume "Elizabeth of Toro" she modeled for leading magazines. The June 1969 edition of *Vogue* featured her in a four-page spread and in November of that year she became the first black woman to grace the cover of *Harper's Bazaar.* In February 1974, less than two weeks after introducing the ban on wigs and trousers for women, Amin appointed Elizabeth of Toro as his foreign affairs minister. With this appointment as Uganda's top diplomat she became the first female cabinet minister in Uganda. Where Amin was scatterbrained and irrational, Elizabeth Bagaya was articulate, witty and cosmopolitan. During her nine-month stint as Uganda's top diplomat she mounted a vociferous defense of Idi Amin, dismissing accusations of racialism, authoritarianism and extreme brutality that were leveled at the regime by Western governments.

One of Bagaya's best moments serving General Amin came on September 26, 1974. She stood before the United Nations' General Assembly in New York. Her speech was caustic towards governments that were critical of Idi Amin's murderous regime. She dismissively characterized them as "imperialists financed by the British and other mass media to carry false and concocted stories about Uganda in order to cover up their own atrocious crimes."[31] The allusion to the prevailing situation in Northern Ireland and Vietnam was not lost on the British and the Americans. Even as she delivered these scathing remarks, she remained poised and skillful, radiating enormous beauty in a tight-fitting glittering golden tube dress— a gift from the Chinese government. Her coiffure was equally dazzling— strands of hair twisted into a glorious birdcage. During a luncheon for African delegates attending the UN General Assembly Bagaya famously lectured U.S. Secretary of State Henry Kissinger on African nationalism. She criticized U.S. foreign policy in Africa. The U.S. was viewed as sympathetic to the apartheid regime in South Africa and an impediment to the struggle to end colonialism. She invited Kissinger to visit Africa and rounded off her long lecture with quotes from Shakespeare. Kissinger took notice of the pretty, intelligent woman. Writing in the *Courier*, a Connecticut College student newsletter, Jack Anderson noted, "Each foreign minister Kissinger met for days thereafter [following his meeting with Bagaya] was greeted with a comment along the lines: 'It's nice to meet you. But I have seen prettier foreign ministers.'"[32] It does not come as a surprise that Idi Amin desired to add Elizabeth Bagaya to his harem of wives and concubines. But Elizabeth of Toro would have none of that.

Upon her return from the UN General Assembly meeting, a dejected Idi Amin placed Bagaya under house arrest. On November 28, 1974, she was subjected to an ignominious firing. Amin cited improprieties and danger to national security as the reasons for dismissing Bagaya from the high-profile ministerial post. Amin alleged that she had brought great shame to Africa when she was photographed having sex with a European man in a Paris Orly airport toilet. The government daily, *Voice of Uganda*, printed a half-length nude picture, purportedly showing the princess' tryst in an airport lavatory. Uganda Television also ran the nude pictures during the evening news broadcast. And for good measure Idi Amin accused Bagaya of consorting with the CIA and British intelligence agents. Leveling accusations of spying against women was a common Amin theme, and he lived in constant fear of foreign spies infiltrating his government. For example, while dispensing wisdom on equality of sexes he had this to say, "If women get responsible jobs or have any other job, they should avoid associating with spies from foreign countries whose aim is to cause confusion and retard development in our country."[33] Amin also accused foreigners of using Ugandan women as their "tools to confuse the people."[34] Elizabeth Bagaya fled Uganda and escaped the fate that had befallen her predecessor, Lieutenant Colonel Michael Ondoga, a cousin to Kay Adroa, Amin's wife. He too had served briefly as the foreign affairs minister before falling out with Idi Amin. His body was found floating in the River Nile shortly after Idi Amin had dismissed and replaced him with Elizabeth Bagaya. According to Dr. John Kibukamusoke, a former personal physician to Idi Amin, an autopsy on Ondoga's body turned up a macabre finding that suggested a ritualistic murder—a missing liver.[35]

Throughout his eight-and-one-half years' rule, Idi Amin worked hard at cultivating an image of a radical and revolutionary Pan-Africanist, and probably believed he was the continent's greatest statesman. Banning the miniskirt, wigs, and the use of perfumes was all choreographed to project an image of a president with impeccable Pan-African nationalist credentials and who stood for traditional African values in face of an assault from an imperialist West. Idi Amin derided the West in colorful language. When he appropriated 85 British firms in January 1973, he declared that, "for a black African like me to kick the British out of the country he must be very strong and tough. I have put an end to the British Empire in Uganda and will now be very friendly to them because they are no longer bwana mkubwas [big bosses]."[36] When Peter Dominick, a conservative U.S. Senate Republican from Colorado, nominated President Richard Nixon as a candidate for the Nobel Peace Prize, Idi Amin lampooned the U.S. president via cable on September 1, 1973:

> I have heard through Press Media of your nomination as one of the candidates for this year's Nobel Peace Prize. I should like to congratulate you for the nomination. However, I have reason to believe that the person or organization that has nominated you merely wishes you to hear of the nomination so that you recover from the worries of the Watergate affair. My reason for holding this view is that it is very discouraging for the real peace makers in the world to hear of your nomination when the record of your administration in the world ... is a long story of human torture, murder and interference in the internal affairs of other states.[37]

Idi Amin's anti-imperialist rhetoric, and ultimately his moralistic legislation, must be viewed within the historical and political reality of the early 1970s sub–Saharan Africa. Most of the continent had shed colonial rule and attained independence. However, stubborn pockets of Western colonialism persisted in Angola, Mozambique, Guinea Bissau and the Cape Verde islands, Rhodesia (Zimbabwe) and South West Africa (Namibia). In South Africa a virulent form of apartheid under white minority rule was firmly in place. Voices challenging the imperial predominance of the colonizing Western powers or demanding majority rule in South Africa were ruthlessly suppressed. Despite the crackdown on revolutionary forces, the struggle to liberate Africa from the yoke of colonial oppression was ongoing. However, the lack of progress in realizing independence and self-determination in the countries still under colonial rule frustrated many Africans. There were a number of charismatic and vociferous African leaders critical of Western colonialism on the continent. Notable among these were Amilcar Cabral, Julius Nyerere and Kenneth Kaunda. Although their voices were significant in keeping the agenda of independence on the radar of regional and international forums, their strategies were not met with immediate results. The people of Africa were impatient and wanted a quick end to colonialism. By appropriating an anti-imperialist rhetoric resplendent with braggadocio militarism, Idi Amin positioned himself as the military leader capable of delivering a fatal blow to colonialism. This seemed to convince many Africans, especially those who were not under his rule. To them Idi Amin became the beau idéal in providing the muscular response needed to liberate the continent from colonialism and rid it of apartheid; he was the image of the "true African patriot, the scourge of imperialists, the true enemy of foreign exploiters who successfully repossessed Uganda for its own people, the friend of liberation movements (who, he has repeatedly said, could crush South Africa in a fortnight if only his advice were followed)."[38] He even earned praise from the legendary Nigerian Afro-pop musician Fela Kuti, whose 1992 "Underground System" song paid homage to what Fela perceived as progressive African leaders, mentioning Idi Amin alongside Nkrumah, Seko Toure, Lumumba and Mandela.

But as Alicia Decker has pointed out, Idi Amin was militarizing "women's bodies while shifting the public attention away from his own improprieties."[39] It was much easier to seek political legitimacy through passage of moral decrees than to deliver on basic services that citizens desperately needed. On ticking off his domestic and foreign accomplishments in the first two years of his government Idi Amin prominently featured his moral agenda—"the abolition of mini-dresses and other clothes that were a disgrace to African culture" and the "reduction of excessive drinking."[40] It is easy to argue that religious zealousness drove Amin's moral decrees. However, in his moral crusade, Amin barely nodded his acknowledgment to religion. As a matter of fact, most of his actions were at odds with the image of the devout Muslim that he attempted to cultivate. In September 1977, a military truck parked in a field of eucalyptus trees just opposite the emblematic Clock Tower (also known as the Queen's Clock) in Kampala, discharging 15 men accused of treason. They were subjected to death by firing squad. This show of extreme cruelty happened during the Muslim Holy Month of Ramadan, a time characterized by virtuous deeds and mercy. This public execution was a message designed to increase fear and demonstrate that the state had the capacity and was indeed willing to kill those that threatened Amin's rule. Religious considerations would not stand in his way.

There is no evidence to suggest that Amin, despite the terror of his regime, had in place a systematic policy to target sexual minorities. Nonetheless, now and again, stories of men impersonating women circulated. Usually it was reported the cross-dressers were out to seduce unsuspecting men, luring them into buying booze or even as a way of getting them drunk and running off with their wallets. One such story of a cross-dresser was reported in *Uganda Argus* in 1972[41]:

> A man who masqueraded as a woman was convicted and fined 75/- [Uganda shillings] at the West Mengo District Court, Entebbe, after pleading guilty to the charge of being idle and disorderly. It was alleged that Mpima ... who was wearing a busuti [a traditional floor-length women's dress with puffed up sleeves] was found at night standing on the verandah of Kennedy's Bar, Kitubulu, near Entebbe. It was assumed that the purpose of the disguise was to attract men. It was further alleged that at the material time, Mpima was standing with another man who posed as a brother and acted as bait. Discovering the trick, soldiers who had gone to the bar to have a drink and to look for good-time girls, arrested him and took him to Entebbe Police Station. "It is disgraceful to see a man that was created as a man presume himself and dress as a woman and go to public places to attract men so as to love him and go with ... another man. This action is very bad, for that behavior the accused must be punished." After the accused had paid the 75/- fine he was taken behind the court by his relatives who gave him a shirt and a pair of trousers.

It is unknown whether this was Mpima's first time soliciting. Although he was never charged of the offense of sodomy, which was a crime under the Uganda Penal Code, I suggest he probably identified as a transgender woman. It is also within the realm of possibility that on previous occasions he had spent intimate time with some of the male patrons of Kennedy Bar, some of whom were probably soldiers. Significantly, the story depicts Mpima's relatives as compassionate, loving and understanding. They did not berate or abandon him. His relatives were in court, and readily bailed him out—they brought him a shirt and a pair of pants.

The casualness with which the phrase *"good-time girls"* was used as a euphemism for prostitutes in the *Uganda Argus* story about the cross-dressing Mpima, suggests a tacit government approval of prostitution. Amin ranted against prostitution but he never undertook any effort to systematically arrest and prosecute prostitutes. The reason for Amin's lack of enthusiasm to have prostitutes rounded up and punished was possibly because he was acutely aware his soldiers and members of his secret police patronized prostitutes. The last thing Amin needed was to antagonize the military and the SRB agents who propped up his murderous regime. There was a well-known brothel community in Mengo, Kampala, which boasted of pretty women from the Congo. It was at the epicenter of a triangle situated between the Army Headquarters, Malire Mechanized Brigade Barracks and the Army Shop. Not far off was New Life Night Club, one of Kampala's premier nightspots at the time. Prostitution, alongside viewing pornographic materials, was not frowned at but seen as spending a "good time," and hence the sanitized and almost innocent euphemism for female prostitutes—*good-time girls*. In the 1970s there was a cyclostyled local pornographic newsletter called *"Ekyama"—The Secret*, which could be snatched up from any street book vendor in Kampala. It was also the most sex education urban kids would ever get. Western adult literature, including *Playboy* and *Penthouse*, was readily available too. Many teenagers in Kampala had read Xaviera Hollander's *The Happy Hooker*, and there were no censors clamoring to ban the book. But in 2001, under General Museveni, the government started arresting and charging people, especially the poor street vendors, for selling *Playboy* and *Penthouse*.[42] This despite the ready availability of hardcore pornographic videos in almost every single video rental store in the country. The hypocrisy of these acts was staggering.

In 2003 Ugandan legislators, mostly members of the Parliamentary Fellowship, coordinated their efforts to ban pornography, which was viewed as a gateway to homosexuality and therefore posing a threat to Ugandan society. It all started off with well-orchestrated public displays of moral indignation and outrage. Soon after, government officials started warning about the evilness of pornography and the urgent need to pass strict morality laws. The most significant moment came when the Family Life Network (FLN), a local Christian conservative group founded by Stephen Langa, organized a seminar on the "Threat of pornography and obscenity in Uganda." Mr. Langa was an elder and pastor at Kampala Pentecostal Church (KPC) of Gary Skinner. He was also given to fringe beliefs. For example, he believed that demons could physically rape men and women and that he had helped many such victims of demonic rape.[43] The FLN seminar, which placed pornography at the center of immorality in Ugandan society, was attended by senior public figures, including legislators, ministers and members of Uganda's judiciary.[44] Participants at the seminar were also told about a Western plot to target the country with pornography ostensibly to corrupt Uganda's culture and language. Earlier, Pastor Ssempa, who had occasionally preached at KPC, led a demonstration against pornography, alleging that pornography was responsible for destroying families and was the cause of rape and incest.[45] It is significant to note that it is the same set of players that railed against pornography who also demanded tough anti-homosexuality legislation.

To bolster support of a pornography-free Uganda, the FLN invited Scott Lively, the president of Abiding Truth Ministries, for a five-day visit to Uganda in June 2002. His wife, Anne, joined him on the trip. Lively had been conscripted by Langa to come to Uganda to help the country fight against homosexuality. Lively described Langa with much fondness, calling him Uganda's "equivalent of Dr. James Dobson."[46] James Dobson is the chairman of Focus on the Family and an influential U.S. evangelical conservative. Mr. Lively talked about the horrors of pornography, sharing a personal story that left a mark on his Ugandan audience.[47] He had grown up in a good family and all was going well. However, this fairy-tale upbringing was upended when his parents embraced pornography. By his telling, Lively's mother was "one of the women who believed that pornography was harmless. It became her Christmas tradition to give a *Playboy* magazine to my father as a gift every Christmas." However, consumption of pornography would by and by have horrendous consequences, tearing the family. Soon the father began molesting his daughters. One of Lively's sisters who suffered the most abuse became a lesbian in addition to developing mental illness. A brother became gay. As for Lively, when he was about 10 or 11 years old, he discovered his father's supply of *Playboy* magazines. He embarked on an addictive path of pornography. He preached that pornography was responsible for child molestation, homosexuality, bestiality and in some cases, sex-related murders. Lively said he was in Uganda "to bring a warning of what is to come, if the [pornography] trend in Uganda is not reversed.... My desire is for Uganda to embrace marriage and family as the means of achieving robust social health.... We need to act because we are not fighting social forces; we are fighting real people who have a goal to advance sexual perversion."[48] Mr. Langa of the FLN would later echo Lively's view on pornography, claiming that a pornography addict is "susceptible to any kind of deviant sexual behavior and, in extreme cases, becomes a criminal or rapist."[49]

In May 2003, Archbishop Nkoyooyo of the COU led a demonstration of hundreds of people protesting publications of pornographic and obscene materials, and calling on government to ban magazines that promoted immorality. The archbishop contended that the protesters represented "millions of Ugandans who are against pornography."[50] The usually tone-deaf government of General Museveni announced it had listened to the calls of Ugandans to ban pornography. Accordingly, in December 2003 the government instituted a select parliamentary committee to study the extent of pornography and advise it on how to respond to what was perceived as a moral crisis. The committee came to be known as the Select Committee on Pornography. It was chaired by Ms. Sarah Kiyingi, a born-again Christian and a member of the Parliamentary Fellowship. As the committee went about its work, security forces stepped up the harassment of people suspected of engaging in "pornography." Two female teenage striptease dancers were arrested and brought before a Kampala magistrate.

They were charged for indecent exposure. While sentencing the duo to an eight-month prison term, the magistrate reprimanded them, saying that the offense they committed was "not only satanic but also criminal" and prayed that they turn to "God to shape your ways."[51] Meanwhile social and religious conservative groups maintained their calls to government to ban pornography. The Uganda Joint Christian Council petitioned Parliament and called upon legislators to enact tough laws against tabloids that supposedly promoted pornography.[52] A group of university students, led by their vice chancellor, marched through Kampala streets denouncing pornography and demanding the institution of tough penalties. The students also claimed they were in support of abstinence and therefore urged the government to ban the use of condoms in the fight against HIV.[53] And Mrs. Museveni waded into the conversation, alleging that democracy promoted pornography.[54] Her husband, General Museveni, was making it hard for democracy to take root in the country.

Ms. Kiyingi's Select Committee on Pornography heard testimonies from representatives of government departments and civil society. But the most significant testimony came from members of Langa's FLN. The legislators commended FLN and noted that the organization had conducted extensive research on pornography in the country. The committee's evaluation of pornography appears to have been based almost entirely on FLN's input. Sarah Kiyingi, in presenting the committee's final report on pornography in Uganda observed,

> According to FLN, pornography in Uganda is found in novels, videos, magazines, some newspapers, tabloids, the internet, some music, FM radio programs and television. Increasingly, live entertainment that depicts nude dancers dancing erotically ... are becoming a common occurrence. The committee was availed with some audio and video recordings of some of the testimonies of people especially the youth who have confessed their consumption of pornography and its consequent negative effects on them. FLN provided the committee with audio and video recordings of some of these testimonies. Going through these testimonies, it became clear to the committee that pornography is already having a serious and harmful impact in Uganda and that some of its negative effects include addiction to the vice, rape, child molestation, abuse and disrespect towards women i.e. seeing them as mere objects of sex, premature sexual curiosity among young people or a desire to experiment with or act out what one has viewed in pornography, deviate sexual behavior such as addiction to masturbation, homosexuality, lesbianism, bestiality and so on. And then inability to engage in intimate relationships thus sometimes leading to marriage breakdown, fear, guilt, shame and so on.[55]

It was not surprising that the Select Committee on Pornography aligned its views on the horrors of pornography with those held by Lively. It appears the American pastor's sad personal experience with pornography struck a deep chord with Ugandan legislators who were sold on the notion that pornography led to homosexuality.

The Select Committee on Pornography had not even concluded its work and reported back to Parliament when Mr. Buturo, who was then minister of information, spoke at a Family Life Network event about a government policy that would soon be implemented to support abstinence and stop pornography. In fact, Ms. Kiyingi's committee was still conducting its evaluation and was largely unaware of an imminent anti-pornography policy.[56] Mr. Buturo was the initial public face of legislators against pornography, playing well the role of the custodian of moral uprightness as seen through the lens of the Parliamentary Fellowship. He claimed that at independence from Great Britain in October 1962, Uganda had entered a covenant with God. Legislating against pornography would therefore help return the country to God. Buturo alleged that pornography was the "most extreme form of human depravity ever known to man" and it "increased cases of adultery, fornication, homosexuality, witchcraft and all other evils are the result of a mind that had been distorted by pornography."[57]

In October 2005, the Select Committee on Pornography concluded its work and presented its findings and recommendations to the Uganda Parliament. The committee's report, which was adopted by Parliament, formed the basis of the anti-pornography bill of 2011, which was presented to Parliament by Father Lokodo, the minister of ethics and integrity. After replacing Buturo as minister of ethics and integrity, Father Lokodo took the fight against immorality to ludicrous heights. He railed against the media for spending inordinate amounts of time on sex, and he wanted the practice stopped forthwith since it led people into comparing "AIDS to malaria, a curable disease" and claimed that there was "a lot of infidelity in Ugandan families."[58]

General Museveni's campaign against the country's LGBT community and "immorality" unfolded against a background of a shifting political reality and a rapidly growing population of empowered young urban women. Stifling the urban young, increasingly shaped by social media, became a priority lest their brazenness and embrace of Western fashion translated to demands for greater political freedom and calls to change the regime. General Museveni's government carefully created and choreographed a belief that its anti-women policies sprung from the community, from the grassroots and was not orchestrated by the leadership in Kampala. First there was the chairman of the ruling party's local chapter in northern Uganda, Mathew Olobo, who banned women from wearing miniskirts and trousers in 2009.[59] Mr. Olobo decreed that women defying the ban would be sentenced to community service. He claimed that women who dressed in miniskirts and trousers were offensive, especially if they still lived at home with their parents. Mr. Olobo's ban, which did not have the backing of Uganda's legislature, received a resounding endorsement from Buturo: "It is good that people now mind the values in their community. The community is entitled to say: this is the way we should behave."[60] Oddly, much of Uganda paid little heed to Olobo's illegal attempt to control women's dress. Mr. Olobo's trouser and miniskirt ban imposed on women of his remote and rural community was a harbinger of a more egregious and nationwide strategy aimed at establishing political legitimacy through the regulation of women's dress. Mr. Olobo's constituency was, so to speak, a social laboratory, used to test the waters and establish how well the Ugandan populace could be corralled to support a cause whose merit was at best dubious and built on a general male insecurity of the urban woman. Targeting the urban woman and attacking her cosmopolitanism was likely to win the president support in the mostly traditional and conservative countryside, a constituency that resented the urban woman's freedom and independence. It also served to further energize General Museveni's base of fundamental Christians whose leaders believed that pornography bred homosexuality.

None illustrated this belief more than Pastor Ssempa, who routinely showed sadomasochist gay pornography at his church, purportedly to illustrate how pornography led to homosexuality. Mr. Bahati attended one of these extreme pornographic screenings.[61] In fact, the pastor's transfixion with gay pornography and his penchant to describe, in graphic detail, violent and degrading sexual acts that he alleged underpinned gay sex, was discombobulating. Speaking at a press conference in his capacity as the chairman of the National Task Force Against Homosexuality, an organization that was obscure to most Ugandans, Ssempa boasted that he had "taken time to do a little research to know what homosexuals do in the privacy of their bedroom," and established that gay sex, in addition to extreme sadomasochist practices, invariably involved "anal licking" where the couple "eat the poo poo [poop]."[62] It is for this latter allegation that Ssempa is also widely known around the globe by the moniker Pastor "Eat da Poo-Poo." Pastor Ssempa readily showed gay pornography to his Christian congregation but he could not tolerate the screening of non-pornographic movies featuring LGBT themes. When Alice Smits, a Dutch art curator, and the American filmmaker Lee Ellickson screened two lesbian-themed movies—the *Watermelon Woman* and *Rag Tag*—at the

Amakula Film Festival in Kampala, Pastor Ssempa was quick to condemn the films. He called upon the government to ban the films on grounds that he could not "allow misguided people to confuse our children through such films. These people do not honour Uganda's laws, culture and values. They had even shown some of the homosexual films."[63] Government swiftly censored the two films but kept a distance when the pastor showed his congregation extreme forms of gay pornography.

The anti-pornography bill was especially designed to curtail the rights and liberties of women in public spaces. Christian clerics represented pornography as a serious danger to Ugandans. The bill defined pornography as "any representation, through publication, exhibition, cinematography, indecent show, information technology or by whatever means, of a person engaged in real or stimulated explicit sexual activities or any representation of the sexual parts of a person for primarily sexual excitement."[64] "*Stimulated* explicit sexual activities" are hard to imagine in the context of this law, but it would appear to have been intended to reference "simulated explicit sexual activities." The broad and ambiguous definition of pornography was extended to justify the arrest of women wearing minidresses and subjected them to an exorbitant fine (that most women would not be able to pay) or 10 years in jail. Once legislators passed the bill, self-appointed moral vigilantes pounced, stripping women purportedly in violation of the dress code. Police turned a blind eye as mothers and daughters were publicly assaulted and humiliated in the streets. Women were left defenseless and could not count on the police to come to the rescue in a nation where moralists had gone berserk.

In July 2013 Uganda photojournalist Colleb Mugume captured this near descent into barbarism when government-backed goons took it upon themselves to uphold the odious anti-pornography bill. His camera zeroed on a fast unfolding scene in a Ugandan street, capturing for posterity the image of a young elegant woman—probably in her early twenties—dressed in a bright yellow tank top and a black miniskirt. A mob of mostly young men besieged the hapless woman. The goons appeared to jeer and mock her, and there was an altogether jubilant atmosphere as this horrifying spectacle of utter humiliation at the hands of moral vigilantes unfolded. It does appear that at one point during this assault, before Colleb's camera had arrived at the scene, the mob had thrown the woman down and dragged her through dirt and gravel, perhaps attempting to undress her. Her right leg was covered with dirt smudges. Despite this terrifying ordeal, which no woman in any part of the world should ever endure, the expression on the young woman's face was one of defiance and courage. She appeared determined to hold on to what was left of her dignity. All this happened in a busy street and in broad daylight. Instead of condemning the vigilantes and prosecuting them for assaulting an innocent woman, the government's position on the matter was lamentable and unsympathetic. Responding to the epidemic of unruly mobs assaulting "indecently" dressed women, the minister for youth and children, Mr. Ronald Kibule, blamed the women.[65] He dispensed the typical General Museveni ministerial wisdom, arguing that women who are raped while indecently dressed have themselves to blame. Mr. Kibule, a polygamist, was not content with blaming female victims but went further and proffered advice to the police investigating future rapes. First and foremost, he argued, the police must carefully investigate the rape. If it is established the female victim was "indecently" dressed, then the male rape perpetrator ought to be set free promptly—perhaps to allow him to go on the prowl for his next female victim. Apparently, the minister had a conviction that Ugandan men would convulse into hysterical fits at the sight of a miniskirt-wearing woman. Apparently, the men's only course of action to save themselves from self-destruction was to commit an act of violent rape. Ugandans were mostly shamed by the minister's misogyny and the online commentary that followed the publication of the minister's views was predominantly an expression of disgust. Arthur Paulo Kamuntu wrote:

> ... he (Mr. Ronald Kibule, the minister for Youth and Children) believes that possession of a penis gives him rights over women's bodies, especially in the South [sub–Saharan Africa], where people ignorantly think covering up one's body is a virtue.... Are men in Kibule's region [constituency] so depraved that no female is safe?

Kajoro Allan summed it up all too well with a sarcastic flair:

> These are the Ministers in this Government. They don't know what to say in public. That is why Museveni is the President, Cabinet, Parliament and Army High Command [the body that has control over the country's military and wields enormous power]. Museveni is very smart in choosing ministers. He chooses buffoons so that they don't oppose any of his schemes.

The anti–LGBT campaign and the war against pornography, and more specifically women's fashion in Uganda, would best be described as a modern-day Inquisition. Of any inquisition, Cullen Murphy observed, it is the "product of a contrary way of seeing things. It takes root and thrives when moral inequality is perceived between one party and everyone else. Inquisitions invite members of one group—national, religious, corporate, political—to sit in judgment on members of another: to think of themselves, in a sense, as God's jury."[66] The ruling National Resistance Movement of General Museveni had appropriated the position of God's jury, sitting on a moral high horse and passing sweeping condemnation like the bishops of the Inquisition. In December 2013, Ugandan legislators overwhelmingly voted to support the anti-pornography bill. This is the bill that once signed by General Museveni into law would ban pornography and set guidelines for how women conducted themselves in public spaces and what dresses they were permitted to wear. It would ban the mini-dress. Ugandan legislators claimed they wanted pornography banned because it was responsible for "sexual crimes against women and children including rape, child molestation and incest."[67] The bill provided for the setting up of a Pornography Control Committee that would, among other things, ensure that all computers in Uganda were fitted with software that blocks pornographic materials. In addition, under the bill, the government would maintain a registry of those engaged in what was deemed as "pornography." The "pornography offenders register" was akin to the sex offenders registry in the U.S.

Given this concerted attack on their sexuality, what could women and the concerned public do? A group of suburban women took to social media. A Facebook group, "END Mini-skirt Harassment," emerged. The group's objectives were existential. It was an "online platform where women have the right to question laws that harm them and are an abuse of their rights." A poster showcased in one of the pictures on the group's Facebook page reads, "Lokodo, hold your libido!" Father Lokodo had not only come to epitomize the destruction of homosexuality in Uganda but he was also seen as the official Museveni government face of the anti-pornography bill's implementation, which disproportionately targeted the urban woman. He seemed to dislike women as much as he hated LGBT people. At one point, Father Lokodo attempted to arrest a fellow legislator, Ms. Proscovia Oromait. She had come to Parliament wearing a dress the minister disapproved of and considered "provocative."[68] He physically participated in security raids on lodges and hotels, arresting women found alone in hotel rooms or suspected to be engaged in sex during afternoon hours. He asserted that such women were prostitutes. Father Lokodo further claimed that the government had formed a special police squad with a specific mandate of enforcing morality.[69] Ugandans were fearful that General Museveni's government was on a slippery slope to curtail their freedoms even further by forming the equivalent of the *mutawwa'in*—the religious police ubiquitous in some Islamic countries—to enforce virtue and prevent vice. In his unyielding misogynist campaign, Father Lokodo had company. There was a segment of urban male youth, well-represented among the thousands of *boda-boda* motorcycle taxi drivers, who felt emasculated by urban women's economic success. These young men were resentful towards urban women, who they believed had unfairly edged them out of jobs once dominated by men. For example, the retail business in Uganda is mostly managed by enterprising women. There was also another sizeable group of prosperous urban women who engaged in international trade, traveling to far-flung places like Dubai, Malaysia and China, where they buy goods for the Ugandan market. Other women, like Ms. Betty Nambooze Bakireke, had emerged as strong leaders and formidable political opponents of General Museveni, mobilizing rural communities to resist the general's increasing authoritarian rule. For her principled stand against General Museveni's quasi-military rule, Ms. Betty Nambooze Bakireke has been in and out of jail, arrested on trumped up charges.[70] Male urban youths, epitomized by the *boda-boda* operators, became eager participants in enforcing General Museveni's anti-women morality laws.[71]

Flooded with reports of women being stripped by men for purportedly dressing indecently, the Uganda Women's Network (UWONET), a women's organization fighting for an end to all forms of gender discrimination, issued a strongly-worded statement in February 2014. It denounced the anti-pornography law for promoting state-inspired violence against women. The organization made an urgent plea to General Museveni's government to keep public spaces safe for women and apprehend those perpetrating acts of violence against women under the pretense of upholding morality and virtuous living.[72] The government hardly batted an eyelid. It appeared resolute in its ongoing persecution of women. A beautiful, young, and talented Ugandan musician, Ms. Jemimah Kansiime, aka *Panadol wa basajja* (*Men's Panadol—Tylenol*), was arrested personally by Father Lokodo. She faced up to ten years in a Ugandan jail. Her crime? Uploading a YouTube music video that Father Lokodo deemed pornographic.[73] YouTube has strict guidelines and does not accept the posting of pornographic and sexually explicit material. It is difficult to arrive at how Lokodo concluded that such material was pornographic. Significantly, most Ugandan music videos on YouTube that have enjoyed sizable viewership feature sensual dancing. Father Lokodo singled out Kansiime for harsh punishment probably because she was a poor and struggling artist without powerful political or military benefactors—easy prey for a self-styled patriarch of morality. On learning that Kansiime faced a stiff sentencing for her artistic creativity, one viewer of her YouTube music video, *Ensolo Yange* (which translates to *My Beast*), bemoaned the ludicrousness of Uganda's morality crusade[74]:

I read that the Ugandan "ethics" minister was "shocked" by this video. But that's not what he really felt when he watched it, of course. No, what he really felt was sexual arousal, and now he wants to punish an innocent human being because he's ashamed of his own sexuality. What a sad excuse of a man he is, and what a terrible political climate that currently exists in Uganda.

General Museveni's morality laws created an environment that encouraged a segment of Ugandan men to intimidate and harass women, irrespective of whether they violated General Museveni's anti-pornography legislation. Undressing women has become an all too common occurrence in Uganda. Female members of the political opposition have been especially targeted for the dehumanizing treatment at the hands of the police. Such barbaric state-sponsored acts of terror elicit a state of extreme fear which dissuades women from freely exercising their rights and participating in shaping the country's political destiny. In May of 1999 the *Monitor*, an independent Ugandan newspaper, carried a front-page photograph of a nude woman, spread-eagled to the ground by soldiers while one of their comrade held a pair of scissors to the woman's crotch. The man holding the scissors was apparently in the act of shaving the woman's pubic hair. The *Monitor* had obtained the photograph from a soldier, a witness to the disturbing incident that was reported to have taken place at a military base in northern Uganda. The woman in the photograph, 24-year-old Candida (her name has also been spelled as Kandida) Lakony, was a girlfriend of an officer in the Uganda army. According to Candida, it all started with an altercation with her boyfriend. General Museveni's government discounted her account of events, insisting the solders in question were not Ugandan and that Candida was not the woman in the picture. But there was overwhelming evidence to the contrary, not least the fact that a high-ranking military officer testified it was routine policy at the military barracks to shave women's heads as a punishment for any number of infractions.[75] Candida was later arrested and charged for giving false statements. She was sentenced to a one-year jail term. The case of Candida Lakony is archetypical of General Museveni's "blame-the-victim" strategy, particularly where women are the innocent victims of state-instigated abuses.

In October 2015, Zainab Fatuma Naigaga, a female member of the opposition Forum for Democratic Change (FDC), was part of an entourage accompanying her party leader, Dr. Kizza Besigye, to address supporters in western Uganda. Police, as is the custom in dealing with political opposition to Museveni's one-man rule, attempted to prevent the motorcade of FDC leaders and party activists from reaching the assembly venue where thousands of supporters waited. Amid arguments between the FDC leaders and the police, a scuffle ensued. It is then that the police officers resorted to a time-tested tactic of intimidation. About eight officers rushed Zainab Fatuma Naigaga, stripping her of her jeans and tank top. She was left stark naked. Her pleas to be treated with civility went unheeded. She asked the police, "Why are you undressing me? You are shaming me ... next time it will be your sister ... it will be your child being treated like this."[76] The disturbing video of Naigaga's arrest, a testimony to General Museveni's war on women, was uploaded on YouTube.[77] Incredibly, despite an abundance of visual and audio evidence, Ms. Naigaga was arrested and charged for "indecent exposure." It was alleged she was a "hired goon" who had intentionally undressed herself. The government demanded that she apologize for her lurid behavior.[78]

Of this incident, *Daily Monitor*, a Uganda daily, reminded its readers that "Ms Naigaga is not the first woman to suffer police brutality.... Hamida Nassimbwa was also stripped and ended up on the ground as police broke up a procession of opposition activists headed to parliament. Nassimbwa was admitted ... nursing an ankle fracture and a swollen index finger. A similar case happened in 2012 when police officers stripped and assaulted political activist Ingrid Turinawe."[79] The online comments on the *Daily Monitor* story of Ms. Naigaga's harrowing experience expressed profound disgust with General Museveni's government's terror against women. James Ndawula, writing in SMS text shorthand, pronounced the violence against women so extreme that it paled in comparison to Idi Amin's brutality:

> Hei u there do not ask yourselves why.... The ans [answer] is if u do not want tear gas harassment, molestation and so on support the sole presidential candidate in ug [Uganda] not only in NRM otherwise expect more. I'm unhappy with whoever compared the regime [of General Museveni] with.... General Idi Amin may be u were young or even unborn so what u may know is hearsay. I'm not undermining u for possibly being young but I want to inform u that.... Amin was 101 percent better than our current regime.

Commenting on an article in the *Observer* on the Naigaga incident, Malakwang Wac provided a somber and hopeful observation[80]: "I hope the Pope is watching these images and should seriously reconsider his pending visit to Uganda." Malakwang Wac's commentary was in reference to Pope Francis' planned two-day visit to Uganda, which eventually happened on November 27, 2015, as part of the pontiff's first African trip. The commentary also highlights the frustration of so many Ugandans with the litany of human rights violations under the leadership of General Museveni. It appears no amount of government repression could galvanize the international community into demanding an end to General Musev-eni's excessive brutality and abysmal human rights record. World leaders continued to reward his government without holding him accountable for the violence against women, LGBT Ugandans, and the political opposition. Incredibly, the plunder and destabilization in the Great Lakes region per-petrated by General Museveni's military, and perhaps orchestrated by his close confidantes, did not elicit punitive responses. The ambivalence and apathy of the international community was baffling. Initially hailed as pro-gressive and inclusive, General Museveni became increasingly erratic as he sought to cling to power at any cost. Faced with increasing opposition to his decades-long rule, the general resorted to populist policies to bolster his support, particularly among rural and socially conservative communities. The ease with which Idi Amin denigrated women without facing any mean-ingful domestic or international outcry emboldened General Museveni's government to enact deplorable moralistic laws for political expediency.

It is argued here that General Museveni's anti-pornography and anti-homosexuality legislation are a continuation of Idi Amin's draconian morality decrees. Significantly, the two leaders relied on morality decrees for the same reasons—to increase their appeal among Ugandans and legit-imize their rule. Indeed, the parallels between Amin's war on women and General Museveni's government's assault on women and the Ugandan LGBT community are remarkable. Where Wazarwahi Bwengye accused urban women of recruiting others into prostitution, Bahati propagated the myth of homosexuals recruiting Uganda school children into homo-sexuality. General Idi Amin and trusted lieutenants like Mr. Abdullah Nasur argued that a segment of women were "immoral" because of how they dressed, looked or their social circumstances, and were therefore criminals. Mr. Buturo, a minister in General Museveni's cabinet, justified banning the miniskirt because miniskirt-wearing women were a danger to the public order—like criminals—since they "can cause an accident because some of our people are weak mentally."[81] The Amin-controlled media's publication of a nude photo, purportedly of Princess Elizabeth Bagaya in a compromised position, was a despicable act of public humil-iation which has its equivalence in Museveni's Uganda, where newspapers, some affiliated with powerful ruling party functionaries, outed LGBT peo-ple. The public undressing of women is common, having been started by Idi Amin and perfected to an exact science by the Museveni government. General Museveni's government uses it as a tactic of choice to intimidate and humiliate women that support opposition parties which seek to use democratic channels to end the general's decades-long rule.

IV

The Uganda Church and Homosexuality

"I am queer, and African, and I am bashed left, right and center by people who claim they know God."[1]—Dr. Paul Semugoma, Ugandan gay activist and recipient of the 2014 Elizabeth Taylor Human Rights Award

Victorian morality laws arrived with British colonialism and Christianization in Uganda. The zealousness with which European missionaries preached Christianity and redemption while at the same time engaging in vicious attacks against the very values and norms that Ugandans had observed for eons caused consternation among the indigenous people. The missionaries worked hand in glove with British colonial administrators, presiding over the systematic dismantling of cultural norms perceived as incompatible to Christianity and British morality. The power of the Bible and the authority of the British colonial administration was pervasive, affecting all manner of transactions in daily life. The locals looked on, impotent to battle the powerful forces of Western imperialism. Same-sex relationships were a particular target of disapproval. As Sarah Coughtry has noted, the alliance of Christian missionaries and British colonial administrators "spread a dominant religious rhetoric that encompassed all areas of life. Over time, the idea that same-sex practices were not only immoral but inherently unAfrican became mainstreamed and normalized as Uganda was turned into a Christian state."[2] Sylvia Tamale pointed out that "the idea of destroying homosexuality came from colonialists. In other words, homosexuality was not introduced to Africa from Europe as many would want us to believe. Rather, Europe imported legalised homophobia to Africa."[3] Or as Roscoe has underscored, "The colonialists did not introduce homosexuality to Africa but rather intolerance to it—and the systems of surveillance and regulation for supporting it."[4]

The Uganda Order in Council of 1902, which in effect was the first constitution of the Uganda Protectorate, led to the promulgation of British laws in Uganda. Under the Order in Council of 1902, the head of the British colonial administration (the Commissioner, and later the Governor of the Uganda Protectorate) received far-reaching powers to enact laws that related to the administration of justice, the raising of revenue and generally for the peace, order and good governance of the protectorate. In the making of such ordinances the colonial administration was supposed to respect native laws and customs unless they were contrary to the British understanding and interpretation of justice and morality. Sexual relationships between members of the same sex were not unusual in Uganda; there was no need to prohibit such relationships as it was an accepted, albeit not openly discussed, aspect of sexuality. However, a provision of the Order in Council of 1902 aligned Ugandan law with the anti-sodomy laws in Britain. This effectively criminalized sodomy, which carried a sentence of life imprisonment. The severity of the punishment was at par with the most serious crimes, such as murder. The Penal Code of 1930 revised the sentencing term for the act of sodomy, repealing life imprisonment and replacing it with a 14-year sentence with hard labor. In 1950, the Penal Code removed hard labor as part of the sentencing for sodomy. However, the 14-year sentencing remained in place. That was the law when Uganda gained independence from Britain in October 1962, and remained in place until General Museveni's government reintroduced life imprisonment as punishment for same-sex intercourse.

Prior to General Museveni's war on LGBT people, there was no evidence of the government arresting and prosecuting gays, and this in spite of the "sodomy" laws. LGBT Ugandans lived in villages and towns across the country without fear for their lives. Significantly, no Ugandan had ever had cause to flee the country because of persecution or discrimination as a result of their sexual orientation. Some people were suspected of homosexuality, and indeed there were high-profile Ugandans widely believed to be gay. But Ugandans appeared overall not intent on interfering with what went on between two consenting adults. In his June 2014 Boston interview with Timothy Lynch Esq., Ugandan LGBT activist John "Long-jones" Abdallah Wambere confirmed this based on his personal experience. He observed that before the rabble-rousing anti–LGBT rhetoric promoted by U.S. evangelicals and the Parliament's passage of the anti-homosexual bill in 2009, homosexuals "were never condemned, never persecuted, no one went to torch their homes, they lived as part of the society, and some of them were appreciated as people of uniqueness, different people. And no one ever called them pedophiles."[5] The first Ugandan gay man tried and sentenced under General Museveni's anti-homosexuality law was Chris Mubiru, a scion of one of Uganda's leading aristocratic families and a national soccer icon. Interestingly, long before General Museveni came to power, Chris Mubiru's homosexuality was common knowledge both inside and outside soccer locker rooms.[6] Then, the police had not found Mr. Mubiru or other Ugandans suspected of homosexuality a threat to public safety. Interestingly, the police in Uganda were baffled at the proposed Bahati bill. They could not recall investigating homosexuality as a crime.[7]

That the LGBT community did not face direct hostility is not to suggest they were under any illusion there was no prejudice against them. Societal stigma against homosexuality was well and alive albeit not translated into open hostility. LGBT people were cautious about openly expressing their sexuality outside the secure confines of their immediate family and trusted friends. Many LGBT Ugandans recount how their parents became conscious about their sexual orientation from an early age. For some in the LGBT community, the family expressed support and understanding, allowing them to be themselves. Some parents believed their LGBT children were possessed by evil spirits of the opposite sex and they did all they could to exorcise the spirits. They turned to traditional diviners and the churches for remediation. After the introduction of Bahati's anti-homosexuality bill in 2009, some families shunned the homosexual children they had once loved and embraced. Michael, a 25-year-old Ugandan student at a U.K. university, found himself disowned by his family because he was gay. An uncle felt the urgency of delivering harsh judgment and distancing the family from his nephew: "I do not even want to hear about that boy. He has been wasted [corrupted] by Western culture and has taken up their way of life as we feared he would because *we always suspected him of being gay for a very long time.* That is why we need a tough law to deter such immoral acts that the bible condemns."[8]

Most LGBT Ugandans remain closeted, living in fear of a brutal government and the harsh judgment of an increasingly intolerant society. In some cases, LGBT people turned to helpful clergy for support, understanding and pastoral care. However, there was a dearth of sympathetic pastors. Nonetheless, despite the political and religious hostility, intolerance and prejudice against the LGBT community there were a few Christian ministries and clergy that showed extraordinary courage, compassion and supported the sexual minorities. These clergymen stood firm as witnesses to Christ's unconditional love, refusing to cave in to popular sentiments to an idiosyncratic morality and condemn, harass and judge people because of their sexual orientation or gender identity. Jesus had embraced the ostracized and socially criticized—the Samaritan woman, lepers, the woman who had committed adultery, those possessed by demons. In the LGBT community, they saw a comparable contemporary group, demonized, harassed and unloved. Bishop Christopher Ssenyonjo of the COU and Father Anthony Musaala, a Roman Catholic celebrity priest, were among the few brave clergy willing to buck the anti-homosexual tone of the national conversation, providing spiritual guidance and counseling to LGBT people. For their love and compassion towards the LGBT community, the two men have had to endure incredible backlash from their churches. Because of his work defending the rights of LGBT Ugandans and offering unconditional pastoral care, the COU denounced and expelled Bishop Ssenyonjo. But expulsion from the church did not deter Bishop Ssenyonjo from his work among LGBT Ugandans, attending to their spiritual needs. He reminded his tormentors, "The Lord taught us to respect each person, however different, as full human beings."[9] Father Musaala, a charismatic and gifted musician, had his detractors. At a press conference that was called by Pastor Ssempa and Pastor Solomon Male, a group of self-confessed gay men accused Father Musaala of homosexuality. It was alleged he regularly held "parties for gays" at his home.[10] Father Musaala denied the accusations, and continues to minister to the LGBT community.

Both the church and the government of General Museveni were complicit in stoking societal angst and creating a climate of fear for the LGBT community. Ordinary Ugandans who see no cause for the harassment of sexual minorities are afraid to speak out. This fear must have been evident to Jeffrey Gettleman, the East Africa Bureau Chief for the *New York Times*, when a Ugandan taxi driver who empathized with the plight of LGBT people said, "I can defend them. But I fear what? The police, the government. They can arrest you and put you in the safe house, and for me, I don't have any lawyer who can help me."[11] What tipped Uganda to move from indifference to a point where open intolerance and hate towards LGBT people became an obsession and a national policy? Both the Museveni government and the church, and in particular the highest echelon of the COU, were responsible for sounding the initial war drums against LGBT Ugandans. With time, the government and the Christian churches fed off each other, each providing the other legitimacy and justification to condemn and persecute LGBT people. In their pursuit of a society based on Biblical values and the Ugandan traditional patriarchal family, they created a perverse environment devoid of safety and dignity for sexual minorities. Many view U.S. evangelicals as the driving force behind General Museveni's adversity towards homosexuals. The influence of American evangelicals in fanning the flames of homophobia in Uganda is the subject of two powerful documentary films—Mariana van Zeller's investigative reporting for Current TV in *Missionaries of Hate* and Roger Ross Williams' *God Loves Uganda*. The general belief is that the American evangelical Scott Lively had considerable influence in shaping the Uganda government's anti-gay agenda. Lively first visited Uganda in March 2002 to speak at a conference on pornography and obscenity organized by Stephen Langa's Family Life Network (FLN). He was back in June 2002, focusing on a message of sexual abstinence and the threat homosexuality posed to society. Lively's views on homosexuality were considered authoritative. A May 2006 editorial in the government-controlled newspaper, the *New Vision*, commended his book *The Gay Movement: How to Recruit-Proof Your Child.* In the book, he outlined methods that the gay movement allegedly used to recruit children into homosexuality.[12] Lively returned to Uganda in March 2009. He was accompanied by Don Schmierer and Caleb Brundidge, two American Christian conservatives. Brundidge self-identified as an ex-gay African-American man who organized and led recovery workshops. The Americans were in Kampala to speak at an anti-gay conference about the "evils" of the gay movement. They met with members of the Ugandan Christian Lawyers Association and Lively also had the opportunity to address a group of Ugandan legislators, most of them born-again Christians. In Kampala, Lively told a Ugandan audience, which numbered in the thousands and had good representation of political and religious leaders, about a "gay movement" and its "agenda" in Uganda. He warned that the gay movement's goal was to "defeat the marriage-based society and replace it with a culture of sexual promiscuity in which there's no restrictions on sexual conduct except the principle of mutual choice."[13] The American evangelicals' propaganda against homosexuality struck a chord with Ugandan legislators, particularly those espousing conservative Christian values. Among these was Mr. James Nsaba Buturo, the minister of ethics and integrity, with whom Lively had a private audience. Apparently, the March 2009 meeting was the first time the two men met. But before Buturo met with Lively, he was an outspoken critic of homosexuality. In 2003, Buturo had already bought into the notion of an international gay conspiracy, and Lively's talk of an "anti-gay movement" must have served to reinforce that belief. At a 2003 impromptu press conference, Buturo, who was then the minister of information and broadcasting, warned of an unnamed nongovernmental organization (NGO) funding the promotion of homosexuality in Uganda. He further alleged that the NGO had paid journalists and some legislators, recruiting them to support the gay cause.[14] It is therefore important to underscore that before Lively arrived in Uganda there was a homegrown toxic anti–LGBT narrative. The COU, more than any other Uganda institution, was instrumental in sowing the seeds of hate and intolerance against sexual minorities.

The 1978 Lambeth Conference, and the subsequent decennial conferences that followed, provide context to understanding the COU's intolerance and hostility towards homosexuality. In 1978, over 350 Anglican diocesan bishops assembled at the University of Kent for the Lambeth Conference. Among those gathered was a delegation of bishops from Uganda led by the Archbishop of the COU, Silvanus Wani (1977–1983). The Ugandan bishops, like many of their counterparts from the Global South (third world countries in Asia, Africa and South America), were mostly on the sidelines at Lambeth 1978. They looked on helplessly and perhaps with a sense of resignation at the deliberations as bishops from the rich Western nations discussed and debated church and worldly affairs without so much as recognizing their presence. A member of the Ugandan delegation best illustrated this powerlessness and alienation when he remarked, "This is not our way of doing things, so we just leave *you* to it."[15] The *"you"* he referred to was what the Reverend Irene Monroe has described as the "white male club of heterosexual power brokers" who had for decades set a Eurocentric agenda and dominated the discussions.[16] When Archbishop Joseph Abiodun Adetiloye of Nigeria rose to contribute to the Lambeth 1978 deliberations, the session chair informed him in a rather off-hand manner that the subject matter under debate had ended. The chair then proceeded to ignore the Nigerian archbishop. But the Nigerian archbishop was not a man to easily give up; he demanded recognition and remained standing for about 20 minutes until the chair reluctantly granted him the opportunity to speak. So much for the Anglican Communion's desire to welcome and embrace diversity! When the archbishop finally spoke, he made history. He became the first black African bishop to address the Lambeth Conference. Perhaps borne out of his frustration and humiliation at the chair's slight, Archbishop Adetiloye made a bold prediction: "For more than twenty minutes I have been standing here and you did not want to recognize me. In ten years, when African bishops come to the microphone at this conference, we will be so numerous and influential that you will recognize us. In 1998, we will have grown so much that our voice will determine the outcome of the Lambeth Conference."[17] Bishops from the Global South patiently listened and prayed for the day when they could raise their voices to defend their interests, challenging the Global North's domineering influence on setting the agenda on theological issues and church practices. Years later, they would find common ground on homosexuality. It was a doctrinal issue that they could own and use to challenge the perceived arrogance, dominance and (spiritual) superiority of the Global North.

Lambeth 1978 deliberated on issues of human greed and self-interest and the urgency of advancing a social gospel. The bishops also discussed homosexuality. In Resolution 10, Human Relationships and Sexuality, the bishops reaffirmed "heterosexuality as the spiritual norm" but also stressed the "need for deep and dispassionate study of the question of homosexuality, which would take seriously both the teaching of Scripture and the results of scientific and medical research. The Church, recognising the need for pastoral concern for those who are homosexual, encourages dialogue with them."[18] Uganda bishops did not voice an opinion either way or another. Nonetheless, that did not stop Idi Amin from mocking and taunting the Christian church. He made public pronouncements bemoaning the spiritual state of the Anglican Church for promoting marriage between men. When the Anglican Communion bishops next gathered in Kent for the Lambeth Conference of 1988, Idi Amin was no longer the president in Uganda. He had been deposed in April 1979 and was living in exile in Saudi Arabia. Archbishop Yona Okoth, the COU prelate from 1984 to 1995, led the Ugandan bishops to the Lambeth Conference of 1988 where homosexuality was again discussed. Resolution 64 reaffirmed the statement of the Lambeth Conference of 1978. The resolution, in a nod to a lack of consensus within the Anglican Communion, urged "each province to reassess ... its care for and attitude towards persons of homosexual orientation."[19]

Again, the COU delegation at Lambeth 1988 did not oppose the resolution on homosexuality, which should not be a surprise. The COU prelate, Archbishop Okoth, was a progressive theologian. He counted among his friends the liberal U.S. theologian John Shelby Spong, the Episcopalian bishop of Newark. Yona Okoth also was friends with openly gay priests in the West. Some of these priests helped raise funds for various community-based church projects in Uganda. At the Lambeth Conference of 1988, the Ugandan church, having emerged from the murderous reign of Idi Amin, had other pressing priorities specific to the country and Africa in general. For example, Ugandan bishops, alongside their African counterparts, wanted the Conference to address the issue of polygamy. Polygamy was widespread in pre-colonial Uganda, and is widely practiced to this day, even among people that self-identify as conservative Christians. Right from their first encounter with Ugandan communities in the latter half of the nineteenth century, Christian missionaries were appalled at the prevalence of polygamy, which they characterized as a manifestation of immorality. The banning of polygamy and enforcement of monogamous Christian marriages became one of the church's priorities. Accordingly, the colonial administration and post-independence Uganda government only recognized monogamous church or civil marriages. However, exemptions were made for Muslim men. They could marry a maximum of four wives. In 1973, Idi Amin issued a decree that legalized polygamous marriages for all religious faiths in Uganda. The Christian churches were in a dilemma. Denouncing and expelling men and women in polygamous marriages from the church was not an option. In fact, the failure to welcome polygamous families as full members of the church had led many to find spiritual succor in churches that dabbled in indigenous religious practices. It therefore was no surprise that Ugandan bishops cared more about addressing the place of polygamy in the church than, say, debating the merits and faults of homosexuality. However, the Global North showed little appetite for the polygamy concerns of the African churches. Miranda Hassett has best summarized Africa's message at Lambeth 1988 as, "Africa has these problems, and the rest of the Communion and the world needs to respond to them."[20] The African bishops showed a rare boldness, demanding a hearing. In the end, the Conference made grudging concessions. The Lambeth 1988 Resolution 26 on the church and polygamy reaffirmed monogamy as God's plan. Nevertheless, the resolution acknowledged that polygamists subscribing to the Gospel could receive baptism and confirmation along with their believing wives and children.[21]

Lambeth 1988 also brought notoriety to Archbishop Okoth. When the conference deliberated on the AIDS epidemic, calling upon the Anglican Communion to show love and be non-judgmental towards AIDS patients, Archbishop Okoth asserted, "We do not have AIDS in Africa."[22] Unfortunately, Yona Okoth was reiterating a sentiment that was strong at the time, which essentially was that the AIDS "epidemic" was non-existent and manufactured by the West. To the bishops and many other people on the African continent it was yet another cynical example of the West demonizing Africans. The archbishop would also state that "Ugandans don't have AIDS and we *don't have gay people*."[23] His statement, which linked homosexuality to the AIDS epidemic, showed that the archbishop, and indeed many others in Uganda at the time, believed that the "exclusively" heterosexual Ugandans could not contract AIDS, a disease thought to afflict gay white men. However, AIDS, or "*slim disease*"—the term in common usage in Uganda because of the extreme weight loss AIDS victims manifest—was well and alive in the country. The disease was decimating entire communities. In fact, one of Uganda's leading HIV/AIDS scientists, Professor David Serwadda of Makerere University Medical School, described the first cases of "slim disease" in Uganda in early 1985.[24]

A Pan-Africanist sentiment to defend a continent vilified for centuries as the epitome of all that is bad about humanity probably informed Archbishop Okoth's erroneous assertion about the absence of AIDS in Africa. Whatever led the archbishop to deny the existence of AIDS, the truth of the matter is that shortly after Lambeth 1988, AIDS delivered a devastating blow. Several people close to and dearly loved by the bishop succumbed to the disease.[25] These highly *visible* tragic events helped turn Archbishop Okoth into a leading crusader against the AIDS epidemic. He even pondered loudly about distributing dildos to AIDS widows as a safe alternative to penetrative intercourse with male partners, hence mitigating the spread of the disease.[26] Yona Okoth was both a spiritual and pragmatic man. He showed love and was non-judgmental towards AIDS patients. However, he must have continued to struggle with recognizing the voices of the marginalized, those *invisible* and vulnerable people living in the shadows of the mainstream society, like LGBT Ugandans. Although Archbishop Okoth denied the existence of homosexuality in Uganda, he deserves credit for not encouraging the harassment of homosexuals. He knew better than to preside over a church that acted as the cheerleader of the LGBT-bashing movement. Unfortunately, that is exactly what his immediate successors did.

Archbishop Livingstone Mpalanyi Nkoyooyo succeeded Yona Okoth. He was the prelate of the COU from 1995 to 2004. Archbishop Nkoyooyo was an important figure in giving impetus to homophobia in the country. The archbishop's paternal grandfather, Eriya Kagiri Musigula, was one of the Christian pages in Kabaka Mwanga's palace. He was destined for execution in 1886, alongside other pages who disobeyed the king. However, a lucky few escaped the ultimate penalty of death by burning at the stake. In return for a royal pardon, they promised fealty and willingness to submit to the king's will.[27] This is a fact that is usually glossed over and not given much attention. Some of the pardoned pages were wary of linking their freedom to satisfying Kabaka Mwanga's sexual needs. This hesitance is understandable. Uganda is overwhelmingly Christian, and the church's teaching is that homosexuality is immoral and antithetical to Christianity. Therefore, any association of Christianity's heroes to homosexuality elicits discomfort and profound denial. Ugandans barely discuss the factors that contributed to the royal amnesty extended to some of King Mwanga's pages—many of whom became influential and much-admired model Christians. Rahul Rao of the University of London observed that for survivors to have dwelled on the sexual shenanigans of Mwanga might "have invited unwelcome speculation about the reasons for which the survivor had been spared."[28] Eriya Kagiri Musigula, Archbishop Nkoyooyo's grandfather, was among the lucky pages. Mr. Eriya, said to have been "over six feet tall with a handsome athletic build" received a royal reprieve at the last minute because of his outstanding performance in his service as a page to Kabaka Mwanga.[29]

In the run-up to the Lambeth Conference of 1998, Anglican bishops from Uganda, Kenya, Rwanda, Burundi and the Democratic Republic of the Congo met in Kampala for a pre–Lambeth conference. At the meeting, Archbishop Nkoyooyo's resentment of the Global North Anglican Communion was evident when he complained that in the past "the West has dominated topics of concern and influenced most discussions [at Lambeth]. This cannot be allowed. We must make certain that our voice is heard and concerns addressed." He went on to assert that "in Europe homosexuality is a problem and the church wants to compromise on it. Some homosexuals are married and ordained as priests. This deserves our attention. As a Christian body, this issue must not be forgotten."[30] The archbishop's remarks were a striking departure from his immediate predecessor, Archbishop Okoth, who was friends with openly gay clergy.

At the Lambeth Conference of 1998 a resolution committing the Church to "listen to the experience of homosexual people" passed.[31] It was further resolved that homosexuals were full members of the Body of Christ. Equally significant, the resolution condemned homophobia. However, that did not deter the Ugandan Anglican bishops who had resolved at their June 1998 pre–Lambeth conference to oppose homosexuality. Bishop Winston Mutebi, representing a central Uganda diocese, told the conference the Bible forbade homosexuality. He urged gays to repent.[32] Meanwhile Archbishop Nkoyooyo joined a group of nine conservative Anglican prelates in issuing a letter that protested the ordination of practicing homosexuals. Archbishop Nkoyooyo went on to become a fierce critic of homosexuality. He had very little patience for those that advocated for love and compassion towards sexual minorities. He viewed any form of recognition of homosexuality as "promoting unbiblical immorality."[33] When the Reverend Gene Robinson, an openly gay minister, was elected bishop coadjutor of the diocese of New Hampshire in 2003, Archbishop Nkoyooyo swiftly severed relationships with the Episcopalian Church in the United States. He justified his decision thus: "We have cut relations with that diocese. They actually cut themselves off because they rebelled against us and the Bible teachings.... The decision the Episcopal Church of United States took to appoint homosexuals as ministers in the church is regrettable and a disappointment.... We shall not favor anyone on this matter."

The archbishop held a firm conviction that the 1998 Lambeth Conference had condemned homosexuality, and the Anglican Church did not have room for gay people. He displayed zero tolerance for gays in the church. Because the Episcopalian Church in the U.S. condoned same-sex relationships, he characterized American Christians as immoral.[34] Archbishop Nkoyooyo also distinguished himself as uncharitable towards those who voiced any form of support for LGBT people. If gay Ugandans were looking to the COU for compassion, love and pastoral care then they were terribly mistaken. The COU took a stance that was antithetical to the spirit of Christ's teaching of love and went against the grain of the 1988 Lambeth call to show love and be non-judgmental towards gay Christians.

The prelates of the COU who have succeeded Archbishop Nkoyooyo (Henry Luke Orombi, 2004–2012; and Stanley Ntagali, December 2012 to time of writing this book) doubled down on the incendiary anti–LGBT rhetoric. It was the centerpiece of a wider push to enforce a strict interpretation of conservative Christian social values. The prelates continued to play a prominent role in the homosexuality debate tearing at the very soul of the worldwide Anglican Communion. The debates pitted the liberals against the conservative traditionalists. At home, the archbishops cheered on the government as it threatened to throw a blanket of oppression against LGBT Ugandans. Archbishop Orombi alleged homosexuality was the reason for the decline of the Western Church: "At the 1988 Lambeth Conference the Anglican Communion declared the 1990s to be the Decade of Evangelism.... While America and Canada debated homosexuality and watched their churches decline, we in Africa took the challenge of evangelism seriously."[35] He urged American Episcopal dioceses that disagreed with the inclusion of LGBT Christians in their congregations to secede from their bishops and submit to his spiritual guidance. His call struck a chord in some U.S. conservative congregations. Across the U.S., conservative Christians embraced Archbishop Orombi's call, disaffiliating with the Episcopal Church and submitting to the canonical jurisdiction of the Ugandan prelate. Orombi's American supporters hailed him as a "wonderfully godly archbishop."[36] This "wonderfully godly archbishop" boycotted the Lambeth Conference of 2008 because of his opposition to the ordination of gay bishops. Because of his opposition to homosexuality, he refused to attend events organized by the Anglican Communion. When Bahati introduced his bill, the archbishop urged legislators to hasten and pass legislation criminalizing homosexuality. He reminded Christians about a time when "the whites had promised to triple the money they were giving us in order for us to accept homosexuality but we refused and broke ties with the Church of England that ordained a gay bishop.... We shouldn't fear to pass the Bill because they [Global North churches] are withdrawing their money."[37]

Archbishop Stanley Ntagali succeeded Henry Luke Orombi as the prelate of the COU. At his December 2012 inaugural ceremony it was evident that homosexuality would continue to be the singular focus of the Ntagali COU. After all, prior to being enthroned to head COU he had distinguished himself as an opponent of homosexuality.[38] General Museveni attended the archbishop's enthronement and proclaimed that the country "cannot accept promotion of homosexuality as if it is a good thing."[39] Meanwhile Archbishop Ntagali made his priorities known—to fight the evils that bedeviled Uganda. High on the archbishop's list of evils was homosexuality. He made no mention of the major ills that Ugandans confronted in their daily lives—an absence of a functioning democracy, deep-seated poverty, crumbling public services, and gross human rights abuses. Apparently, none of these issues mattered more than fighting against homosexuality. In his homily, he made a conscious decision to choose retribution over love and judgment over inclusion. Archbishop Ntagali championed hate and called for the criminalization of LGBT Ugandans. His mantra was that the "battle against homosexuality is not our battle; it is the Lord's battle."[40] His tone was in stark contrast to other global Anglican leaders like the Uganda-born Dr. John Ssentamu, the 97th Archbishop of York. Dr. Ssentamu preached a message of love and hope, and reassured LGBT people that they too were God's children.

It is instructive to note that the Christian church in Uganda has evolved in surprising ways. Considerations of virtues of love and human dignity, even for the least of God's children, are often lacking. The church has embraced disturbing aspects of the secular Ugandan body politic and has become more oppressive and restrictive especially towards sexual minorities. In attacking LGBT people, it is common to hear Christian clerics use militant language as they urge their followers to "wipe out," "demolish," "fight," "battle," homosexuals. The Uganda church's anti–LGBT rhetoric is not any different from the hateful speeches that spurred Hutu militias and extremists in neighboring Rwanda to kill hundreds of thousands of Tutsis and moderate Hutus in the 1994 genocide. Unconditional love and inclusiveness characterizes Christ's church. If this is accepted as a critical premise of Christianity, then why did the leadership of the COU in their attitude towards homosexuality take on a rigid stance that smacked of religious bigotry? There is no doubt that theological interpretations partly inform the COU's anti-gay posture that eschews same-sex relationships, arguing such relationships are unbiblical and inconsistent to the church's teachings. However, this is unlikely to be the singular factor behind the COU's vituperative and unfettered promotion of homophobia.

Part of the church's anti-gay attitude comes down to an unglamorous sense of shame. The first Christian missionaries to Uganda were unequivocal in equating homosexual relationships with paganism. Missionaries urged and encouraged Ugandans to shake off any traces of "pagan" practices, which included many of their customs. To fit into a modern and Christian mold, Ugandans denounced almost every aspect of their culture and tradition that faintly resembled practices that risked interpretation as belonging to the realm of "paganism." This fear of being associated with paganism is pervasive even to this day. Ugandans take offense when they or recent ancestors are called "pagan," a word considered a slur laden with weighty negativity—primitive, unsophisticated, ignorant, savage. The Ugandan martyrs, the forbearers of Christianity in the country, are celebrated as enlightened, prophetic and principled religious heroes. That some of them engaged in homosexual liaisons is undeniable but nonetheless a subject that Ugandans do not readily acknowledge. The reason for this wall of silence is rooted in a hesitancy to admit that the genesis of Christianity in Uganda owes much to the time-honored practice of same-sex relationships at Kabaka Mwanga's palace. Archbishop Nkoyooyo boasts of an impressive Christian pedigree like no other prelate in Uganda—his grandfather was a page at Kabaka Mwanga's court. Asked by Rahul Rao about Mwanga's homosexuality, Archbishop Nkoyooyo retorted, "That is a bazungu [white men] story which Ugandans do not believe."[41] This is a curious assertion by the archbishop and a perplexing ignorance of the history of Christianity in Uganda. The archbishop was using his ecclesiastical bully pulpit to negate or conveniently ignore historical fact, and distance himself and Ugandan Christianity from any association with homosexuality, a behavior that the church, from its inception in the country, had inveighed against as pagan, evil and vile. Was the archbishop perhaps motivated to deny homosexuality in Kabaka Mwanga's court as a calculated strategy to deflect speculation as to the reasons that led the king to pardon a Christian convert grandfather condemned to death? There is no contention that Archbishop Nkoyooyo's grandfather was a committed Christian who was ready to lay down his life for the faith that he professed. Whether he ever recounted stories of homosexual practices at the king's palace after his pardon is a matter of conjecture. It suffices to reiterate that Ugandans have shown an almost deliberate selective memory bias when narrating the story of the martyrs, placing emphasis on the "political questions of power and the limits of obedience ... whether one's first loyalty is to an earthly, possibly despotic, ruler, or to God, the King of the Universe."[42] This came at the expense of negating homosexuality in the story of the brave and courageous Ugandan martyrs, just as the archbishop did. The Victorian morality had coalesced with the Christian message, spewing intolerance towards gays, making acknowledgment of homosexuality in the cohort of early Ugandan Christians a potent taboo to embrace. In a 2012 interview with Gloria Haguma, Archbishop Nkoyooyo named two Ugandan Christian leaders for inspiring him to become a church minister.[43] Curiously, in spite of enjoying a pioneer Christian status, the archbishop's courageous grandfather, a page at Mwanga's royal court, did not play a significant role in the grandson's career choice to serve the COU.

The COU is possibly insincere when it insists that its desire to uphold biblical teaching and promote a Christian-based moral and virtuous society is the sole reason for its opposition to homosexuality. If this were the case, they would surely apply a consistent standard in opposing all "immoral" behavior perceived as incompatible with Christian teachings. The clergy's personal biases and prejudices, and even shameful opportunism, partially drive the church's obsession and fascination with homosexuality. The extramarital shenanigans of high-ranking Christian government officials are fodder for the Uganda tabloids. Take as an example the 1999 wedding of the 37th king of Buganda, Kabaka Ronald Muwenda Mutebi II, to Sylvia Naggina Luswata, a former World Bank employee. The marriage ceremony at St. Paul's Cathedral in Kampala was an opulent and lavish affair, presided over by Archbishop Nkoyooyo. Over the years, the King and his Queen exemplified the true meaning of a Christian monogamous marriage. Then this happened. In January 2012, the 56-year-old king acknowledged fathering a love child with a 24-year-old barely literate girl in the deep countryside. The Uganda press moved swiftly to elicit comment from COU leadership. The clergy mostly kept silent. As for Archbishop Nkoyooyo, his lackadaisical response spoke volumes about the church's double standards, "I am the one who wed them and I cannot comment about it."[44] Ugandans have an acute sense of smell and can smell hypocrisy from afar. Online commentaries on the *New Vision's* publication of the article "Church Speaks Out on Kabaka's Son" was proof Ugandans had seen through the church's demagoguery and duplicity. The church became intimidated when it came to taking a principled stand against powerful entities, preferring to harass the marginalized and vulnerable instead. This was the general theme of the online comments following the breaking of the story.[45]

Martin expressed a sense of betrayal: "Oh! Hypocrisy of the highest order. We should learn to call sin in its real name. Why should men of God fear to speak the right thing?" Desire highlighted the church's cowardice, observing with a twist of irony that the appropriate title for the article in the *New Vision* newspaper should have read, "Anglican Church Fears to Speak Out on Kabaka's Sin." Mark Bukenya in Kampala was right on the money with an incendiary comment that showed his disgust:

> Church of Uganda was very vocal when it came to consecration/ordination of gay reverends/bishops. COU broke away from other Anglican groups in UK and America based on what they called practices contrary to biblical teachings. Now, the same Church of Uganda has closed its eyes, pretending they can't see and condemn infidelity. What a double-standard!!!

Beyond religious conviction and both personal and institutional shame, a number of observations appear at play and critical to the understanding of the church's antagonism towards homosexuality and LGBT people in general. The COU had not recovered from Idi Amin's mockeries following Lambeth 1978, where the first discussions on homosexuality within the Anglican Communion took place. At the conference, it was evident to the bishops from the Global South that they had never really been invited to attend as equal partners in the first place. There was a glaring absence of mutual acceptance and respect, best illustrated by the slight of Archbishop Joseph Adetiloye when the session chair at the 1978 Lambeth Conference ignored the Nigerian prelate. That entire humiliating episode smacked of condescension. It was a critical inflexion point in the relationship between the rich Global North and the poor Global South, with the latter viewing the former as a purveyor of imperialist power. Over a period of years, the Global South, and particularly the African Anglican Church, grew in self-confidence and was ready to challenge any vestiges of a patronizing Global North Church. In this battle of recognition and increasing assertiveness between the North and the South, homosexuality became the unsuspecting cause célèbre as was evidenced during the 1998 Lambeth Conference. The primates of the Anglican Global South had found a voice, and they were ready to show their prowess in defining church doctrine. As one African proverb has it, when two elephants fight the grass suffers. Where the European and American churches were calling for accommodation and the welcoming of gay Christians to serve the church, the COU balked at the prospect. Claiming to champion an orthodoxy grounded in Christ's teachings, the Ugandan church has unashamedly used its opposition to homosexuality as a testing ground for the African church's growing influence and power within the Anglican Communion. The obsession with banishing homosexuality in the name of remaining true to Biblical teachings allows the Church in Uganda to claim moral and spiritual superiority over the financially powerful Global North Anglican churches. Just like Idi Amin's moralistic decrees of decades before, a desire to break with a perceived patronizing West informed the COU's stance against LGBT people. The COU rejected and resisted calls for human rights and dignity for LGBT Ugandans, viewing such show of sympathy for sexual minorities as part of the West's imperialist hegemony.

Another factor that helps place the church's anti–LGBT zealotry in perspective relates to declining numbers in church attendance. Congregations in the traditional Christian denominations started seeing a significant drop in attendance around the mid–1980s. It is significant to note that around this period, the country was in the throes of a devastating AIDS epidemic, with entire communities decimated. It would be decades before the current cocktail of antiretroviral drugs would be available to Ugandans. In the 1980s and 1990s, a diagnosis of AIDS was tantamount to a death sentence. With no prospect for a cure, many of the patients diagnosed or people suspecting infection with HIV turned to the Pentecostal Church. The Pentecostals approached the AIDS epidemic with a lingua that resonated with most ordinary Ugandans. A considerable number of Ugandan Christians, irrespective of their educational and socioeconomic status, still believe in the power of witchcraft and sorcery—and the attendant evil spirits believed to be the source of all illnesses and misfortunes. It is for this reason that ritualistic human sacrifices, especially involving the murder of children by businesspeople seeking to create or consolidate wealth, is on the rise.[46] The Christian churches have not condemned this barbaric practice as passionately and voraciously as they have attacked LGBT Ugandans. Even members of the mainstream traditional

Christian clergy are not immune to superstition and can display the most irrational belief in evil spirits, defying logic. For example, Archbishop Orombi found time to come out of retirement to claim that demons manifesting themselves as black cats infested St. Paul's Cathedral in Kampala, the seat of the Archbishop of the COU.[47]

With an emphasis on spiritual healing, and presenting life's vicissitudes, including AIDS, as a battle between the Holy Spirit and the old evil spirits that ordinary Ugandans knew too well, the Pentecostal message had its allure. The evil spirits, under their master Satan, were responsible for disease and misfortune, and only the Holy Spirit could prevail in this battle. The Pentecostal church could claim mastery over exorcising evil spirits, which hitherto had been the domain of witch doctors. Although many Ugandans consulted witch doctors, most, especially the religious and educated, felt shame in openly admitting soliciting the services of witch doctors since this was equated with being "pagan" and certainly not "modern." Because the Pentecostal pastors essentially offered the same services as witch doctors, spiritual Ugandans gravitated towards Pentecostalism, which provided a sanitized and Christianized belief in the pervasiveness of evil spirits. Ugandans wholeheartedly embraced the Pentecostal movement. However, not everybody was celebrating. The traditional Christian denominations were alarmed at the ease with which the Pentecostals made inroads into people's spiritual lives. Everywhere, makeshift churches had emerged. Deafening ululations of praise as the Pentecostals spoke in tongues characterized the nights. Their message had touched the hearts of Ugandans. With more and more Ugandans flocking to Pentecostal churches, revenue in the traditional churches slumped. The hemorrhage had to be stanched.

Pentecostal churches in Uganda are profitable businesses. Most of the Pentecostal church "ministries" are managed more like big business ventures than churches. Pastors at the helm of these churches rank among the wealthiest Ugandans, living in palatial homes, driving luxurious expensive cars, and shamelessly flaunting their riches. When a Uganda newspaper printed a list of the wealthiest Ugandans, there was a liberal representation of Pentecostal church pastors. The newspaper provided some insight into how they had amassed their huge fortunes: "Religion is big. It sells and the new breed of God's men and women know how to get the money rolling in. They don't stand at the pulpit and give boring sermons. They excite, dazzle and woo the congregation. And when the time comes for the congregation to make their offerings, they dig deep into their pockets."[48] Rivalry and intrigue is commonplace in Pentecostal churches, with accusations and counter-accusations rife. In 1995, *Uganda Confidential*, a newsletter that claimed to propel investigative journalism to new heights in Uganda, published a scurrilous story, which alleged that Handel Leslie, the influential black Canadian founder and chief pastor of Abundant Life Faith Center, in Kampala, was gay.[49] Handel Leslie preached the gospel of prosperity, stressing material success, personal enrichment and indulgence in comfort and luxury. The congregation at Abundant Life Faith Center was wealthy, elite, and included many high-ranking government and military figures. It was the Sunday playground for the rich and powerful. During his sermons, the pastor openly called upon the congregation to donate generously in order to receive God's blessings. The congregation did not let the pastor down. Propelled by abundant spiritual enthusiasm, they came forward with their tithes, donating lavishly to the church in hope of receiving blessings to acquire even more wealth and dispel misfortune. At St. Paul's Cathedral, Kampala, the COU priests were more subdued and did not place tithe-giving above sedate sermons on the path to salvation through humility and rejection of worldly treasures. The Sunday collection paled in comparison to the financial harvest at even a modest Pentecostal church in Kampala's slums. Abundant Life Faith Center became one of the most successful Pentecostal churches in Uganda and its pastor a wealthy man. Did the COU seize upon the *Uganda Confidential* allegations to ratchet up its critique of homosexuality as an indirect way to discredit and dethrone a Pentecostal rival? With accusations of homosexuality, it became difficult for Handel Leslie to defend himself against those that would question his moral integrity and commitment to a Christian faith that denounced homosexuality as a sin.

I argue that the Anglican Church in Uganda used homosexuality as a cheap form of spiritual propaganda to wrest back its position as the arbiter of God's moral standards. By mooring homosexuality central to its moral and theological teachings, the COU had found the perfect bogeyman on which a spiritual revival would be born, countering the growing influence of Pentecostalism. It was indeed a cynical attempt to employ spiritual populism by sacrificing the rights of LGBT Ugandans. However, that strategy would backfire. Ugandan Pentecostalism validated its homophobia by the support of American Christian conservatives like Scott Lively, usurping the COU to become the leading anti–LGBT crusaders. The Pentecostals had access to the corridors of power, using that advantage to maximum benefit. They held a firm conviction that Christian values must shape and influence politics, and anything short of that was evil. The Pentecostals also subscribed to the notion that the traditional family and Christian morality was central to Uganda's re-emergence from its dark past and in its efforts to address the challenges the nation faced. The HIV epidemic was of particular concern and seen as evidence of God's disfavor because Uganda had veered away from pursuing God's righteous ways. Using their influence, the Pentecostals called on the government to legislate morality and criminalize sexual laxity and license.

Paradoxically, the Ugandan Christian church viewed sexual immorality as a product of Western influence that threatened to destroy the traditional Christian family. Battling Western immorality became a calling. On the other hand, General Museveni played on this narrative for political expediency, placing Western immorality on a continuum of the West's neo-colonial manifestation. General Museveni constructed Western immorality, trashed and denigrated by Ugandan Christian churches, as an assault on national sovereignty. By presenting himself as a revolutionary opposed to neo-colonial and imperialist forces of immorality, the president latched onto a populist theme that had the promise of bolstering his image as a Pan-Africanist while diminishing focus on the restive Ugandans eager to see him leave power. Therefore, the Christian churches in Uganda and General Museveni built a mutually beneficial ecosystem curiously united in their anti–LGBT campaign. The Pentecostals in particular upped homosexual hate, elevating it to even scarier heights. LGBT Ugandans were in mortal danger, scared for their lives and, much to their horror, not even the traditional churches were welcoming—they were complicit in the push to strip LGBT Ugandans of their humanity and dignity.

Pentecostal churches did not begin building their presence in Uganda by singling out the LGBT community for condemnation. Their initial message encouraged people to repent their sins and accept Christ as their personal savior. It was an uplifting message of hope and salvation that resonated with many Ugandans. The anti-gay rhetoric crept up insidiously and over many years. Prior to General Museveni's 1999 order to the police to hunt down and arrest homosexuals, nobody took Pentecostal pastors seriously when they inveighed against sexual immorality, which they were apt to do. The pastors railed against homosexuality, and ordinary Ugandans interpreted their admonishment as moralistic absurdity, just like Uganda Pentecostalism's prohibition of alcohol and smoking. To understand the Pentecostal church's fascination with homosexuality and its relationship with Uganda's political elite, the Kampala Pentecostal Church (KPC) provides a good starting point. The Rhodesian-born Canadian Gary Skinner and his wife, Marilyn, founded KPC, an offshoot of the Pentecostal Canadian Assemblies of God (PAG), in 1983. They located their church in the heart of Kampala, in a building that once hosted the city's foremost cinema theater, the Norman Cinema. KPC was an English-language church, which distinguished it from other Pentecostal churches in the country. For this reason, the church attracted a large segment of government officials and college students. Gary Skinner, who is the church's senior pastor, is generally considered among the most influential people in Uganda.[50] The faith movement influenced the pastor and his sermons reflected conservative Christian values, including the promotion of heterosexual marriage-based Christian families. Gary Skinner was homophobic, and viewed homosexuality as inhuman.[51] Frank Mugisha, a Ugandan gay rights activist, has said that Gary Skinner is among the most homophobic people in the world.[52] In March 2009, Scott Lively, Don Schmierer and Caleb Brundidge spoke at KPC. According to the flyer announcing their three-day seminar, the Americans were in the country to provide "reliable and up to date information to Ugandans and nationals from Africa so that they can know how to protect themselves, their children, families and can make informed decisions on this global subject [homosexuality]."[53]

President Museveni's wife, Janet Museveni, is currently a member of the Covenant Nations Church, a Pentecostal church founded and managed by one of her daughters who in 2007 famously dedicated Kampala City to God.[54] Prior to worshipping at Covenant Nations Church, Mrs. Museveni was a regular at KPC. Janet Museveni is arguably the most powerful first lady Uganda has ever had. She was a legislator and a minister in her husband's cabinet. The appointment of Mrs. Museveni to a senior cabinet post was in keeping with General Museveni's reliance on close relatives and allies to implement and entrench his hold on power. General Museveni's brothers, children, numerous cousins, including his wife's relatives and associates, form a core group of supporters appointed to key political, civil and military offices.[55] Mrs. Museveni said that she owed her political career as a legislator representing a rural southwestern Uganda constituency to her obedience to a personal call from God, who instructed her to contest for electable office as a legislator.[56] However, some have contended that her appointment to a cabinet post in her husband's government was to broaden her access to "state resources and perks."[57] Unquestionably, Mrs. Museveni wielded greater influence than most ministers and senior army officers and had the whip hand in shaping some of General Museveni's policies.[58] She also had significant leverage over legislators from the ruling party. Bahati, the man generally believed to be the architect of the anti-homosexuality bill, enjoyed a close relationship with

Uganda's first lady.[59] He would later assume the chair of the Parliamentary Fellowship, which was described as a caucus of God. Janet Museveni was perhaps *the* most prominent member of the fellowship.

The Uganda Parliamentary Fellowship, which is the Uganda chapter of "The Family," was founded in 1986 by Balaki Kirya, the first Pentecostal minister in General Museveni's government. Jeff Sharlet has written extensively about the Uganda Parliamentary Fellowship and its close ideological and personal links to "The Family," which also is called "The Fellowship" or the "International Foundation."[60] The Family is a powerful secretive Christian fundamentalist group in the United States, and Nancy Goldstein writing in the *Nation* described it as a major background player in American and global politics for decades. Its founder, Abraham Vereide, claimed God had provided him the inspiration to go and minister "to other powerful men, introduce them to Jesus, and together create a leadership headed by God. Consequently, Family members' most heartfelt prayers, as their legislative interests indicate, concern dismantling healthcare reform, shredding the social safety net, busting unions, promoting deregulation, making abortion illegal and enriching themselves."[61] Professor Paul Gifford of the School of Oriental and African Studies (SOAS) of the University of London observed that Kampala Pentecostal Church (KPC) stood for "the reform of Uganda through total personal integrity on the part of Christians who take on leadership positions."[62] KPC, just like the Family, targeted Christians in leadership. Mr. Balaki Kirya helped General Museveni win trust among Western governments, which were weary and suspicious of his Marxist ideology when he captured power in 1986. In addition, Mr. Kirya was critical in introducing the Family to Uganda's leaders. Janet Museveni, Bahati and Buturo were active members of the Parliamentary Fellowship. Following in the footsteps of the American Family, the Uganda Parliamentary Fellowship organized an annual prayer breakfast every eighth of October. The first such gathering took place in 1997, attracting a modest 20 people. At the 2015 event in Kampala, over 1,500 people attended. General Museveni speaks at these events, liberally sprinkling his speeches with Biblical quotations as the audience in attendance nods in both acknowledgment and appreciation. Besides the national prayer breakfast, the Parliamentary Fellowship holds a weekly prayer session, which Mr. Buturo regularly chaired at one point.

Mrs. Museveni's KPC membership provided Gary Skinner and his church a unique and easy access to the very pinnacle of power in Uganda. Therefore, KPC enjoyed a privileged political position unlike any other religious institution in the country. Some of the most powerful and influential political figures in the country subscribed to KPC's strong Christian conservative message on moral purity. Given the significant power that KPC had over its faithful, it is conceivable that the church's moralistic extortions against homosexuals shaped Mrs. Museveni's sentiments about LGBT people. Like her husband, she was born into a western Uganda pastoral community where homosexuality was an accepted norm especially among the aristocracy. Therefore, her opposition to homosexuality, coming years into her husband's presidency, could not be attributed to tradition and the "un–Africanness" of homosexuality. I argue here that KPC's morality sowed the seeds of Janet Museveni's homophobia. Also, significantly, she wielded considerable clout over Uganda's Pentecostal movement.[63] Like her pastors at KPC, Mrs. Museveni variously ranted against homosexuality, which she alleged sought to "destroy the family setting as it was defined by God."[64] Central to her homophobia was a claim to protect conservative Christian values and the traditional African family. She variously warned Ugandan youth not to "experiment these new sex fashions in town, like homosexuality and others. Please, I warn you youth of Uganda, that it pays to stay pure sexually, respect your life and guard it well."[65] In the eyes of Mrs. Museveni, homosexuality was an unnatural evil lifestyle that impressionable Ugandans chose. Her opposition to homosexuality was grounded in a curious theology, which she shared during a speech congratulating the COU bishops' firm opposition to homosexuality, "We must listen to God and obey him.... If cows did not practice homosexuality, how could we, the human beings, start arguing over homosexuality?"[66]

When a local journalist turned-vigilante boasted that his organization planned to hunt down homosexuals and close their meeting places, he claimed General Museveni was behind their anti–LGBT crusade. He also alleged that even "Mrs. Museveni is openly against homos. She supports our crusade."[67] Organizations founded by or affiliated to Uganda's first lady, such as the Uganda Youth Conference, made it a point to condemn homosexuality in the strongest terms possible.[68] Janet Museveni and like-minded legislators, chiefly members of the Parliamentary Fellowship, were apologists for theocratic rule, striving for a "God led country and God led policies."[69] According to leaked diplomatic cables from WikiLeaks, Mr. John Nagenda, an advisor to General Museveni, told Mr. Jerry Lanier, the U.S. ambassador to Uganda, that Mrs. Museveni was a "very extreme woman" and was "ultimately behind the bill [Bahati's anti-homosexuality bill]."[70] The "extreme woman" is possibly a reference to Mrs. Museveni's radical brand of Christian fundamentalism she sought to impose on

Ugandans. For example, in 2005 Ugandan women organized to stage Eve Ensler's play, the *Vagina Monologues*. The government put an immediate halt to the artistic enterprise. It alleged the play promoted homosexuality and was therefore not suitable for performance in Uganda. In actuality the play raises awareness of sexual abuse against women. In neighboring Kenya, the play had run for years to packed audiences without provoking moral outrage. There are claims that Mrs. Museveni lobbied her husband to order the government censors to ban *Vagina Monologues*.[71] A statement issued by the Uganda women organizers of the play condemned the ban, highlighting the irony that "a vast amount of energy and resources has been spent on condemning the use of the word vagina rather than condemning the actual violations that the play clearly addresses. This is tantamount to silencing women's voices and is and has always been, the major obstacle in addressing violence against women in a substantive way."[72]

As for the "Kill the Gay" bill, Mrs. Museveni denied being the initiator of the frightful legislation. However, if Mr. Nagenda's allegation about Mrs. Museveni's central role in Bahati's anti-homosexuality bill is correct, and given Nagenda's longtime association as a confidante of General Museveni there is no reason to doubt his assertion, then the first lady was content to stay in the background as the bill was active in Parliament. Buturo, and later Bahati, rose through the stable of born-again legislators that were trusted as standard-bearers of a moralistic Christian-centric agenda shaped by Ugandan and American Christian fundamentalists. Despite the braggadocio, Bahati did not wake up one day and dream about sponsoring the anti-homosexuality bill. Rather, he was willing to act on behalf of a number of interests as the face of the draft legislation in return for political and personal favors. Behind the bill were powerful conservative religious and political influences acting collectively to persecute LGBT people but for different reasons. Bahati has credited the Parliamentary Fellowship for initiating the anti-homosexuality and anti-pornography bill.[73]

The COU had staked out their position on homosexuality, and so had the Pentecostals. Other traditional religious leaders—Muslims and Roman Catholics in particular—did not fare any better in terms of extending a welcoming hand to the homosexual community; they were decidedly hostile. The leading Muslim cleric, Sheikh Ramathan Shaban Mubajje, joined the ranks of the anti–LGBT camp. He appealed to General Museveni to round up homosexuals, banish them on a Lake Victoria island and leave them to die off.[74] In 2014, the U.S. denied the Muslim cleric a visa, allegedly for his anti-homosexuality views.[75] By contrast, that same year,

Archbishop Ntagali of COU, whose name is synonymous with stoking paranoia against LGBT Ugandans, visited the U.S. Anglican Diocese of New England. Archbishop Cyprian Lwanga of the Roman Catholic Church, believed by many to be the calm voice of sanity in a country where Christian teaching was increasingly leaning towards an intolerant ideology driven by religious fanatics, gave conflicting opinions on the national conversation on homosexuality. He initially spoke out against the Bahati "Kill the Gays" bill in his 2009 Christmas message to the faithful. However, following a 2012 ecumenical meeting with the prelates of COU and the Orthodox Church, he appeared to support the statement issued on behalf of the religious leaders calling on legislators to speed up the passage of the "Kill the Gays" bill since homosexuality was supposedly "an attack on the Bible and the institution of marriage."[76] However, in a 2013 interview with *The Observer*, a Ugandan newspaper, Archbishop Cyprian Lwanga revealed a more reconciliatory position towards homosexuals: "Although homosexuality is indeed a troubling moral and social phenomenon, homosexual persons should be helped to overcome this anomaly in their lives, through counselling and spiritual formation."[77] Another Catholic archbishop, John Baptist Odama of the northern Ugandan diocese of Gulu, was more caring. He spoke directly to his fellow citizens, calling upon them to show mercy and not dwell on fractious social issues. He urged Ugandans "to love God's human creatures" and "not take the laws into our hands to harm and hate the homosexuals because we all have weaknesses."[78] Archbishop Odama's compassionate words echoed Pope Francis' memorable and refreshing reply to a journalist's question on gay priests: "If someone is gay and he searches for the Lord and has good will, who am I to judge?"[79]

Historically speaking there is an astounding unawareness about LGBT issues. Both political and religious leaders exploited the people's ignorance, ratcheting up fear and creating an environment of anxiety in Ugandan communities. Every pastor or imam could throw every outrageous accusation at the LGBT community and Ugandans would bite bait. Pastor Solomon Male alleged homosexuality "is bad, it is dangerous. I don't want it because of what it causes. Hemorrhoids, prolapses, bowel damages, incontinence, oral gonorrhea ... there are many complications."[80] Meanwhile, Pastor Ssempa claimed lesbians insert bananas, carrots and cucumbers into their private parts as substitute for a male member. This act, he further alleged, caused "ripping" of the "urinary tract area" and perforation of intestines.[81] Not to be outdone, Sheikh Siliman Kasule Ndirangwa—later appointed to the position of Supreme Mufti—blamed homosexuals for the long period of drought affecting the country.[82] The sheikh should have done well denouncing government's dismal environmental policy. In 2007, General Museveni ordered the transfer of Mabira, one of Africa's last remaining tropical forest, to a transnational corporation, which would cut down trees, including rare species, to grow sugarcanes.[83] The logic behind the general's degradation of a national heritage appeared to be that "Uganda should not have to import sugar while forest land lies idle, or hosts trees that cannot be eaten, exported or taxed."[84] The general's spokesperson, Mr. Tamale Mirundi, underscored that perception when he infamously declared that the government "can grow trees anywhere but we cannot establish a factory anywhere. We cannot relocate a factory but we can relocate a forest."[85]

General Museveni is a skilled and canny man who saw political capital in exploiting the anti–LGBT paranoia and hatred orchestrated by religious leaders. Initially General Museveni was happy to cling onto the tailcoats of the religious fanatics as they bashed LGBT people. However, he would seize the momentum from church zealots and chiefly through his political proxies, choreograph the anti–LGBT movement. General Museveni, although nominally a Christian affiliated with the COU, seemed not to take Christianity seriously. He has claimed he became a born-again Christian in 1962, the year of Uganda's independence. The born-again message of moral rectitude, puritanical discipline and personal responsibility appealed to him. He broke with the born-again Christian church in 1966 partly because of "public confessions, and their exposing of one's personal life."[86] That he shows the occasional apathy towards Christianity is not surprising given his strong roots in Marxist ideology. Sometimes General Museveni displays a startling ignorance and a limited understanding of Christianity in the country, making bewildering gaffes. Speaking at the June 3, 2015, Uganda Martyrs' Day Celebration, General Museveni, the chief celebrant at the Anglican martyrs' shrine, confessed to a gathering of tens of thousands that he had not been aware of Anglican martyrs, believing that all Ugandan Christian martyrs were of the Roman Catholic faith.[87] Even the general's ardent Christian supporters were at odds to explain the president's ignorance. The basic school curriculum intensively covers the story of the Uganda Martyrs. The president did not care for Christian history. He was more interested in the Pentecostal movement and how best to harness their obsession with morality to further his political agenda.

Because of their mass appeal and sizeable following, Pentecostals are a critical constituency for General Museveni. In an interview with Richard

Downie of the Center for Strategic and International Studies, an evangelical Christian summarized the importance of the Pentecostal movement to Uganda's politicians: "The Pentecostal church is the only church in Uganda that is well organized. One call from a pastor can determine whether people don't vote or do vote, for example. This is because Pentecostal people are so much attached to the church, rather than just going once a week. It is an integral part of their lives."[88] Indeed, Pentecostal pastors routinely mobilize their followers to rally behind General Museveni. The pastors use extravagant and flattering language extolling the general's virtues such as elevating him to a near mystical pedestal. Some preached to their congregations that God chose the general to heal Uganda's political problems and emancipate its people.[89] In turn, General Museveni has extended preferential treatment to "born-again" Christians, fast tracking them for jobs in the civil service and security organs.[90] Some "born-again" Christian security agents have gained notoriety as the worst perpetrators of human rights abuses, actively participating in the torturing of Ugandans in what is reminiscent of Idi Amin's rule of terror.[91] At the surface, it would appear as though the Christian churches, particularly the Pentecostals, wielded a disproportionate influence on government and its policies. In reality, the government viewed them as a godsent ally, a partner prone to easy manipulation by feeding on their over-bloated sense of moral righteousness. Pentecostals, wittingly or unwittingly, became an arm of General Museveni's regime.

The General's Impunity
and the Politicization
of Sexuality

"Homosexuals are the ones provoking us. They are upsetting society. We shall not allow these people to challenge society."[1]—General Yoweri Kaguta Museveni, President of the Republic of Uganda

General Museveni was sworn in as president of Uganda in January 1986. The event was remarkable in that it was the first time at a swearing-in ceremony of a Ugandan president where prayers were conspicuously absent.[2] General Museveni's ascent to Uganda's highest political office was the culmination of a five-year protracted guerrilla war in which his rebel force, the National Resistance Army (NRA), routed government troops. The NRA's victory marked the first time that a guerrilla force had overthrown an African government. Libya's Muammar Qaddafi provided General Museveni's rebel army with guns and money. The NRA also bolstered its fighting force by recruiting child soldiers. General Museveni justified the use of child soldiers thus: "In Africa here, even by the age of four, you learn how to fight. This is our tradition.... So if you are trying to think this may disorientate them [children] psychologically ... that is not the case."[3] General Museveni's view on the use of children in combat perpetuates a fallacy in asserting that it is all right for African children to engage in military combat because they are shielded from the traumatic effects of war, ostensibly because of their emotional and psychological maturity which is unlike that of children in other parts of the world. The uniqueness of the African that sets him apart from all other races, as highlighted by General Museveni, is also a theme repeatedly used to propagate the myth that Africans are exclusively heterosexual.

Like Idi Amin before him, General Museveni's rise to power was greeted with great jubilation. People held on to a hope for a better future— a truly democratic government that treated its citizens with dignity and respected the rule of law. General Museveni vowed that under his watch pervasive corruption, tribalism and lawlessness that had dogged previous governments were passé. His high-minded aspirations for the country were spelled out in a simple but clear 10-point program, a progressive social and political agenda. Ugandans were ecstatic when he promised to promote the ethics of frugality while castigating the culture of material excesses of his immediate predecessors. He also pledged to prioritize the investigation of widespread atrocities committed by past governments. There was a strong emphasis on the right of the people to have a demo-cratic government, and he swore his government was "quite different from the previous people in power, who encouraged *evil* instead of trying to fight it."[4]

The *evil* that General Museveni referred to was generally interpreted as a reminder of gross human rights abuses that characterized both the Amin and post–Amin regimes. However, with the passage of time and spurred on by a desire to hold onto power under any circumstances, there has been a broadening of the definition of the "evil" General Museveni spoke about so passionately in 1986—it now encompasses LGBT people. General Museveni's first decade in office distinguished itself by several spectacular successes and important failures as he worked on an ambitious agenda to address the country's pressing problems. HIV/AIDS had emerged as an existential threat, and Ugandan communities were reeling from its disastrous effects. The sheer scale of the human cost was astounding, pos-ing significant challenges to the very viability of the socio-economic pro-grams that General Museveni had promised. Unlike other African leaders, General Museveni did not play down the public health significance of the HIV epidemic. He used every available avenue to caution his people about the dangers of unsafe sex. He strategically partnered with local and inter-national experts to put in place robust preventive measures. Education was central to the HIV prevention strategy, which meant dispensing with the reluctance to talk about sex. For the first time, sex issues left the closet and were mainstreamed. It is this candidness, and much more besides, that coalesced to enable Uganda to successfully roll back the HIV epi-demic. But despite the newfound openness to discuss sexual matters, there was no recognition of the needs of homosexuals and they were left out of all HIV/AIDS programs. Perhaps this oversight was intentional. Homo-sexuality was illegal in the country. It is in this new era of openness on sexuality that Archbishop Nkoyooyo of the COU began castigating homo-sexuality. It did not take long for the leaders of the Pentecostal movement and other self-styled arbiters of moral authority from various walks of life to join the chorus of LGBT condemnation.

The anti–LGBT obsessions and ranting of leaders of Uganda's Chris-tian fundamentalist community would have been empty rhetoric lost in the dry winds of the savannah grassland had it not been for the imprimatur of General Museveni. The general was initially content to let the religious leaders spew hateful anti-gay speech, refraining from joining the conver-sation. He preferred to use the church's anti-gay push as a sounding board to test the country's mood on homosexuality. Sensing the popularity of the anti-homosexuality rhetoric and the potential political capital that could be reaped, General Museveni seized the moment and made common cause with the church. He eventually came to own the anti-gay agenda, appropriating it as official ideology in a calculated attempt to bolster his standing among Ugandans. With time, General Museveni had become an expert at delivering populist schlock of a kind that a largely peasant and uneducated society could buy in, and quite frankly, enjoyed. And he chose his targets carefully—LGBT Ugandans and urban women were selected for marginalization. General Museveni must have known that targeting LGBT people and urban women would make him unpopular in the West, where he was often hailed as a hero—a man that had saved his country from decades of misrule by a succession of dictators that had come before him. But it was a risk General Museveni was willing to take since it poten-tially guaranteed to shore up support for his unpopular government. The LGBT community and the urban women were the low hanging fruit, an easy scapegoat.

In September 1999, the *Sunday Vision*, a government-controlled paper, ran a story alleging a marriage had taken place between two gay men in Wandegeya, a Kampala suburb.[5] One of the alleged "gay" men was a celebrity barber. His client list read like a who's who of Ugandan politics. These included the country's attorney general, powerful cabinet ministers and top civil servants. General Museveni's response was not immediate, as was his usual modus operandi. He waited for over two weeks to make known his disapproval of the reported gay marriage: "I have told the CID [Criminal Investigation department] to look for homosexuals, lock them up and charge them."[6] What is intriguing is that General Museveni did not issue the order because he believed homosexuals had violated Uganda's existing "sodomy" laws. He wanted them imprisoned because homosex-uality was "abominable" and "God created Adam and Eve as husband and wife but not man to marry fellow men."[7] Clearly, Archbishop Nkoyooyo's message against LGBT people had resonated with General Museveni and he deemed it politically prudent to align his thoughts with the cleric. Following General Museveni's directive to apprehend homosexuals, Mr. Muruli Mukasa, the minister for security, claimed homosexuality was at the center of the downfall of great civilizations and "God has decreed that homosexuals be stoned to death."[8] Mr. Mukasa promised that security personnel would enforce General Museveni's order and launch a crackdown on the LGBT community.

Questions were raised as to why General Museveni was speaking out now against homosexuals, a marginalized group that did not present a threat to his then 13-year rule? And how credible was the gay wedding story reported in the government-controlled newspaper? To try to answer these questions we would have to provide some background on Uganda's evolving political landscape in 1999. On June 14, 1999, Nelson Mandela resigned as president of South Africa, opting not to run for re-election and fulfilling a pledge he had made in 1995. Mandela's resignation after serving one term in office bucked the trend of African leaders who once in office sought to find ways, mostly through repression, to entrench themselves in power and rule for perpetuity or until deposed by a restive military. Ugandans followed Mandela's resignation with intense interest. In 1999, their own president had been in power for a very long time—13 years. A new constitution had been adopted and ratified in 1995, and it limited the president to a maximum of two five-year terms. The next presidential elections were scheduled for March 2001, and General Museveni was already canvassing for support. If General Museveni won the 2001 presidential election he would be serving his final five-year term, and would leave office in 2006. However, rumors—which turned out to be true—were rife that the general would seek to amend the constitution to award himself a life presidency, just like Idi Amin before him. It was too tempting for the general to want to forego the trappings of power—an extensive security detail of crack elite presidential guard, a personal ambulance that accompanied General Museveni on every trip in Uganda, not to mention a 15-plus vehicle presidential convoy that included a silver Mercedes Benz SUV hauling the prized portable toilet for the president's exclusive use.

The life-presidency scheme had its detractors. Notable among them were grandees of General Museveni's ruling party, the National Resistance Movement (NRM).[9] It was an intriguing observation that a number of NRM big-wigs opposed to General Museveni's life-presidency project were clients of the "gay" barber who had allegedly married his partner, "Joyce."[10] Was General Museveni playing a cynical game of Machiavellian intrigue, readying to smear those critical of his life-presidency project by manufacturing salacious rumors or even instructing the CID to "lock them up and charge them" for suspected homosexuality? The previous year, Malaysia had set such a precedent. There was a rift between two very good friends—Prime Minister Mahathir Mohamad and the deputy prime minister and finance minister, Anwar Ibrahim. The disagreements, which were initially over policy, took on an ominous twist, with the government-controlled press accusing Anwar Ibrahim of shocking improprieties. In September 1998, Mahathir Mohamad dismissed Anwar Ibrahim following accusations of a grievous and immoral act—sodomizing his wife's driver. General Museveni's "war" on homosexuals in Uganda appears to fall within a broader pattern of political opportunism—stifling political opponents while drumming up support by rallying people behind a popular cause. As for the alleged Wandegeya gay marriage, it never happened.[11] That it was all fictitious did not in any way lessen General Museveni's newfound enthusiasm to hunt down and arrest homosexuals. General Museveni's ruling party, the NRM, through Mr. James Magode Ikuya, the party's director of information and public relations, made it clear it would never accept homosexuality and disparaged Ugandan elites and intellectuals who dared defend gay rights: "The greatest drawback of our elite and intellectuals is that they have never actually bothered to understand and base themselves on the society in which they are born ... they only articulate things by rote, blindly replicating white society under the cover of pursuing liberal life.... The starting point is that homosexuality has, hitherto, not been known nor practiced in our communities. There is even no word for it."[12] Mr. Ikuya wanted the world to believe him, that homosexuality was not practiced by his community.

Truth is one thing and falsified narrative another. Mr. Ikuya is a member of the Gisu (or Bagisu) tribe whose ancestral home is on the slopes of Mount Elgon in eastern Uganda. The Gisu people do have a term for same-sex relations—*inzili*. Further, traditional Gisu recognized the *bayazi*—transwomen. The *bayazi's* behavior was attributed to either witchcraft or possession by evil spirits (known by the Bagisu as *bamakombe* or *bisimu*).[13] Mr. Ikuya further alleged that in traditional Ugandan communities, the act of homosexuality would "overwhelm even the most insensitive criminal. The elders would hand ropes to the culprits to hang themselves.... Any adult person who does such unnatural things [homosexuality] *deserves no life*, even if such a person were a lunatic."[14] Contrary to Mr.

Ikuya's assertion neither did the Gisu elders or community condemn or ostracize the *inzili* and *bayazi*. They were part of the tribe. In the early twentieth century, Felix Bryck, a renowned Swedish anthropologist and entomologist, observed that among the Gisu men, "cases of homosexual acts occur" and they are an "expression of true homosexual love."[15] The truth of the matter is that Mr. Ikuya was the one guilty of failing to understand his own local community. His spurious hyperbole and inept appreciation of the richness in the sexual and gender diversity of his Gisu culture lent a disturbing dimension to the nascent homophobia in Uganda. For the first time, we document evidence of a Ugandan political leader suggesting homosexuals did not deserve to live; in other words, "kill the gays."

In Uganda, the official September 1999 policy was to "look for homosexuals, lock them up and charge them." There were Ugandans prepared to heed that call, and they burned with nationalistic fervor and moral righteousness. A secret vigilante group headed by Bart Kakooza sprang into action, sending a violent message to gay Ugandans. The group had a singular goal—raiding local venues where gays were known to network and socialize. Mr. Kakooza affirmed that his anti-gay organization had the backing of General Museveni and his wife, Janet.[16] Significantly, Mrs. Janet Museveni did not deny supporting Mr. Kakooza's anti-gay offensive. Kakooza, an internationally recognized journalist who has contributed to CNN's *World Report*, had zero respect and tolerance for gays: "We are working against these immoral fellows who are duping the public that they are exercising human rights. What rights does one man have when it comes to having carnal knowledge of his fellow man?" Kakooza's anti-gay rhetoric, coming from a well-respected journalist, opened the floodgates to the tabloid's harassment and humiliation of gays. Apparently, some people can never learn from history, even after watching it unfold at close quarters. Kakooza was in Rwanda in 1994, reporting on the shocking killings as one ethnic group turned against the other because of its "Otherness." The extremist Hutus killed Tutsis and moderate Hutus because they were the "Other"—dangerous "cockroaches" that had to be exterminated. Bart Kakooza failed to see the irony in his crusade to hound and harass sexual minorities because of their "Otherness."

About a month after General Museveni's 1999 directive to arrest gays, five men and women, all gay activists, were apprehended by government agents. They were blindfolded and held in illegal secret detention centers—the so called "safe houses." General Museveni's security agents operate "safe houses" in and around Ugandan towns. People accused of opposing General Museveni's policies and authoritarian rule are commonly locked up in these safe houses and subjected to torture.[17] The activists were sexually and physically abused. One of the detainees, Christine, described her ordeal at the hands of General Museveni's security agents: "Coming midnight, they said 'we want to show you something.' They took my clothes off and raped me. I remember being raped by two of them, then I passed out."[18]

Uganda-watchers were appalled at the extent to which General Museveni's government was prepared to go in humiliating and terrorizing Uganda's LGBT community. It was yet another example of a recurrent pattern of flagrant disregard and abuse of human rights perpetuated by the State. But General Museveni, as was his policy when defending his abysmal human rights record, deflected criticism. He insisted his government did not persecute LGBT people, claiming they were welcome to live in the country provided they refrained from revealing their sexual orientation.[19] In other words, it was all right to be gay if you exercised self-censorship and denied yourself the right to be who you are. At the 2002 Commonwealth Heads of Government Meeting in Coolum, a beachside Australian resort, General Museveni sent a contradictory message, claiming there were no homosexuals in Uganda.[20] Which begs the question: If the country did not have homosexuals or LGBT people then why did the general order the arrest and prosecution of a non-existent group?

LGBT Ugandans were not a figment of the imagination; they were real people, from all walks of life, living and working in Uganda's cities and villages. These were the people hurting under a well-orchestrated repressive state machinery, which exploited their sexual orientation and gender identity as a political tool to win support in a country with a record of failure to deliver on basic services and where corruption, rampant human rights violation, and ill-advised military adventurism had become the norm. Roads were in a sorry state, hospitals without medicines, poverty on the rise, and infrastructure crumbling. The supply of power in the main cities was erratic, and entirely absent in most of the country. A jigger infestation borne of poor hygienic conditions gripped an entire rural district in the east of the country, affecting tens of thousands of people. Against this background, there was growing discontent with General Museveni's government and the calls for his removal became louder. Meanwhile, General Museveni built a political and economic network centered on nepotism, cronyism, corruption and perverse fear. Those that dared challenge the general's hold on power were ignobly sidelined— "placed on *katebe*" in Uganda parlance. The less fortunate were mercilessly strafed. For the favors extended from his presidential largess, General

Museveni expected and demanded blind political fealty in return. General Museveni's intemperate character and disdain of political rivals was evident when dealing with political opponents, who were routinely beaten, imprisoned and sometimes killed. To many Ugandans this arbitrary use of state power and heavy-handedness from a government that had claimed to respect human rights was an eerie flashback to the dark era of the country's past. There was a narrative, especially perpetuated by the international media, that Uganda under General Museveni had made gigantic leaps in terms of introducing meaningful and durable political, social and economic reforms. Nothing could have been further from the truth.

There were the widespread atrocities that Ugandans were concerned about—abuses that had left in their wake unspeakable crimes that went largely unreported in Western media. In northern Uganda, a two-decade war between government troops and myriad rebel groups, including the Lord's Resistance Army (LRA) of Joseph Kony, unleashed immense suffering and death. Tens of thousands of civilians were killed and an estimated 1.8 million people displaced from their homes and confined to internal refugee camps. The rebels conducted a campaign of extreme viciousness—raping, mutilating and killing innocent civilians, destroying homes and crops, abducting girls for use as sex slaves, and forcibly recruiting boys into their ranks. Government troops were equally merciless, killing, plundering and laying the land bare. Some incidents that shocked Ugandans and which represented everything wrong with General Museveni's government stand out for the sheer gruesomeness of the carnage.

In 1986 General Museveni's 35th Battalion was deployed to Namokora sub-county in Northern Uganda. In August, the soldiers rounded up about 100 villagers, cramming them onto the back of a military truck. After a short ride to the town's outskirts, the truck halted. The civilians were ordered to stay on the truck as the soldiers disembarked. Without warning, the soldiers opened fire with machine guns on the unsuspecting civilians. When the guns fell silent, 71 people had been massacred. A day before the Namokora massacre, one of the male survivors had been subjected to severe beating while detained inside a church. Later, the soldiers dragged him onto the church veranda where he was repeatedly raped.[21] This incident of rape must not be seen in isolation; there are many accounts of soldiers deliberately raping men. Appearing before a Ugandan magistrate in 1999, a woman from the war-ravaged northern Uganda part of Gulu testified that some "soldiers force their fellow men into homosexuality. They call it *ogung* in our language, meaning bending for sex."[22] An Amnesty International report on human rights violations by General

Museveni's army in northern Uganda listed allegations of homosexual rape of civilians by soldiers.[23] The Ugandan military has used sexual violence against the civilian population, both men and women, as an instrument of war, to terrorize, humiliate and dominate. In July 1989, government troops rounded up over 300 civilians in Mukura, a town sitting on an old railroad track in eastern Uganda. The civilians were beaten and accused of collaboration with militants opposed to General Museveni's rule. They were herded into a disused train wagon without windows or vents. The door was bolted for four hours, and it was over 100 degrees outside. The wagons became a charnel house. Hundreds of innocent civilians suffocated and roasted to death.[24]

Equally, General Museveni's military adventurism in neighboring countries, in the main, has been detrimental. Indeed, the unilateral military adventures in the countries that General Museveni's army has invaded and occupied increased instability in the Great Lakes region. The Second Congo War (1998–2003) ranks among the world's bloodiest since World War II. It all started in 1998 when Uganda and Rwanda invaded the Democratic Republic of the Congo (DRC, or the Congo) in a bid to oust the president, Laurent Désiré Kabila. Between July and September 1998, the Uganda military deployed an estimated one quarter of its manpower inside the Congo—about 40,000 troops.[25] Soon, nine African national armies and at least 20 rebel groups aligned to the various countries engaged in vicious fighting. They plundered the Congo's rich natural resources—gold, diamonds, coltan and many other minerals in high demand in the West. The human toll was staggering. General Museveni's army provided support to some of the rebel factions that have been accused of being behind the worst atrocities. The International Rescue Committee (IRC) estimated the death toll at 5.4 million.[26] And a United Nations investigation implicated Ugandan officials, including members of General Museveni's close family, for organizing crime syndicates that caused general mayhem and plundered the Congo's natural resources.[27] The report named General Museveni as one of the "main sponsors" of the war, and alleged the general had given criminal cartels a "unique opportunity" to exploit the mineral wealth of the Congo.

Even after General Museveni had manipulated Parliament, forcing legislators to amend the country's constitution to allow him run for office in perpetuity, the country's problems continued to pile. This went in tandem with heightened repression of real and imagined political opponents. The dissenting voices grew louder, restive, and bold.[28] General Museveni and his loyalists were caught off-guard by the emergence of a new media phenomenon that Ugandans called *"ekimeeza,"* which followed the liberalization of the media. The *"ekimeeza"* was a roundtable discussion conducted by privately owned radio stations and was a combination of live public debate and phone-in talk shows focusing on topical issues. It was a good barometer of prevailing public mood. To the government's ire much of the conversation on the radio talk-shows was critical of General Museveni and the ills of his government—runaway corruption, nepotism, injustice and increasing repression. Government responded by claiming that these public debates created public disaffection, promoted tribalism, sectarianism, divisive tendencies and generally led to confusion among the public.[29] Much to the frustration of Ugandans, outspoken opposition politicians were arrested for participation in these public debates that had stirred up political passion among ordinary people.[30] Predictably, General Museveni, threatened by the emboldened masses, ordered a total ban on the *"ekimeeza."*

It was no longer enough to rely on the hackneyed messages and the empty sloganeering that General Museveni had frequently relied on to deflect criticism of his rule and rally the masses. One approach that he used successfully was to play on the people's fear, reminding Ugandans that he had liberated them from the fangs of past dictatorships. At the core of this logic was that because of his "sacrifices" fighting in the "liberation" guerrilla war that had brought him to power he was justified to hold on to the presidency, and the country owed him gratitude and allegiance. General Museveni also relied on an age-tested populist message, cynically playing on popular societal resentment to perceived interferences by imperialist (Western) forces in the internal affairs of African states. Bashing the West and accusing Western governments of imperialism and neo-colonial policies that supposedly suppressed Africa's growth is a message repeated by every African dictator to shore up shrinking support. And yet it is the financial aid from these very vilified western countries that provided a significant percentage of Uganda's budget. Despite this, General Museveni relished in spiting the West, a message that appealed to his domestic audience. When the U.K. expressed concern over the arrest of General Museveni's political opponents and his intolerance of democracy and the rule of law, the general issued a caustic retort charging that "Europeans really have bad manners. Don't lecture to me."[31]

General Museveni's distrust and disdain of western society was not new. An understanding of this provides insight into what informed his decisions in the run-up and the aftermath of the anti-homosexuality bill. General Museveni catapulted to regional recognition as a young, militant

student at the University College, Dar es Salaam, Tanzania, where he studied from 1967 to 1970. He was initially disappointed because the student
body lacked militancy and displayed a perplexing hostility to socialism,
an ideology that he cherished. He disapproved of "watching decadent
Western films" and did not hide his distrust of imperialists. General
Museveni would join other students to form the University Students'
African Revolutionary Front (USARF), which aimed to "encourage revolutionary activities at the College, and to transform the college from being
a center of reaction ... to a hotbed of revolutionary cadres, cadres that
would dedicate themselves, unto death, to the cause of African revolu-
tion."[32]

The leftist students at University College, Dar es Salaam, were heavily
influenced by the teachings of Marxist scholars such as Walter Rodney,
Stokely Carmichael, Angela Yvonne Davis and Jim Mellen.[33] The latter
went on to co-found the radical leftist group, the Weather Underground,
that was active from 1969 to 1977. The Weather Underground was dis-
satisfied with the Establishment, and conducted a series of bombing campaigns in the United States as a means to realize social and political
change. At University College, General Museveni was the chairman of
USARF, which published an anti-imperialist and Marxist-Leninist magazine, *Cheche* (which in the Swahili language means "Spark"). The magazine's title was an apparent wink to *Novaya Zhizn* (New Life), the Leninist
journal of the Russian Bolsheviks.[34] The magazine took a hostile stance
towards perceived imperialist and neo-colonial forces. As part of its militant anti-imperialist mission, the magazine published a list of alleged CIA
agents operating in Tanzania.[35] Decades later, Ugandan tabloids would
take to outing homosexuals in a manner very reminiscent of *Cheche* magazine's praxis. The USARF leftist ideology was considered extreme even
by the standards of Tanzania's ruling socialist party. Both the organization
and *Cheche* magazine were banned in November 1970.[36]

Ugandans were taken aback when General Museveni's government,
as part of its newfound obsession with fighting "immorality," introduced
laws that were an outright assault on women's rights. In particular, the
criminalization of wearing of miniskirts was generally viewed as a sad
throwback to Idi Amin's rule. I argue here that General Museveni's assault
on women's bodies borrowed partly from his own experience living
through the Tanzanian "decency" campaigns of the 1960s and early 1970s,
which saw the banning of miniskirts, wigs, tight pants and cosmetics.
These items of fashion and beauty were represented as "symbols of imperialist infiltration from the decadent West."[37] Young party male militants

were mobilized under Operation Vijana (Swahili for "Youth") with instructions to enforce the ban on Western fashions and beauty products. They particularly targeted urban women, attacking and arresting those wearing miniskirts, wigs and cosmetics. Urban women were a source of resentment, especially among male youth and traditionalists. The urban woman, with her miniskirt, wig and whiff of perfume, posed a challenge to a patriarchal society as she related to and utilized urban space. She was the ultimate symbol of female independence, eliciting male anxieties and resentment in a society where women's labor participation was hitherto limited to working the fields or performing domestic chores. Andrew Ivaska has pointed out that Operation Vijana's focus on women's bodies and fashion was "an opportunity to air profound anxieties about women, sex, work and mobility."[38] The decency campaign tapped into a "common nationalist trope in underscoring that Tanzanian women literally embodied national culture and thus could protect the integrity of the national family by adhering to 'tradition' in dress and comportment."[39] In other words, attacking urban and feminized decadence as represented by women embracing western fashions and beauty products was a critical part in the definition of an evolving nationalistic cultural identity. Similarly, General Museveni's assault on women's bodies and LGBT people exploited similar anxieties that were at play in the 1960s Tanzania.

Informed by precedent, General Museveni cared little about accountability for his actions, however unpopular or repressive. The international community lacked the will or appeared to fear reprimanding him. That gave him a hyper-inflated sense of pride, self-assurance and impunity. In the Congo, an estimated 5.4 million people had died from direct or indirect consequences of the Uganda's military involvement in that country. Back home the military had left a sad trail of human rights abuses while fighting an armed rebellion in the north and northeast of the country. Rights of free expression, association and assembly were heavily curtailed, and opposition figures and journalists were subjected to regular harassment, intimidation and arrest. There was an absence of strong condemnation. Instead, General Museveni has been the recipient of resounding commendations and many in the West hailed him as a leading member of a new breed of African leader. The "new breed" of African leaders were a "motley collection of presidents whose stated vision for their individual countries marked a radical departure from past leadership methods" and were "held in high esteem by Western intellectuals, media, and governmental and intelligence circles."[40] In February 1993 General Museveni hosted Pope John Paul II, and Pope Francis came calling in November

2015. Oloka-Onyango recognized General Museveni's wiliness, noting that he is "able to hobnob with all sides of the political divide" and was "great friends with Libya's Muammar Qaddaffi" while maintaining "close relations with all the British prime ministers ... from Margaret Thatcher through John Major and up to Tony Blair."[41] President Bill Clinton visited the general in March 1998, and expressed regret over the United States' role in African slavery. George W. Bush was in Uganda in July 2003, praising General Museveni for his leadership in the fight against HIV. Citing the general's "personal commitment" to addressing the HIV epidemic in Uganda, the Secretary General of the Commonwealth of Nations awarded him the Commonwealth Award for Action on HIV/AIDS for Government, Policy and Advocacy. During his acceptance speech, General Museveni laid the blame of the HIV epidemic on the West: "Our societies were very strict on sex, this liberalism that has facilitated the spread of AIDS, was brought by our European partners."[42] At the same time, this celebrated hero of the fight against one of the formidable epidemics of modern times did not hesitate to use AIDS as a political tool to stigmatize political opponents. He suggested that HIV-infected people could not compete for public office. General Museveni alleged that his long-standing political nemesis, and one-time personal physician, Dr. Kizza Besigye, had AIDS. Therefore, the general argued, Dr. Besigye was disqualified to seek the presidency.[43] Incredulously, General Museveni was mentioned as a possible candidate for the Nobel Peace Prize, ostensibly for his role in bringing about peace in the very region where his soldiers stood accused of heinous atrocities.[44]

The international community's seemingly unconditional support for and dalliance with General Museveni despite overwhelming evidence of gross human rights was a carte blanche to the general to introduce and enforce repressive laws without fear of consequences. Thus, the NRM ruling party prioritized the rise of anti–LGBT sentiments, stoking societal angst as a deliberate policy to politicize sexuality in order to deflect criticism of General Museveni's declining popularity. LGBT people became a convenient state machinery to blindside people and distract their attention to the country's pressing needs. The initial official instrument for the persecution of LGBT people and prescription of strict social mores was the Ministry of Information. The ministry was led by Dr. Nsaba Buturo. Later, General Museveni appointed Buturo to head the Ministry of Ethics and Integrity. As the minister of ethics and integrity, Buturo's vitriolic pronouncements against homosexuality were elevated to deafening decibels. The first minister of ethics and integrity, Miria Matembe, was a fiery woman who relentlessly pursued corrupt officials. Although she attempted to close LGBT-friendly bars and venues, she did not make LGBT witch-hunting a sport or obsession.[45] Mr. Tim Lwanga, her immediate successor, was notable for his ineptness in combating corruption. He is best remembered for calling Gaetano Kaggwa, the 2003 Uganda *Big Brother Africa* housemate, "immoral" for participating in a reality TV show.[46] A flirtatious racy scene between Kaggwa and Ms. Abergail Plaatjes, the South African housemate, during a *Big Brother Africa* episode, was interpreted by many viewers as a depiction of "live sex." Because of this, Kaggwa earned the ire of Uganda's minister of ethics and integrity. Mr. Kaggwa was extremely popular among urban youth. After his eviction from the *Big Brother Africa* house in South Africa, thousands of cheering Ugandans welcomed him home. The popularity of Kaggwa and reality TV among ordinary Ugandans on one hand, and the resentment of politicians like Mr. Lwanga on the other, exposed a chasm between the urban youth and the aging, predominantly male, politicians. Ugandan youth were consumers of a global culture that embraced reality TV, Facebook, Twitter, WhatsApp. The youths' worldliness frightened the leadership, which was hopelessly out of step with the socially interconnected global world. They therefore sought to disengage the youth from the influences of the modern world, shackling Ugandan millennials to an "African" culture that demanded unquestioning obedience to masculine, heterosexual authority. Lwanga was another anachronistic moral crusader, whose obsession was to criminalize pornography and ban Kampala's burgeoning striptease (*ekimansulo*, in local vernacular) scene.[47] The harassment of LGBT Ugandans and the persecution of women, be it dressed in miniskirts or because of their opposition to General Museveni's government, cannot be divorced from the larger and more deliberate political scheme that aimed to entrench the general in power and help him to establish a dynastic rule.

Dr. Buturo is a man of contradictions and a good study of political sycophancy and naked opportunism behind the anti–LGBT campaign. Buturo was first appointed to General Museveni's cabinet as a minister of information in May 2003. This was a time of unprecedented assault on print and broadcast media.[48] The Ugandan press, which was reeling from government censorship, intimidation and arrest of journalists, welcomed Buturo. Members of Uganda's media fraternity believed Buturo would be a much better minister than his predecessor, a hardline ruling party fanatic. On his appointment, *The Monitor*, an independent local newspaper, ran a favorable editorial which referred to him as "a known gentleman in all senses of the word" while expressing hope that his "political approach to politics will rub off the rougher types we know populate the cabinet."[49] But it did not take long before Buturo disappointed the press. He proved that he was just another lackey, a sycophant singing General Museveni's praise. Buturo had the right pedigree and the stellar record of a loyal and unquestioning enforcer of unpopular repressive policies. In the 1980s he had served as District Commissioner for Kampala in the second Milton Obote government (December 1980–July 1985). Obote's government of the 1980s was characterized by mayhem and bloodshed, and widespread arrests and disappearance of civilians. It has been alleged that as District Commissioner Buturo oversaw the infamous 1980s *panda gari* operations.[50] A senior adviser to General Museveni described Buturo as a "very bad guy."[51] *Panda gari* was an ill-conceived security strategy instituted by the Obote government to turn the tide against General Museveni, who had launched a guerrilla war to oust the government. People suspected of sympathizing or supporting General Museveni's antigovernment guerrillas were randomly picked off the streets and bundled onto military trucks. Many were never seen again. Buturo has denied any involvement in the *panda gari* operation.

Buturo was initially not taken seriously. Ugandans dismissed him as one of those sycophants, a dime a dozen, who sang General Museveni's praise irrespective of anything. His defense of General Museveni's unpopular policies earned him a comparison to "Comical Ali"—Mohammed Saeed al-Sahhaf, the Iraq information minister in Saddam Hussein's government.[52] When General Museveni started in earnest to manipulate the constitution to grant him a life presidency after serving out his presidential term in 2006, Buturo was the first cabinet minister to endorse the life-presidency mission.[53] He would urge Ugandans to rally behind General Museveni because he was "God-sent" and warned that opposing the president was tantamount to disobeying God.[54] He defended General Museveni from internal and external voices critical of the general's maneuvers to prolong his stay in power with the zealousness he would display in condemning LGBT people. He was yet again another cog in General Museveni's perpetual wheel of power. The media that had held out hope and appealed to his supposedly objective sensibilities became a victim to his viciousness. Buturo accused the media of harboring an anti-government agenda, and oversaw further curtailing of press freedoms.[55] He also accused the media of abusing "media freedom" by promoting a pornography agenda to "feed this unsavory and immoral menu to Ugandans."[56] This was a not-too-subtle message to Uganda's media fraternity, used as it were to the government's heavy-handed approach when dealing with the press. The government was getting creative: it was ready to use the "promotion of pornography" as a justification to limit the media's freedom.

Buturo portrayed an image of a born-again Christian fundamentalist, a loyal government official on a spiritual mission to save the very soul of a country at risk of collapsing under the weight of secular evil. He shared his moralistic beliefs through regular opinion pieces published in the government-controlled *New Vision*. This in and of itself gave his perspective an official imprimatur. Buturo decried the proliferation of "profoundly immoral practices" and called on responsible "moralists" to "oppose ... the ... pernicious demands to affirm homosexual acts as both a moral and human rights issue."[57] He invoked God, reminding the country that a "resurgent nation must have God" at its core and appealed to the people to refrain from engaging in "ungodly" practices such as homosexuality.[58] Before David Bahati's rise to international infamy, Buturo, more than any other Ugandan politician, kept homophobia alive. He accused international non-governmental organizations (NGOs) of giving money to journalists and legislators to buy their support of homosexuality in the country. He did not name the NGOs, and there was not a scintilla of evidence to back his assertion that journalists or legislators—generally interpreted as referring to opposition members of Parliament—had received foreign money to support the gay cause. All this bore the hallmark of a sophisticated government campaign aimed at finding new avenues to discredit political opponents and justify clamping down on the media. The press and political opposition were vocal in their denunciation of a possible lifting of presidential term limits to pave way for General Museveni's life presidency, and getting them out of the way was a government priority. In fact, some legislators questioned Buturo's sincerity about fighting pornography. It was common knowledge that the government or its agents owned the country's widely circulating tabloids, whose salacious tittle-tattle and racy pictures were popular with the public.[59] It is incongruous that General Museveni's government through its spokesperson, Buturo, would accuse anybody of receiving a bribe to support a cause. Barely a year after Buturo accused the press and some legislators of taking bribes, General Museveni's government bribed legislators with $1,500 in exchange for voting to lift the presidential term limits.[60] This money was doled out from funds that were supposed to finance public projects.

Nsaba Buturo's rabid anti–LGBT rhetoric alarmed many in Uganda and overseas. General Museveni's government was aware of these concerns, especially from Western governments. To contain possible criticism from Western governments, General Museveni's government launched a pre-emptive strike. Foreigners were accused of funding the political opposition in the 2006 elections in order to encourage public disorder and overthrow the government.[61] Basically, as General Museveni maneuvered to sell his life-presidency agenda to the country, he sent out a nationalistic message to Ugandans, that is, unnamed foreigners, ostensibly the very ones demanding human rights for LGBT people, planned the overthrow of a legitimately elected democratic Ugandan government. The Netherlands Embassy was not intimidated. A Dutch diplomat in Kampala expressed dismay at the treatment of homosexuals in Uganda. He called for recognition of their human rights. A strident Buturo dismissed the Dutch, accusing them of interference in the affairs of a sovereign state. He reminded the Netherlands Embassy that just because they provided significant financial support to Uganda that in itself did not grant them a right to lecture Uganda on moral issues.[62] This dismissive and almost reckless pride towards the West's substantial financial aid would be echoed by many secular and religious anti–LGBT campaigners.

In his unrelenting persecution of homosexuals, Buturo was patently emphatic. He maintained that homosexuality was unnatural and the government would never grant any rights to homosexual Ugandans. Through a combination of intimidation, bribery, and threats of violence, General Museveni finally succeeded in getting his prized life presidency. In July 2005, Ugandan legislators concluded debate on the Constitution (Amendment) Bill No. 3, which lifted presidential term limits. The same bill stipulated that there would be no legal recognition of gays and lesbians, and it also prohibited same-sex marriage.[63] The bill was codified into law on September 26, 2005, with the appendage of General Museveni's signature. Hence, by the stroke of the general's pen, the government had erased recognition of the Uganda LGBT community—a sexual minority. The law had decreed they did not even exist. It appeared the law aimed to provide the perfect legal justification to General Museveni's 2002 contentious assertion at the Commonwealth Heads of Government meeting in Australia that "we don't have homosexuals in Uganda."[64]

In the 2006 presidential and parliamentary elections, General Museveni was elected to yet another five-year term in office. Meanwhile the parliamentary contest in Ndorwa West, a rural southwest Uganda constituency, was won by Bahati. His personal story is compelling, and speaks to the courage and determination of a young Ugandan man who triumphs in spite of inordinate life's vicissitudes. He was three years old when his mother died during childbirth. Three years later, his father died from what was believed to be poisoning. Raised by relatives, Bahati eventually graduated from Uganda's prestigious Makerere University and Cardiff University in Wales. In 2004 he was awarded a certificate in campaign leadership after completing a short course at the conservative Leadership Institute in Arlington, Virginia. In Arlington, he met an American politician who introduced him to the Family and its Ugandan affiliate, the Parliamentary Fellowship.[65]

Prior to contesting in the 2006 parliamentary elections Bahati had not held public office. His first months as a legislator were not entirely unremarkable. He advocated for a peaceful resolution of the Joseph Kony rebellion, which had been going on for two decades in northern Uganda. He talked passionately about the plight of internally displaced people from the Kony war and decried the poor conditions in refugee camps. That he made it a point to remind Ugandans of the raging Kony war of attrition was outstanding for a country that is usually divided along north-south sectarian fault lines. Bahati was a politician representing a southwest Uganda constituency; but that did not deter him from doing the right thing—championing ways to end the long-running insurgency and bring peace and stability to northern Uganda. In a July 2006 *Monitor* op-ed Bahati listed the peaceful resolution of the Kony rebellion as one of the major issues he cared about. Homosexuality was not on that list.[66] He cared about children, especially the underprivileged, and sought to uplift their living conditions. He was passionate about education and worried about the slackening reading habits among Christians as reading was "very important in evangelism of the Gospel of Jesus Christ."[67] It therefore comes as no surprise that he was elected to the executive body of the ruling party's parliamentary caucus. He became the caucus' treasurer. A loyal supporter of General Museveni and the ruling NRM party, Bahati treaded carefully; he did not contradict the president's policies, however unpopular. When a group of mostly youthful NRM parliamentarians staged an internal rebellion over internal party democracy, Bahati avoided his fellow "Young Turks" as the plague. In due course, he rose to greater prominence in Uganda politics and was generally considered a trusted confidante of General Museveni. General Museveni had mastered the art of operating through proxies, choosing loyal NRM parliamentarians to shape his political and legislative agenda. He could rely on Bahati to advance his anti–LGBT campaign, which on the one hand pleased the Christian churches and their Western conservative supporters, and on the other was an opportunity to direct the country's restiveness towards a common "enemy" and drum up support for the government. Religious leaders in Uganda hold inordinate power over the faithful. They routinely advise their congregations on how to vote. General Museveni knew that. By giving the religious leaders what they were asking for—intolerance to homosexuality, pornography and women's "indecent" dress—General Museveni would be perceived in religious circles as a dependable ally. He could therefore claim to be a champion of righteous Christian living. In turn, the clergy would mobilize the faithful to support the president's political agenda.

In September 2006 Lift Up Jesus Church, a Ugandan Pentecostal ministry, hosted its Annual World Revival Conference. Lift Up Jesus Church emphasized the miraculous. And the church alleged to be a witness to many miracles. According to church accounts, a prayer session in 2005 had achieved an almost impossible feat—prayers had delivered a fatal blow to demonic forces responsible for countless vehicular accidents along a much-traveled highway. Like so many Pentecostal churches in Uganda, Lift Up Jesus Church claimed to heal HIV/AIDS in addition to curing infertility and many other illnesses that had defied medical science. The September 2006 conference was planned as a week of prayers during which the congregation would beseech God to end Kony's brutal war. Bahati was an invited guest and he addressed the conference. It was the first time for Bahati to publicly share his incredulity about the rampant immorality in the church: "Can you imagine a situation where some people want to legalize prostitution, homosexual and lesbian marriages? Pray for the church so that such bad behavior is abolished."[68] With that pronouncement, Buturo had found an ally in the young first-term legislator. Both became actively involved with the Uganda Parliamentary Fellowship where they advanced Christian values and bemoaned the country's perceived immorality.

David Bahati, ignorant or uneducated on the historical and cultural constructs of homosexuality in Uganda, embraced the role of the self-righteous zealot, contesting what was an integral norm within his own Ugandan culture. He denounced homosexuality in forceful and unforgiving terms. He viewed homosexuality as a "vile evil" which was "spreading in schools, churches and NGOs." Bahati feared that if no action was undertaken to legislate against homosexuality then the country faced the prospect of electing gay legislators who would "criminalize all morals and legalize all manners of perversion."[69] Bahati lashed out at the "rich ill-intentioned perverts," invariably foreigners, who he claimed were forcing homosexuality on morally upright Ugandans. This was consistent with General Museveni's beliefs that "European homosexuals are recruiting in Africa."[70] General Museveni and Bahati painted a picture of an African country caught in the crosshairs of Western homosexuals whose hidden agenda was to promote immorality and annihilate the exclusively hetero-sexual Ugandans. Dr. Sylvia Tamale noted that homosexuality presented a "challenge to the deep-seated masculine power within African sexual relations and disrupts the core of the heterosexist social order."[71] The het-erosexist social order saw women as subservient and submitting to men's sexual needs. Mr. Muruli Mukasa, General Museveni's minister for secu-rity, provides a good example of the heterosexist male privilege when he questioned the mental state of gay men for their disinterest in Ugandan women who were supposedly given to a "good degree of permissiveness" and therefore easy prey to any self-respecting man.[72] This sexist, misog-ynist and scornful attitude towards Ugandan women, especially those in urban areas, was one shared by many top ruling party functionaries. With such views prevalent, it was an easy matter for the government to pass anti-women laws in the name of defending morality. Buturo's successor as minister of ethics and integrity, Father Lokodo, was particularly active in pursuing the morality laws. The priest had an unhealthy fixation to homosexuality and was known to drive around the country hounding homosexuals and physically breaking up their private gatherings.

What really motivated some Ugandan legislators and government officials to passionately embrace and pursue the politics of hate against peace-loving Ugandans just because of their "Otherness"—their sexual orientation and gender identity? What was the overriding moral impera-tive, if they had any? Many anti-gay politicians and public officials justified their vitriol against LGBT people on cultural, religious and even nation-alistic premises. Mr. Buturo identified as a born-again Christian. He had been in public office for a long time, holding positions of seniority. There is no record of him waxing and waning against homosexuality prior to joining General Museveni's cabinet in 2001. Buturo's homophobia seems to be less a result of his Christian born-again beliefs on immorality but more a product of political opportunism. A senior adviser to General Museveni, Mr. John Nagenda, provided insight into Buturo's motivation. Nagenda claimed that Buturo's anti-gay stance was motivated by a desire to ingratiate himself with General Museveni and thus expunge any asso-ciation to participation in the brutal *panda gari* campaign under past gov-ernments. Nagenda further noted that Buturo would "do anything in his power to be a populist."[73] On several occasions he demonstrated a readi-ness to do anything to please General Museveni.

Uganda had managed to register dramatic decline in HIV infection rates through its ABC approach—Abstain, Be faithful, using Condoms.

HIV infection rates dropped from a high of 15 percent in the early 1990s to about five percent in 2001. Despite the success of a multipronged approach in HIV prevention, Christian conservatives were unhappy with the emphasis on condom use and were eager to see it dropped altogether. Their preference was an abstinence-driven public health campaign, arguing that condom promotion increased promiscuity and premarital sex. Swayed by American Christian conservatives and with the support of his wife, General Museveni's government abandoned the successful ABC approach in favor of abstinence and fidelity in the fight against HIV. It fell to Buturo to vigorously defend the new policy. He also indicated he would introduce legislation to criminalize premarital and extramarital sex.[74] In tandem, Mrs. Museveni taunted a so-called multipronged program that would replace the ABC approach—behavior development, behavior reinforcement, and behavior change. She was a fierce critic of sex with condoms, which she equated to killing and theft.[75] Further, Mrs. Museveni called for a census of virgins in Uganda as a starting point in government's new emphasis on abstinence.[76] Meanwhile, Pastor Ssempa staged a burning of condoms while invoking the name of Jesus Christ. The pastor is a fiery preacher with an idiosyncratic Christian zealotry, and was at one point close to Pastor Rick Warren, the conservative evangelical leader of Saddleback Church, a California megachurch. In fact, Warren's wife, Kay, said endearingly of Ssempa: "You are my brother, Martin, and I love you."[77] Helen Epstein noted that Ssempa's sermons condemned "homosexuality, pornography, condoms, Islam, Catholics, certain kinds of rock music, and women's rights activists, who he says promote lesbianism, abortion, and the worship of female goddesses."[78]

Buturo, Bahati, Muruli, Father Lokodo and many other anti–LGBT legislators may have strongly identified themselves as members of the Uganda Parliamentary Fellowship who subscribed to the notion that Christian values shaped politics. But they were first and foremost quintessential sycophants, too eager to sacrifice principles of common decency for the sake of winning personal favors from General Museveni. Showing unconditional support to authoritarian leaders is mostly rewarding, and is a stepping stone to career advancement and job security. As General Museveni's spokesman rightly pointed out, most Ugandan legislators rely on the general for their survival.[79] *The Daily Monitor*, a Ugandan newspaper, cited a WikiLeaks cable attributed to Jerry Lanier, the U.S. ambassador to Uganda, in which the ambassador characterized some of General Museveni's ministers as people with "no conscience" who were too eager to undertake anything, including "dirty tricks" to ensure their master maintained his hold on power.[80] Indeed, at the root of the most toxic anti-gay rhetoric were legislators motivated by naked political opportunism. According to the internationally acclaimed Ugandan journalist, Onyango-Obbo, what drives General Museveni's loyalists' excesses is best summarized as an "irrational fear of loss of privileges."[81] Fortified by anti–LGBT messages from American Christian fundamentalists, opportunistic political leaders felt vindicated in their hate towards LGBT Ugandans. It must be stressed that American Christian fundamentalists built on an already pre-existing hostile LGBT environment in Uganda. The COU had led the initial assault, and the Pentecostals followed shortly after, becoming the dominant religious voice against LGBT people in the country.

VI

From the Closet to a Kuchu *Identity*

"In my country, in Buganda, my great grandfather, the King of Buganda, was a known homosexual and he was respected. Today they are using my culture to condemn me."[1]—Kasha Jacqueline Nabagesera, Ugandan LGBT activist

It was not easy to live as an LGBT person in Uganda, even before General Museveni infamously ordered the police to hunt down and lock up homosexuals in a dramatic turn that propelled anti–LGBT sentiments to become ingrained in the political and social discourse like at no other time in the country's history. Prior to General Museveni's assault on the homosexual community, there is no evidence of anyone having been convicted of homosexuality in Uganda.[2] This despite Uganda's Penal Code in existence before the rule of General Museveni, which prescribed harsh punishment for "carnal knowledge against the order of nature." Although this was generally interpreted as reference to "sodomy," the law was criticized for not spelling out what constituted "carnal knowledge against the order of nature." Indeed, a notable Ugandan blogger and LGBT advocate argued that in "a strict sense, therefore, homosexual sex is illegal but not homosexuality because it is possible to be homosexual and one doesn't engage in any carnal knowledge or, indeed, any sexual activity whatever. As a result, the only realistic way of enforcing the sodomy law would be for the police to rely on eavesdroppers and a peripatetic sex-brigade hiding in closets of both heterosexual and homosexual couples to catch offenders in flagrante delicto."[3]

Cultural attitudes, ignorance, legislation and a prevailing Christian doctrine that characterized homosexuality as immoral, all conspired to create a Ugandan society that was intolerant and hostile towards homosexuals. Same-sex intercourse or identification as a homosexual was taboo. Although homosexuals were generally not actively persecuted and hounded, they could not freely show their sexual orientation and be who they really were. For most, their sexual orientation had to be kept a secret from family, friends and the wider community. There was the constant fear of societal disapproval, rejection and ostracization. Society demanded that men had to marry and get children. So, many gay men ended up marrying and having children. Gay men who chose to avoid entering heterosexual marriages had to find excuses, such as creating a fictitious girlfriend. Sylvia Tamale, the human rights activist, noted, "It is not surprising that most homosexuals find it difficult to 'come out' of their closeted lives or to be open about their sexual orientation. Most blend within the wider society and even live under the cover of heterosexual relationships while maintaining their homosexual relationships underground. The tendency is to construct 'comfort zones' where they complacently live a different and segregated lifestyle until they are rudely awakened."[4]

Not surprisingly, LGBT Ugandans have struggled with sexual orientation and gender identity issues and the attendant psychological, emotional, and spiritual stress. Seeking love and understanding, and finding none in the community, some of them lapsed into depression and contemplated suicide. Paul, a young Kampala resident, was confronted with such a dilemma. His parents were distraught on learning about his homosexuality. He was taken to a psychologist who claimed he could change the young man's sexual orientation. The conversion therapy did not help, and he considered committing suicide. Fortunately, his mother came around and accepted him for who he was.[5] In the Kampala suburb of Nsambya, an 18-year-old high school student named Paula Rwomushana could not stand the humiliation of being outed publicly. The school administration had found her in possession of love letters from other women. She was promptly accused of being a lesbian, a "crime" for which she was whipped in front of a crowd of assembled schoolmates. She could not bear the public humiliation and assault on her privacy and dignity. She committed suicide.[6]

As long as they kept a low profile, conducted their relationships discreetly, and self-policed themselves into invisibility, Ugandan society appeared not overly concerned about what homosexuals did in the privacy of their bedrooms. LGBT activists claimed there were at least 500,000 homosexual Ugandans in 2007.[7] However, the clear majority remain closeted, keeping in line with societal expectations. General Museveni wanted it that way; a Uganda with closeted LGBT citizens. He said that gays and lesbians were free to lead their sexual lives as long as they "did it quietly" and refrained from flaunting their homosexuality.[8] And during one of his famous flip-flops, he conceded that pre-colonial Ugandan societies had homosexuals, but his major issue with homosexuality was "exhibitionism of homosexual behavior," which must be punished because in Uganda it is "forbidden to publicly exhibit any sexual conduct (kissing, etc.) even for heterosexuals," and adding an interesting and curious twist that if he kissed his wife of 41 years in public he would lose elections in Uganda.[9] Again, one sees the obsession of the general with morality issues and their impact on elections and his longevity holding the reins of power. Although the general seemed to imply that public kissing is forbidden in Uganda this happens not to be supported by existing laws. Public display of affection in the form of holding hands or putting arms around the waist among same sex friends is culturally acceptable, and a common sight on Ugandan streets. Two gay men can therefore show their affection for each other by holding hands in public spaces without running the risk of condemnation. However, acts such as public kissing, be it between homosexuals or heterosexuals, elicit much discomfort and strong disapproval. They are generally seen as a display of decadent Western behavior. Writing in *Transition*, Richard Ssebaggala remarked that "while there is nothing wrong or novel about same-sex loving, it is unfortunately un–Ugandan to put it out there in public bars, on the streets, on radio, or on television talk shows. Indeed, when Ugandans say that same-sex loving is a Western import, what they really mean is that 'flaunting' it is a Western import, since talking about any kind of sex, sexual practices, or sexuality is a Western phenomenon that many Africans are still clumsily trying to grapple with."[10]

LGBT Ugandans struggled in the realization that their community was out to marginalize and punish them just because of their sexual orientation or gender identity. In a similar manner that minority groups all over the world have fought against prejudice, injustice and discrimination, some courageous LGBT people did not accept the status quo. The first well-publicized incidents of LGBT people challenging and testing long-standing unspoken cultural taboos that confined them to the closet, involved two brave young men who were probably transgender women and a gay man who claimed space in Uganda's media, albeit operating covertly. These trail-blazers in the Uganda LGBT movement challenged the notion that their gender or sexuality had to be confined within the narrow interpretation of government moralists or religious clerics, or indeed, the wider community.

In October 1998, Brenda Kiiza, biologically born a man but employed as a housemaid, put on make-up, straightened his hair, picked a bra and slipped into a beautiful dress. The teen proceeded to walk in the streets of a Kampala suburb. Shortly after, he was accosted by a group of burly policemen who roughed him up and kicked out his teeth. He was detained and later forcibly undressed in the presence of journalists who had been invited by the police to a press conference. It was a dehumanizing experience for the defenseless teen as police peeled off his underwear and removed the bra. This humiliation was purportedly to show to the assembled journalists that Kiiza was a man. Throughout this humiliating ordeal, Brenda's soft feminine voice pleaded with his molesters to show lenience. But the police bullies towering over his frail body answered back with cold mockery and derisive laughter. Since Uganda did not have laws that forbade cross-dressing, the police charged Kiiza for being "idle and disorderly" and for conducting himself in "a manner likely to cause a breach of the peace." He was also accused of having "intended to annoy the constable on duty."[11] Police appeared to treat Kiiza as a security threat, stating it was urgent to establish if sinister intentions were behind the cross-dressing: "Why should a man deliberately perm hair, wear a bra to look like a woman? ... We need to establish if there is no ill motive behind the act."[12] A friend of Kiiza's implored the police to release him, claiming they both belonged to an innocent but hitherto unknown cult called *Abamerika*—the Americans. He alleged the cult had about 25 cross-dressing men who also straightened their hair and wanted "to look like Michael Jackson."[13] But the police were having none of that. Kiiza was held in police detention for seven days. In 2008, a decade later, Kiiza, turned LGBT activist, was arrested again. This time, together with another activist, he was charged with the offense of "recruiting homosexuals."[14] The two activists were detained for several days during which they were subjected to severe beatings.[15] The *Abamerika* organization, however rudimentary and lacking a coherent structure, was one of the first attempts by the Ugandan LGBT community at organizing themselves albeit clandestinely.

In May 2001, Mr. Sebudde Lule formed the Gay & Lesbian Alliance of Uganda (GALA).[16] GALA aimed at giving a voice to Ugandan gays and lesbians, and demanded for their recognition and equal treatment under the law. GALA was principally a one-man effort, hiding behind a clandestine media operation. When some doubted the very existence of L.G.B.T Ugandans, Lule countered with the publication of a letter in the government-controlled newspaper, the *New Vision*, affirming LGBT people were part of the country's fabric. In an impassioned plea, he told Ugandans that "arresting or criminalising us because we are gay and lesbian is not a solution. We are also normal human beings who pay taxes and hold responsibilities in different sectors. We also contribute to the development of our country. We need our freedom and the right to be free."[17] In 2003, Lule wrote a letter to the minister of justice and constitutional affairs, Mrs. Janat Mukwaya, appealing for constitutional recognition of gay rights. The minister dismissed the request outright: "I don't think gays have a right in our Constitution."[18] Lule's enduring hope was that one day LGBT Ugandans "will be recognized. Maybe I won't be around but I have made [laid] the ground[work]."[19]

Shaban Amanda was a Ugandan transgender woman. Not content with remaining in the shadows, she opted to go out in the open and live her dream as a transgender woman dancer. She originally gained fame as a dancer for one of Uganda's popular music groups, the KADS band. In early 2003 she formed a dancing group, Amanda's Moonlight Angels. Within a very short time, Amanda's group ranked among the most successful striptease act in the country. They performed to sold out shows at venues around Kampala. Amanda was a favorite with the audiences. Her stripping act sent the crowds clapping wildly and screaming lustily. She was tall, elegant, beautiful and with profound charm, a true belle. The crowds loved her. Revelers at her performances had a hard time determining her gender or sexuality. It has been said that many a man followed Amanda to the restroom under the pretense of giving her money as a commendation of her dancing skills when in fact their intent was to put to rest the speculation and mystery around her gender.[20] During the group's debut performance at Kampala's upscale Speke hotel in April 2003, police arrested Amanda and six of her dancing girls. They were arrested for "indecent" dress and charged with performing "sex acts" and staging a "nude show."[21] Some welcomed the arrest, alleging that Amanda and her dancers had been "terrorizing especially men in different bars in the city suburbs."[22] After several run-ins with the police and numerous stints in jail, Shaban Amanda called it quits to the world of Kampala's showbiz. She returned to her ancestral home, a fishing outpost on the shores of Lake Albert. In 2014, NTV, a Uganda TV station, tracked her down. Not wanting to draw publicity to herself, she declined to be interviewed. However, the TV journalists interviewed locals who spoke proudly of Amanda, narrating that she had displayed female mannerisms from a very early age. Importantly, they indicated their support for Amanda and at no time did they show unduly concern about her gender or sexuality—she was just another Ugandan.[23]

The arrests of both Brenda and Amanda owed more to their transgender status than violations of non-existent moral codes of indecent dressing. In Amanda's example, she was not the only striptease act in town. Police did not hound other strippers as much as they did Amanda. That Amanda's hometown welcomed her is evidence that ordinary Ugandans could rise above the hatred projected by the politico-religious establishment and show open-mindedness, acceptance and generosity towards LGBT people. Homophobic sentiments among Ugandans are exaggerated—ordinary Ugandans have better things to worry about than spending inordinate time caring about which two consenting adults are having sex with each other. The acceptance of Amanda in her hometown further goes to illustrate that government and religious clerics were chiefly responsible for engineering the hatred against LGBT Ugandans, with the media fanning the flames of intolerance. This fact was not lost on LGBT Ugandans, and certainly not on Kasha Jacqueline Nabagesera, an indefatigable LGBT activist. She noted, "When you go to Kampala and ask about gays they'll say: 'Kill them!' And when you ask why, their answer is, 'Because my preacher in church says that it's a sin against God. Because politicians say it's a crime. So we should kill them.'"[24] The government stepped up its persecution of LGBT people, and the clerics upped their condemnation of sexual minorities. LGBT Ugandans struggled to understand the mounting and unprecedented level of homophobia in the country. Before 2003, there was no coherent national LGBT movement capable of defending the rights of sexual minorities. However, by 2003, several conditions and circumstances had coalesced to galvanize the Ugandan LGBT community to organize overtly and oppose state- and church-sponsored repression and demand for a recognition of the community's fundamental civil and human rights.

First and foremost, the constant intimidation and harassment by government agents, clergy and sections of the media emboldened LGBT people to put up resistance in the form of countering the anti–LGBT toxic and misleading narrative. In 1999, General Museveni had ordered the arrest of homosexuals. This in itself, and subsequent pronouncements from civic and religious leaders, had a chilling effect on the Uganda LGBT community. After the general's directive, vigilante groups, the police, and even government ministers upped the ante of anti–LGBT sentiments and conducted raids on LGBT-friendly bars and cafes in and around Kampala.[25] Meanwhile, General Museveni's surrogates in the media revved up the crusade against the LGBT community, deliberately sowing misinformation calculated to increase homophobia. For example, Robert Kabushenga, who would later be appointed to head the state-controlled newspaper, the *New Vision*, alleged that homosexuality affected "intellectual disposition and creativity" and arrested "personal development." He further promised to make "Uganda extremely unsociable" for homosexuals.[26] Others appeared to equate sexual defilement and rape with homosexuality, calling for harsher punishment. In October 1999, Hajati Janat Kayondo led a group of Ugandan Muslim women in a demonstration against sexual defilement and rape. While addressing the demonstrators, she recommended to government that "every [sexual] defiler be executed, homosexuals be arrested and sentenced to life imprisonment while prostitutes be put in camps and counseled."[27] It is around this time that LGBT Ugandans, fearing for their lives, started fleeing the country. The most notable LGBT person to go into exile because of General Museveni's government's persecution was a 32-year-old Ugandan physician. His homosexuality was known to his family. Following General Museveni's orders to arrest homosexuals, family members warned the physician to avoid wearing accessories, such as earrings and necklaces, that risked exposing him as a gay man. He kept a low profile until he fled to South Africa, where he sought asylum.[28] South Africa forbids discrimination based on sexual orientation. Many more LGBT Ugandans fled the country, seeking asylum mostly in northern Europe and the United States. A few went to neighboring Kenya, which was relatively a better place for LGBT people than Uganda.

Another factor that would give impetus to the emergence of an organized LGBT movement were the voices critical of Museveni's stance against Uganda homosexuals. Criticism came from some Western countries, such as the U.S. and Sweden; international NGOs, and most importantly from a group of heterosexual Ugandans. These groups and individuals perceived General Museveni's onslaught on the LGBT community as unwarranted. They positioned their pro–LGBT support as based on respect for human rights. Notable in this group of LGBT advocates were Bishop Christopher Ssenyonjo, Dr. Sylvia Tamale, Professor Joe Oloka-Onyango and progressive journalists like Charles Onyango-Obbo and Andrew Mwenda. But the first challenge to General Museveni within Uganda came from Professor Ali Mazrui, a respected Kenyan scholar who lectured at Uganda's Makerere University before joining the University of Michigan in 1974 as professor of political science. In widely publicized remarks while on a visit to Uganda in October 1999, soon after General Museveni had ordered the arrest of homosexuals, Mazrui took issue with General Museveni. He argued that the intrusion in the "private lives of individuals is unconstitutional" and that the government can "support the values of the African family without using homosexuals as scapegoats."[29] He drew parallels between General Museveni and Zimbabwe's president, Robert Mugabe. Robert Mugabe was very dismissive of homosexuals, declaring that they were worse than pigs and dogs.

Perhaps emboldened by Professor Mazrui, Andrew Mwenda, a Ugandan journalist, rhetorically mused as to why Ugandan clerics were spending an inordinate amount of their time talking about homosexuality. He reflected that if homosexuality was not practiced by a substantial number of Ugandans then the subject would have attracted little attention. Mwenda is an astute political observer. He postulated that General Museveni's war against homosexuality correlated with an absence of democracy in Uganda. Mwenda argued that "homosexuality has a lot to do with liberal democracy and its opposite, authoritarianism…. There is no dictatorial or authoritarian system in this world where homosexuality is tolerated. And all liberal democratic societies in the world today tolerate it."[30] When Bahati introduced his anti-homosexuality bill, Mwenda took him on, exposing the hypocrisy of the anti-gay advocates: "Those opposed to homosexuality argue that it is un–African. But they do not point out any specific traditional and cultural sanctions against gays in any particular pre-colonial African society. Instead, they turn to Christianity—a religion that is not African and is indeed against many African traditions." And he further argued that "African cultural fundamentalists" railing against LGBT people, from "the president down have second and third wives. Bahati tolerates adultery and fornication but is hostile to homosexuality. Why?" Bahati had famously said that in "other countries … adultery is criminal—it is unbelievable in America, but here it's tolerated."[31] In fact, some of the leading self-declared morality crusaders were known for their adulterous liaisons, with some of the men keeping harems of women with whom they had children. Mwenda postulated that profound prejudice, and not so much a desire to uphold Christian teachings and values, was behind the persecution of the Ugandan LGBT community at the hands of Bahati and his fellow anti–LGBT campaigners.[32] Another Ugandan journalist who came out strongly to criticize the government's anti-homosexuality pronouncements was Charles Onyango-Obbo. Onyango-Obbo was an award-winning journalist and a 1992 Nieman Fellow at Harvard. For many years, he wrote a progressive column, "Ear to the Ground," in the *Monitor*. His writings were thoughtful, witty and provocative. He was one never to shy away from holding General Museveni accountable and he built a reputation for kvetching against the ills of the general's regime, particularly its penchant for authoritarianism and crony politics. Onyango-

Obbo was perhaps the first journalist to lay bare the political opportunism behind General Museveni's sudden interest in homosexuality after being in power for more than thirteen years. In his characteristic tongue-in-cheek style, he noted, "In Zimbabwe, when President Robert Mugabe went gay-bashing, he was preparing the country for his second marriage. He managed to make the point that however much people criticized his marriage to his far younger secretary and the extravagant wedding, it was still a distinctly better alternative than being gay. Since Museveni has been looking happily married, perhaps then his eyes are on an election? There are two around the corner: the referendum next year and the general election thereafter."[33] Both Andrew Mwenda and Charles Onyango-Obbo have over the years criticized and challenged General Museveni over his civil and human rights record, and continue to oppose state and church-sponsored homophobia. For their unwavering stance in support of freedom and democracy, the two men have endured constant harassment at the hands of General Museveni's security forces and subjected to multiple arrests over banal and trumped-up charges.

The Reverend Christopher Ssenyonjo was a retired COU bishop who encountered LGBT Ugandans through his counseling work. Unlike other clerics of the COU he did not condemn or pass harsh judgment against LGBT people. In 2001 he founded Integrity Uganda, providing pastoral care and counseling to LGBT Christians. He counseled them and provided comforting words—although they were different from the predominant heterosexual culture, God loved them just the way they were. Bishop Ssenyonjo was the first Ugandan cleric to openly minister to the LGBT community. He became an outspoken critic of the failure of the Christian church to practice what it preached when relating with sexual minorities. The widespread misunderstanding and discrimination of LGBT people in the country disturbed him, and he decried the absence of compassion and love for sexual minorities in the Ugandan Christian church. Unsurprisingly, the COU leadership condemned Bishop Ssenyonjo's pastoral outreach to the LGBT community. The prelate of the COU, Archbishop Nkoyooyo, alleged that Bishop Ssenyonjo had compromised Christian values and morals by serving homosexuals. Archbishop Nkoyooyo claimed that Bishop Ssenyonjo was indigent, having retired from a financially rewarding position as a bishop of the COU, and was therefore apt to be "tempted to do anything" to shore up his meager pension.[34] The archbishop was implying that Bishop Ssenyonjo's choice to minister to the LGBT community was motivated by a desire to receive substantial personal financial benefits from pro-gay Western individuals or institutions.

Archbishop Nkoyooyo would later brand Bishop Ssenyonjo a "rebel" and claim that the bishop had enlisted "all the reverends, whom the church fired because of misbehaving, into his followers in the same manner in which Satan gets his followers."[35] For offering pastoral care to LGBT Christians, Bishop Ssenyonjo was excommunicated from the COU in 2006. He maintained that working with the LGBT community did not mean that he was "practicing or even preaching gay relationships, or even alienating myself from the Anglican Church. On the contrary, I am simply implementing the Lambeth resolutions of 1998, which require all provinces to put in place a support system for gay folks in the church before the next Lambeth, in an effort to study and pray for one another."[36] Undeterred by the absence of charity from the COU leadership, Bishop Ssenyonjo continued his work among the LGBT community, counseling and providing pastoral care in a climate hostile to his show of concern and compassion to a segment of Ugandan society that had been and continue to be the target of government and church-sponsored harassment and intimidation. In recognition of his courageous work promoting equal rights for LGBT Ugandans, former U.S. President Bill Clinton awarded Bishop Ssenyonjo the Clinton Global Citizen Award in 2012.

In February 2003, Dr. Sylvia Tamale was invited to speak at a workshop discussing the drafting of principles that would guide the Equal Opportunities Commission (EOC). The EOC had been formed by an Act of Uganda's Parliament. The workshop was a brainstorming session to further define and elaborate on the EOC's guiding principles, which centered on eliminating discrimination and inequalities against individuals or a group of people and implementing affirmative action policies in favor of groups "marginalized on the basis of gender, age, disability or any other reason created by history, tradition or custom."[37] Dr. Tamale argued that homosexuals were a marginalized group, just like women and the disabled. She therefore urged the government to recognize them as such: "I know President Yoweri Museveni is against gays but that does not mean they should be denied their rights to a sexual orientation of their choice."[38] Just like Bishop Ssenyonjo before her, Dr. Tamale was mocked and vilified for her support of the LGBT community. Some openly called for her "lynching" and "crucifixion."[39] Conservative readers of the government mouthpiece, *The New Vision*, weighed in and voted her the "worst woman of the year." Although Dr. Tamale was aware of the challenges she would likely encounter in her work defending the rights of sexual minorities, she expressed shock at the profound prejudice displayed by a sector of Ugandans against LGBT people and the caustic vitriol directed at her, admitting that "the degree and extent of this bias came as a nasty shock to me; such bigotry and injustice I had read about only in history books on slavery and apartheid. That society could vilify the harmless, private, victimless acts of consenting adults defies logic."[40] As testimony to her extraordinary courage, Dr. Tamale has remained undaunted in her support of the rights of LGBT people and is steadfast in her fight for issues that pertain to human and civil rights. To her conservative critics, Dr. Tamale had this to say: "Homosexuals are not asking for your pity, love, approval or redemption. They only want you to affirm their humanness and their right to exist and be different."[41]

Bishop Ssenyonjo and Dr. Sylvia Tamale, and others who continue to speak out against homophobia, further illustrate that Uganda has a vocal group of activists that detest the government's and church's anti–LGBT policies. These prominent pro-gay advocates, the overwhelming majority of whom are heterosexual, have objected to the criminalization of LGBT Ugandans. They view the state-orchestrated harassment of the LGBT community as a gross abuse of fundamental civic and human rights. Senior government and political figures, on the other hand, have contested this argument. For example, Ms. Bako Christine Abia, a Ugandan legislator, discounted the notion that "human rights" could be applied to LGBT people. She expressed her opinions on same-sex relationships in an interview with *Deutsche Welle*, Germany's international broadcaster, saying, "Even animals, beasts, have not degenerated that far. How come, people with conscience, physiologically disoriented themselves, and then call it, 'We are a certain sexual orientation.' No! You have just disoriented yourself then pretend it is a human right. No; for goodness sake it is a human wrong." Ms. Bako Christine Abia, quite well-known and respected in the West for her defense of women's rights, went on to suggest how best to deal with sexual minorities: "Throw them in the water to let them be eaten by good fish."[42]

With the government and church coming out to strongly oppose LGBT Ugandans, the community grappled for answers to understand the new concentration of homophobia. It is in this desire to unpack and comprehend the toxic homophobic environment that led several members of the community to turn to the internet, seeking answers and solutions to a vexing problem. The contribution of the internet as a source of information on educating the Uganda LGBT community cannot be overemphasized. Richard Lusimbo, a LGBT activist called the internet an "open window" and a platform "where we [the LGBT community] have been freely sharing information; where we are freely connecting with each other."[43] For Kasha Jacqueline Nabagesera the internet helped her learn more about homosexuality in Uganda, including the shocking and painful realization that her beloved country criminalized homosexuality.[44] Therefore, the internet provided the community with information that they could not access through traditional media. In internet cafes across the country they explored different themes relating to their sexual orientation and gender identity outside the prying eyes and disapproval of puritanical government agents and religious clerics. While surfing the internet, LGBT Ugandans became aware that they were not alone. They learned about sexual minorities in different parts of the world. They also discovered that many sexual minorities, particularly those in other African countries, had to contend with the same kind of fears and anxieties that confronted their Ugandan community. But beyond learning that there was a bigger community out there, LGBT Ugandans were introduced to individuals and organizations that provided them with encouragement and nurtured the impetus that led them to fight for the recognition of their rights and oppose laws that criminalized people on basis of their sexual orientation and gender. Of importance were contacts with well-organized LGBT advocates and organizations in South Africa and the West. LGBT Ugandans were now able to feel they were part of a global movement, which campaigned for the recognition of their rights and putting an end to the discrimination and harassment they faced. The internet, along with access to mobile telephony, also enabled LGBT Ugandans to find each other, share experience, mobilize and form social support networks. These modes of new media, especially in the major towns where people could free themselves from the constraints imposed by traditional conservative values, gave birth to an urban LGBT subculture. They began referring to themselves as *kuchus* (sing. *kuchu*)—an all-encompassing local term for LGBT people.

Precedent from courageous LGBT Ugandans like Brenda Kiiza, Sebudde Lule and Shaban Amanda, the support for LGBT rights from brave heterosexuals, and the new media's reach and impact in educating and fostering communication, all contributed to equipping LGBT Ugandans with the tools required to mobilize into a coherent organization to respond to the state and church-sponsored anti–LGBT climate. On July 4, 2003, three valiant and well-educated lesbian women—Kasha Jacqueline Nabagesera aka "Bombastic," Victor Juliet Mukasa, and Taz Musisi (pseudonym)—founded an organization called Freedom and Roam Uganda (FARUG). Kasha was a princess of the Buganda kingdom and a great-granddaughter of Kabaka Mwanga, the nineteenth-century gay king of

Buganda. She had been openly lesbian from an early age, and was fortunate to have a supportive and understanding family. FARUG was the first LGBT organization in Uganda to operate openly. It had an activist agenda, aiming to use legal avenues to advocate for and protect LGBT rights. The organization also sought to empower the Ugandan LGBT community and educate Ugandan society, providing a counter-narrative to the incendiary anti–LGBT rhetoric from government and religious leaders. The initial phase of FARUG's evolution was not easy. The organization faced multiple headwinds, not least from some within the LGBT community itself. Some within the community were wary to join FARUG, believing that open support would unmask their sexual orientation and expose them to unwelcome scrutiny. After all, some who were outed had been evicted from their homes and disowned by families. Others had lost jobs and were even subjected to lynching by self-righteous homophobic mobs. Victor Mukasa, a co-founder of FARUG and who now lives as a transgender man, had suffered it all. He faced daunting challenges that could have crushed a lesser soul. While still living as a female, he came out as a lesbian at an early age, which led his family and circle of friends to abandon him. Mukasa narrated his frustration with family and societal ostracism: "They threw me out and never wanted to have anything to do with me. My family requested me to stop using our family name because it embarrasses our dead father who was called Mukasa. To my family, my dead father is more valuable to them than me; who is still alive and well. This always makes me think that homosexuals are taken to be deader than the dead. I have been beaten or physically thrown out of public places on more than ten occasions—just because I am a lesbian. I have been abused and insulted on streets, in restaurants, discotheques and bars."[45]

The emergence of FARUG emboldened others in the LGBT community to mobilize and organize. At the end of 2003 numerous LGBT groups had sprung up. Most of the organizations acted as social support networks and a few engaged in activism. The groups did not coordinate their activities and were independent of each other. In some cases, the founders of the various groups were oblivious of the existence of other organized LGBT initiatives in the country. This is not surprising since homosexuality was criminalized and LGBT people feared for their lives. Therefore, the groups had to organize clandestinely. Inevitably, there were duplications and redundancies in efforts and activities since most of the groups shared the same objectives. On the plethora of groups representing LGBT Ugandans, Richard Ssebaggala observed that "you would be hard-pressed to find three gay Ugandans who can differentiate between them, what they were set up to do, and whether they are actually doing it."[46] Nonetheless, some of the LGBT organizations serve a differentiating need, and there are groups that work on specific issues, such as HIV/AIDS prevention advocacy, providing health services to members living with HIV, and housing those fleeing violence and persecution. To provide coordination and focus attention to advocacy, a group of LGBT activists led by the charismatic Victor Juliet Mukasa founded Sexual Minorities Uganda (SMUG) in March 2004. SMUG is an NGO bringing together numerous LGBT organizations with a mission to "monitor, coordinate, and support member organizations to achieve their objectives aimed at the Liberation of LGBTI people."[47] It aimed at uniting disparate groups into an organized and coherent organization that could better advocate for LGBT rights. At a very early stage in its existence SMUG enlisted the support of civic organizations, partnered with global human rights groups and canvassed for support from Western governments. SMUG would later form an important alliance with the Civil Society Coalition on Human Rights and Constitutional Law (CSCHRCL), a conglomeration of numerous Ugandan civil society organizations. The alliance with CSCHRCL proved to be critical as the organization came out in full force to challenge the legality of Bahati's "Kill the Gays" Bill.

As the sexual minorities organized into a more cohesive movement to resist repression and discrimination, General Museveni's government was determined to crush and stop their momentum, upping the intimidation and harassment. In 2004 Nsaba Buturo, the minister of ethics and integrity, ordered the police to investigate and "take appropriate action" against a gay organization at Makerere University in Kampala.[48] On August 26, 2004, three LGBT activists appeared on a local Radio Simba talk show, "Olutindo"—the Bridge. The activists discussed the everyday challenges they encountered, including discrimination and barriers to accessing HIV services. The government censor was not all too pleased. Radio Simba was fined more than $1,000 for contravening General Museveni's Electronic Media Act, which "prohibits any broadcasting that is contrary to public morality."[49] Subsequently, leaders of the nascent LGBT organizations were systematically targeted, humiliated and brutalized. Several activists fled the country, seeking asylum overseas. In July 2005, government agents raided Mukasa's home, taking away documents related to SMUG's activities. Mukasa, who was the chairperson of SMUG at the time, was not home during the raid. However, a visiting friend, Ms. Yvone Oyo, was taken into police custody where she was undressed and her breasts fondled to "prove that she was a woman."[50] A local government agent claimed the raid on Mukasa's home was in response to complaints from his neighbors, who accused him and his friends of engaging in homosexuality: "They don't dress like women. They wear shoes that are for men."[51] Fearing for his life, Mukasa fled the country. Nonetheless, he was determined to correct an injustice and seek affirmation of his constitutional right as a Ugandan who also happens to be an LGBT person. In an unprecedented turn, Mukasa and Yvone Oyo sued the government for trespassing, theft of property, illegal arrest, and inhuman and degrading treatment. *Mukasa and Another v. Attorney-General* (2008) was a landmark civil suit in the annals of Uganda's judiciary. It was the first time that LGBT people had used the courts to challenge government over harassment and discrimination. During the court proceedings, a rowdy group of anti–LGBT Pentecostals, led by Pastor Ssempa, were a constant presence inside the courtroom. Most of them dressed in T-shirts printed with anti–LGBT slogans such as "Anal Sex is Abominable." In December 2008, Judge Mary Stella Arach-Amoko, widely respected in Uganda for her impartiality and professionalism, ruled in favor of Mukasa and his friend. In her ruling Judge Arach-Amoko said, "The case is not about homosexuality. It is also not about abuse of office. It is about abuse of the suspects' human rights by the Police."[52] The two plaintiffs were awarded about $7,000. It was not only a victory for Victor Mukasa and Yvone Oyo but for the entire Ugandan LGBT community.

Although operating under difficult conditions, the LGBT organizations labored on. Against the odds, they undertook several successful and significant initiatives. On August 17, 2007, Victor Mukasa and other activists working under the umbrella organization SMUG embarked on a public media campaign. They held the first ever LGBT press conference in Uganda. In a show of moral support, some of the country's leading human rights activists, including Jessica Nkuuhe, Sarah Mukasa and Beatrice Were, attended the briefing. Most of the LGBT activists wore masks to hide their identity. The activists spoke passionately to the assembled press about the violation of their human and civil rights because of their sexuality and gender, and the widespread humiliation and prejudice they encountered. They asked government to rein in the police, and appealed for peaceful co-existence, "Please, let us live in peace. Stop persecuting us. God created us this way. We are children of God as well."[53] But the patriarchal Ugandan society, edged on by religious clerics and politicians, was not ready for peace. Bitter condemnation of the press conference followed. In a mixture of feigned conniption and total disgust, Pastor Solomon Male, a harsh critic of the LGBT community, denounced the press conference alleging that "homosexuals and lesbians aim at promoting this confusion in the country through their activities like press conferences and planned demonstration by these misguided and confused people. They are the ones who need to change, not change our laws to suit them."[54] On August 21, 2007, four days after the SMUG press conference, Pastor Ssempa rallied his anti–LGBT troops under an umbrella organization called the Interfaith Rainbow Coalition Against Homosexuality, supposedly composed of "devout" Christians. The pastor and hundreds of his followers assembled at Kampala's rugby grounds, chanting anti–LGBT slogans and waving banners condemning LGBT people. Some banners read "Arrest all homos." The pastor demanded swift and firm government action against the "well-orchestrated effort by homosexuals to intimidate the government."[55] Particular ire was reserved for the 22-year-old Katherine Roubos, a Stanford University journalism student on a three-month internship at the independent Ugandan newspaper the *Daily Monitor*. Ms. Roubos had earned Pastor Ssempa's wrath because of her coverage of LGBT issues in some of her *Daily Monitor* articles. Pastor Ssempa and his crowd demanded her immediate deportation to the United States.[56] It was ironic and preposterous that Pastor Ssempa, a dual Ugandan and American citizen, clamored for the deportation of a fellow American for fulfilling her journalistic duties. Would Pastor Ssempa, if he was to live in his adopted country with his white American wife, Tracey, petition Congress to deport LGBT Americans? Ssempa's mendacity and sheer cruelty was bewildering and troubling, more so for a man that claimed to be inspired by Christ's message of love.

Responding to the same SMUG press conference, Sheikh Multah Bukenya, a leader of the Islamic Tabliq sect, announced during Friday prayers at Noor Mosque in Kampala that he was forming an "Anti-gay Squad" forthwith. He emphasized that the intent of the squad was to "wipe out all abnormal practices like homosexuality."[57] The Tabliq or Tabligh, a radical Salafist sect, formed in Uganda in late 1980s. The Tabliq seek to establish an Islamic state in Uganda, and engaged in frequent showdowns with Ugandan security forces in the 1990s. A splinter radical faction of the Tabliq formed the Allied Democratic Force (ADF) which waged an armed insurrection against the Uganda government. The ADF unleashed horrific acts of terror, including random grenade attacks around Kampala which killed and maimed several people. In one of their most brazen and cruel attacks, on June 8, 1998, the ADF raided a vocational training school in western Uganda. The rebels torched three student dormitories. About 80 people died in the ensuing inferno. The ADF rebels also abducted over

100 students.[58] Sheik Multah Bukenya's declaration of war on the LGBT community aligned the interests of militant Islam with the morality of Ugandan Christian fundamentalists.

As the activities of the LGBT organizations took on more visibility through courageous public debates and social mobilization the government increased its repression. LGBT Ugandans were subjected to arbitrary arrests and the voices of LGBT advocates muzzled. The climate of fear was heightened and all but a few brave people retreated even deeper into the closet. Homophobic religious clerics and sections of the print media ratcheted up their anti–LGBT rhetoric. On August 8, 2006, the *Red Pepper*, a scurrilous Ugandan tabloid edited by Mr. Deo Arinaitwe Rugyendo, printed the first names, place of residence and work of 45 alleged Ugandan gay men. The list included men from all walks of life—the military, clergy, legal professionals, entertainers. The paper denounced homosexuality, claiming it was a "mortal sin that goes against the nature of humanity." It justified its editorial decision to out gay men as, "To show the nation how shocked we are and how fast the terrible vice known as sodomy is eating up our society, we have decided to unleash an exclusive list of men who enjoy taking on fellow men from the rear."[59] The following month, the *Red Pepper* continued its outlandish and distasteful McCarthyism, publishing the names of 13 alleged Ugandan lesbians. The paper claimed the outing of lesbians was necessary to "rid our motherland of the deadly vice, we are committed to exposing all the lesbos in the city [Kampala]." More ominously, and displaying profound insensitivity, the paper appealed to its readers to send in the names and occupations of lesbians for shaming in print.[60] The *Red Pepper* continued outing gays under sensational headlines like, "Ugandan Homos Cabinet List Leaks" or "Exposed! Uganda's 200 Top Homos Named," or "This Gay Monster Raped Boys in School but Failed to Bonk Wife." It is suspected that General Caleb Akandwanaho aka Salim Saleh, General Museveni's all-powerful half-brother, owned the *Red Pepper*. He officiated, amid much fanfare, at the paper's launch.[61] The gutter journalism took on new lows in October 2010 when Giles Muhame's *Rolling Stone* (no relationship to the U.S. *Rolling Stone* magazine), another vituperative tabloid, printed the photographs, names, occupations and residential addresses of 100 alleged homosexuals without regard to safety and right to privacy.[62] The front page of that *Rolling Stone* issue prominently featured two pictures of alleged gays—Bishop Christopher Ssenyonjo (he is heterosexual) and David Kato, a consummate LGBT activist and the first openly gay man in post-independent Uganda. Kato had come out in 1998. Above their pictures, *Rolling Stone* ran a chilling caption: "Hang them." The paper gleefully wrote:

A 12 months clandestine investigation into the dark world of homosexuality and lesbianism in the country has led to the full exposure of the facial appearances of leading gays in this nation. The mighty Rolling Stone is glad to reveal some of the most horrible secrets in community, which is bent on recruiting at least one million members by 2012. Threateningly, gays are after very young kids, who are easily brain washed towards bisexual orientation. Our investigators have secured 100 pictures and more are coming in.... The leaked pictures of Uganda's top homosexuals and lesbians have rendered calls for the strengthening of the war against the rampage that threatens the future of our generation by hanging gays. Unless government takes a bold step by hanging dozens of homosexuals, the vice will continue eating up the moral fabric and culture of our great nation.

Muhame promised to start raiding LGBT Ugandans in the privacy of their bedrooms, boasting that he would soon acquire "sophisticated cameras" to out them.[63] He was calling for nothing short of total annihilation of an entire community. His violent anti–LGBT propaganda displayed a coldness that was at once shuddering and frightful. In November 2010, Muhame, who had previously worked as a reporter at the *Red Pepper*, continued his vile and hateful campaign, printing more pictures of alleged LGBT Ugandans in the *Rolling Stone*.[64] This was the tipping point for the LGBT activists. With the support of the Civil Society Coalition on Human Rights and Constitutional Law, Jacqueline Kasha, David Kato and Onziema Patience (better known as Pepe Julian Onziema) sued Giles Muhame and *Rolling Stone*. The activists alleged that by publishing their pictures, *Rolling Stone* had infringed on their right to privacy, which they were entitled to under Uganda's constitution. After several fits and starts, the court heard the case. During the court proceedings, Pastor Solomon Male confronted the LGBT advocates, haranguing and shouting them down with demeaning commentary. Pastor Male's singular resolve appeared to hinge on ridding Uganda of moral turpitude. He saw LGBT people everywhere, and he had to stop them before they could destroy the future spiritual health of the country. On January 3, 2011, Justice Vincent Musoke Kibuuka, described as "one of the most experienced" and "independent-minded" judges, ruled in favor of the LGBT activists.[65] He reaffirmed the plaintiffs' right to human dignity and protection from inhumane treatment. *Rolling Stone* was ordered to pay a hefty fine. Ugandan media, including independent newspapers generally believed to be progressive, was silent on this epoch-making victory for the Ugandan LGBT movement.

The LGBT community savored the court victory, which afforded them a degree of reprieve from the ever-present harassment. But other challenges, perhaps even more potent and diabolical than *Rolling Stone* and *Red Pepper* outings of LGBT Ugandans, loomed. On the night of January 26, 2011, a few weeks after the historic court victory over Muhame, David Kato, a co-founder of Sexual Minorities Uganda and an intractable fighter for LGBT rights in Uganda was bludgeoned to death. Kato, a brave, jovial man of boundless energy, had dedicated enormous time fighting the injustice and prejudice faced by the LGBT community. He worked tirelessly to find ways to stop Bahati's anti-homosexuality bill. He had this to say about the egregious piece of legislation: "This Bill is a blow to the progress of democracy in Uganda. It goes against the inclusive spirit necessary for our economic as well as political development. Its spirit is profoundly undemocratic and un–African."[66] Dr. Oloka-Onyango, a professor of law who has extensively studied the LGBT movement in Uganda, noted that Kato's death was a "pivotal landmark in the struggle against homophobia in contemporary Uganda."[67] He highlighted that it was the first high-profile event affecting the Uganda LGBT movement, and one that garnered intense domestic and international scrutiny of General Museveni's freewheeling abuse of LGBT rights. There was widespread domestic and international condemnation of Kato's murder. U.S. President Barack Obama issued a statement mourning Kato's death: "I am deeply saddened to learn of the murder of David Kato. In Uganda, David showed tremendous courage in speaking out against hate. He was a powerful advocate for fairness and freedom. The United States mourns his murder, and we recommit ourselves to David's work."[68] The U.S. secretary of state, Hillary Clinton, condemned Kato's murder emphasizing that the "tragic death underscores how critical it is that both the government and the people of Uganda, along with the international community, speak out against the discrimination, harassment, and intimidation of Uganda's LGBT community, and work together to ensure that all individuals are accorded the same rights and dignity to which each and every person is entitled."[69] Kato's brutal death also served to rally the resolve of the LGBT community to fight for their civic and human rights.

As Kato's family and friends grieved, Muhame displayed a total absence of moral scruples and self-introspection. Even in death, he could not let David Kato rest in peace, assailing his departed soul with hateful insults. Muhame claimed that because of Kato's homosexuality, "God is going to roast him."[70] And he was quick to deny that his anti–LGBT campaign could have in any way contributed to Kato's murder. He instead said that his paper had advocated for Kato to be "arrested, tried, sentenced, hanged."[71] It may be an understatement to say that Muhame was an inept and irresponsible young man who distinguished himself by the inability to demonstrate even a bit of common decency. He clearly knew nothing about journalistic standards, let alone professional ethics, despite *Rolling Stone's* boast as "Uganda's leading investigative political newspaper." Muhame appeared to have operated without the backing of powerful government officials or religious figures. It is possible he had hoped that his vehemence against the LGBT community would win him a berth as an advance guard, or at least a position as a favorite errand boy, in General Museveni's war against the LGBT community. Anti-LGBT politicians and clergy largely ignored him. *Rolling Stone,* which was reeling from the financial cost of the court's ruling in favor of the LGBT activists, shut its doors.

The Uganda *kuchus'* movement has weathered many rough storms. But despite repression the *kuchus* worked with resolve and resilience to realize a society within which their human rights, and indeed the rights of every Ugandan, could be respected. The struggle was punctuated by a victory here and a defeat there, and optimism vacillated with pessimism. In February 2012, Kasha Jacqueline Nabagesera, ever the courageous human rights activist, organized a LGBT leadership training workshop. Father Lokodo, the ethics and integrity minister, flanked by police, stormed the workshop, forcing its premature closure on grounds that it was illegal and Ugandans "do not accept homosexuality."[72] He ordered Kasha's arrest. The *kuchus* refer to the incident as the "Valentine's Massacre."[73] Fortunately, Kasha escaped and evaded arbitrary detention. Amnesty International condemned Father Lokodo's heavy-handedness and called on General Museveni's government to "end its outrageous harassment of people involved in lawful activities."[74] Writing in *The Daily Monitor,* Ugandan journalist Daniel Kalinaki cautioned his fellow countrymen: "It is easy to thumb one's nose at the gay rights activists and call for them to be jailed and the keys cast into Lake Victoria but the same people who will arrest the gays will one day return to arrest the teachers and doctors asking for better conditions. We should not let our moral convictions interfere with our legal obligation to respect the rights of all."[75]

The U.S. Alien Tort Statute (ATS) of 1789 (also known as the Aliens Tort Claims Act) allows foreign nationals to sue in U.S. district courts for alleged violations of international law. In March 2012, the New York–based Center for Constitutional Rights (CCR) invoked the ATS. CCR filed a lawsuit in Massachusetts on behalf of SMUG against Scott Lively for his role in persecuting the Uganda LGBT community. The lawsuit also named four Ugandan co-conspirators—Pastor Martin Ssempa, Stephen Langa, David Bahati, and James Buturo.[76] Lively called the lawsuit "absurd" and "frivolous," and claimed he had never advocated for violence against gay people. He asked the court to dismiss the case.[77] At the time of writing, the lawsuit was ongoing. In August 2012, activists staged the first Gay Pride event in Uganda. Over 100 *kuchus* attended the exuberant and peaceful event on a Lake Victoria beach in Entebbe. They marched and partied, celebrating their sexual and gender identity. The revelers held signs that read: "We are gay and proud" and "Killing gay people solves nothing." It was by all accounts another momentous achievement for the LGBT movement. Late into the festivities, the police descended, beating and arresting some participants. Despite the enormous headwinds, the LGBT activists have labored on, demanding recognition for their fundamental human rights. Since 2012, the *kuchus* community has organized an annual Gay Pride. Unlike the first ever Gay Pride in 2012, there has not been hostile police action at subsequent Gay Pride events. The enterprising Kasha Nabagesera launched *Bombastic* in December 2014. It was the first magazine for sexual minorities in Uganda. The magazine aimed at countering the misinformation about the community through the presentation of stories about the lives of lesbian, gay, bisexual, transgender and intersex Ugandans. And in December 2015, SMUG celebrated a decade of existence at the frontline of fighting for *kuchu* rights. SMUG crowned the celebration with a gala dinner at one of Kampala's top hotels. The fête was notable for the presence of straight Ugandans from all walks of life—clerics, politicians and internationally-recognized and award-winning musicians. The guest of honor at SMUG gala was Dr. Specioza Kazibwe, who had served as Uganda's vice president from 1994 to 2003, the first woman to hold the post. SMUG also supported the participation of *kuchus* in "mainstream" activities as a way of combating societal alienation and reasserting their position as equal and responsible citizens. For example, SMUG sponsored *kuchus* to run in the November 2015 MTN Kampala marathon. These and many other initiatives are significant developments and victories for Ugandan *kuchus*.

These victories have been made possible by a team of dedicated LGBT advocates—*kuchus* and straight. These men and women have shown endurance and resolve to challenge and defeat unjust laws that unfairly target, discriminate against and punish *kuchus* for their sexuality and gender. For their courage and steadfastness, several Ugandan LGBT organizations and activists have received worldwide commendations and are recipients of prestigious awards. Frank Mugisha, SMUG's soft-spoken and thoughtful leader, was the recipient of the 2011 Robert F. Kennedy Human Rights Award. In 2011, SMUG was awarded the Rafto Prize. In honoring SMUG, the Norwegian Rafto Foundation for Human Rights prize highlighted the importance of respecting human rights for minority communities: "By awarding the 2011 Rafto Prize to SMUG and Frank Mugisha's fight for sexual minorities, the Rafto Foundation wishes to underscore that human rights encompass everyone and that it is unacceptable to persecute or discriminate against anyone based on their sexual orientation or gender identity. SMUG and Frank Mugisha's fight for the human dignity of a particularly vulnerable group is also part of a greater fight for democracy and social justice."[78] Kasha Jacqueline Nabagesera's work fighting LGBT injustice and calling for tolerance in Uganda was recognized worldwide, and in June 2015 she was featured on the cover of *Time* magazine's European edition. She has received multiple awards, including the 2011 Martin Ennals Award (MEA) for Human Rights Defenders. The MEA has been referred to as the Nobel Prize for human rights. Kasha was also the recipient of the International Nuremberg Human Rights Award. Pepe Julian Onziema, a transgender man and a SMUG executive, gave a profoundly thoughtful interview in June 2014 on HBO's *Last Week Tonight with John Oliver*. The interview won him the 2015 GLAAD Media Award for Outstanding Talk Show Episode. The award was presented to him by Jussie Smollet, an actor on Fox's hit TV drama *Empire*.

VII

Unraveling of the Anti-Homosexuality Law

"This is my home.... Go back to your home."[1]—General Museveni, reprimanding U.S. President Barack Obama in 2014

When Mr. Bahati first introduced the anti-homosexuality bill on October 14, 2009, on behalf of the conservative Christian Uganda Parliamentary Fellowship, he portrayed the bill as a fulfillment of his Christian moral obligation and duty. Bahati considered homosexuality a cardinal sin, arguing that "God's law is always clear, that the wages of sin is death."[2] He compared homosexuality to criminality and terrorism, asserting that in such cases, governments had a mandate to intervene and bestow rule of law and protect the public order: "If two thieves were in the bedroom, would you stop government from going there? If two terrorists were in the bedroom, would you stop government from going there?"[3] Bahati believed that his "Kill the Gays" bill would not rankle the international community, bragging that there was no country "in the world that will cut aid because of this issue of homosexuality."[4] He further boasted that no amount of pressure or intimidation would deter him from protecting Ugandan children against the vice of homosexuality and defending family values.

But no sooner had Bahati presented his anti-homosexuality bill than there arose significant opposition. A diverse group of Ugandans raised their concern. LGBT advocates launched an effort to collect signatures petitioning the Uganda Parliament to jettison the bill. By the end of the initiative almost half a million signatures were collected.[5] There was scathing condemnation of the bill from liberal Ugandan journalists, academics, civil rights groups and prominent Ugandan voices overseas. The Civil Society Coalition on Human Rights and Constitutional Law, which represented nearly 20 Ugandan advocacy groups, issued a strongly worded statement on international Human Rights Day, December 10, 2009, calling for the withdrawal of what it deemed a discriminatory and oppressive bill: "We can either turn further towards an agenda of divisionism and discrimination, and pay the costs in terms of internal suppression of our own citizens coupled with international isolation and marginalization, or we can embrace diversity, human rights and constitutionalism."[6] Solome Nakaweesi-Kimbugwe, the head of *Akina mama wa Afrika*, an NGO advocating for the rights of African women, together with Frank Mugisha of Sexual Minorities Uganda (SMUG), lambasted the bill as an "alarmingly retrogressive piece of legislation ... legalizing hatred against a section of the Uganda citizenry." They pointedly noted that the bill's real purpose was to divert the country from the "serious issues facing Uganda's policymakers today in the lead-up to the 2011 [presidential] elections ... poverty and lack of jobs," among others.[7]

Mr. Opiyo Oloya, a Ugandan living in Toronto and who had once led Uganda's student movement in the 1980s, appealed directly to Mr. Nsaba Buturo, the then minister of ethics and integrity, to end his bigotry against LGBT Ugandans and treat them with respect and dignity. Opiyo Oloya observed that he too had once harbored prejudice and fear against LGBT people. But this changed after learning of the sexual orientation of some wonderful people in his circle of friends. He underscored his belief that the "gay and lesbian struggle is very much a human rights issue that ought to be taken up by people who believe that no human being should live under oppression." He encouraged Buturo to "take time to understand your own fear and angst about homosexuals—you might learn something about yourself and about them."[8] Another Canadian-Ugandan, Dr. Muniini K. Mulera, could not help but expose the bigotry of those at the forefront of pushing for the criminalization of homosexuality in Uganda, noting a fact that was shared by many others that "among those who support the criminalization of homosexuality are some of Uganda's most prolific fornicators and adulterers. These are Pharisees whose increasingly pious appearances in places of worship and public displays of support for religions are testimony to man's infinite capacity for hypocrisy. How often have we heard them lecturing Ugandans about the dangers of promiscuity, even as they themselves add to their collection of female conquests and offspring?"[9]

International condemnation of the anti-homosexuality bill was equally swift. The Canadian government described the proposed anti-gay law as "reprehensible, vile and hateful" and an "infringement of human rights in Uganda."[10] Sweden, a major development partner and contributor to Uganda's budget, indicated it would consider discontinuing development aid to the country if the bill was signed into law.[11] Britain, Norway, and the United States joined the countries that threatened to cut aid if the anti-homosexuality bill was passed. Over 110 British members of Parliament signed an Early Day Motion, condemning Bahati's bill. They called upon General Museveni's government to "uphold international humanitarian law by abandoning the Anti-Homosexuality Bill, decriminalizing same-sex acts between consenting adults in private, and outlawing discrimination against gay people."[12] Further, the U.K. government threatened slapping a travel ban on Bahati.[13] And in a rare display of bipartisanism, a U.S. Senate resolution urged Ugandan legislators to reject the anti-homosexuality bill and to repeal laws that criminalize homosexuality.[14] The European Union expressed deep concern about the draft legislation, warning that "international donors, non-governmental organizations and humanitarian organizations would have to reconsider or cease their activities in certain fields should the bill pass into law."[15] Against the backdrop of the anti-homosexuality bill, the Permanent Missions to the United Nations of Argentina, Brazil, Croatia, France, the Netherlands, Norway and Sweden hosted a panel discussion at the December 2009 United Nations General Assembly to "explore grave and extreme human rights violations and discrimination occurring on the basis of sexual orientation and gender identity. Such violations include attacks on the security of lesbian, gay, bisexual, and transgender (LGBT) people, extrajudicial, summary or arbitrary executions, the practice of torture and other cruel, inhuman and degrading treatment or punishment, and arbitrary arrest or detention."[16] Victor Mukasa, a Ugandan LGBT activist, appeared before the UN panel. He shared a personal story of harassment at the hands of Uganda police. He made an impassioned plea for governments to do more for LGBT people, and particularly in Uganda where they faced a state-sponsored hate campaign. Mukasa called upon the UN to extend its "human rights promotion work to all the corners of the earth" and warned that the world "cannot claim that we have been successful in our human rights work when people are still killed because they are gay, transgender, intersex, albino, indigenous, black, or poor." Mukasa made a final urgent appeal to the UN in his own personal experience as a "Ugandan homosexual and transgender person" and "on behalf of all Ugandan LGBTI people" to publicly denounce Bahati's anti-homosexuality bill.[17] Father Philip J. Bené of the Permanent Observer Mission of the Holy See to the United Nations read a statement to the UN panel expressing the Vatican's opposition to "all forms of violence and unjust discrimination against homosexual persons, including discriminatory penal legislation which undermines the inherent dignity of the human person."[18] Although the statement did not explicitly mention Uganda, it took a swipe at the country when the Vatican criticized countries that have created an environment that perpetrates violence against LGBT people: "The murder and abuse of homosexual persons are to be confronted on all levels, especially when such violence is perpetrated by the State."

If Bahati had counted on the larger Christian world to endorse his harsh bill, then he was mistaken. Some of the blistering criticism of the anti-homosexuality bill came from Christian churches and leaders from across the world. Clearly, there were Christians that saw in his bill much that was misaligned with the compassion and love that their faith represented. They were dismayed and urged Ugandan legislators to respect human rights and vote to throw out a draconian and hateful bill, which they saw as antithesis to Christian tenets. The Archbishop of Canterbury, Rowan Williams, found Bahati's bill to be of "shocking severity" and said he had a hard time seeing how it "could be supported by any Anglican who is committed to what the Communion has said in recent decades" and that apart from "invoking the death penalty, it makes pastoral care impossible—it seeks to turn pastors into informers."[19] The archbishop was apparently referring to the bill's stipulation obligating citizens to report known acts of homosexuality to the police within 24 hours. The World Council of Churches (WCC), an influential body of about 350 Protestant and Orthodox Christian groups widely respected in Africa for its fight against South Africa's apartheid system, expressed its concern about the anti-homosexuality bill. The organization's General Secretary, the Reverend Samuel Kobia, wrote a letter to General Museveni in which he beseeched him to join "African church leaders and fellow people of faith, to abstain from supporting any law which can lead to a death penalty; promotes prejudice and hatred; and which can be easily manipulated to oppress people."[20] A strongly worded statement from the Rt. Rev. Mark S. Sisk, the bishop of the Episcopal Diocese of New York, did not conceal the anguish, dismay and pain evoked by the "Kill the Gays" draft legislation: "To put the matter bluntly: for a Christian, no matter how many carefully culled Bible passages might be cited, no matter how lofty the spokesperson, there are no circumstances whatsoever that justify such oppression. Such tyranny is an offense to God." Bishop Sisk's statement further added, "I do understand that in some places, Uganda being one of them, homosexuality is considered either a sin or a sickness (it could not be both); never-the-less neither understanding remotely justifies these terrible laws. I urge all Christian communities in Uganda to join together with a single voice in opposition to this outrage. Further I urge that each and all of us examine and reexamine our own lives and repent of those injustices of which we are witting and unwitting participants."[21] The respected retired archbishop of Cape Town, Desmond Tutu, took his plea directly to Ugandan legislators, drawing parallels between on one hand apartheid and Nazism and on the other Bahati's "Kill the Gays" bill which would legalize the "persecution, discrimination, hatred and prejudice" of LGBT Ugandans. He reminded legislators that "God does not discriminate among members of our family. God does not say black is better than white, or tall is better than short, or football players are better than basketball players, or Christians are better than Muslims ... or gay is better than straight. No. God says love one another; love your neighbor. God is for freedom, equality and love."[22] Archbishop Tutu believed if Ugandan society harbored profound prejudice against LGBT people, then it was incumbent upon legislators as part of their duty and responsibility to "clarify the fundamental misunderstandings in communities about what it means to be lesbian, gay, bisexual, transgender or intersex (LGBTI)."

The domestic and international appeals to Ugandan legislators to reconsider and reject the anti-homosexuality bill did not appear to sway the advocates of harsh penalties against LGBT people in the least. As for the warnings that passage of the bill would lead some of Uganda's Western financial backers to reconsider their aid to the country, the anti-homosexuality bloc took a stance that was bewilderingly belligerent and reminiscent of Idi Amin. Faced with the prospect of an economic meltdown due to financial mismanagement and a looming Western trade embargo, Idi Amin shrugged off the threat, reminding Ugandans theirs was a nation of peasant farmers and if push came to shove, everyone could fall back on a subsistence existence.[23] This was very much the message that the anti-homosexuality crusaders adopted. They urged Ugandans to pour cold water on Western financial aid that supports the country's agriculture, education, health services, and improvements to a colonial-era rickety and crumbling infrastructure. Ugandans were told to stand firm despite the economic woes that would certainly arise if the West followed through with the threats and imposed sanctions. A Ugandan legislator dismissed Western financial aid, claiming that most of that support was inconsequential and was anyway used for insignificant "things like workshops and seminars."[24] Bahati and several other antigay crusaders such as the notorious Giles Muhame, the managing editor of the defunct Uganda tabloid *Rolling Stone*, maintained that the West's suspension of financial aid would be easily offset by dizzying revenues from Uganda's 2006 oil finds in the Lake Albert region.[25] The estimated three billion barrels of recoverable oil buried in the region had the potential of turning Uganda into a mid-sized oil producer, and if well managed could spur economic growth and create immense benefits for the people of this poor nation. There were many in the country that believed the oil wealth could be used as a powerful cudgel to defy the will of the international community. After all, this school of thought contended, Western nations were unlikely to criticize the bad policies and the human rights record of a significant oil producer.

The Archbishop of the COU, Henry Orombi, dismissed the West's threats: "We shall not associate with them [Western countries] even if it means losing aid. We rather remain poor than accept aid which will in the end lead to moral decay of society." Another COU bishop, Yona Katonene, argued that homosexuality was not about human rights but sin, and that Ugandans should be ready to accept any hardship resulting from a halt in Western financial aid. Such suffering, the bishop avowed, was justifiable before God: "We should prepare to suffer for our faith.... They can take their money and leave us with our faith."[26] Indeed, in 2006, the then archbishop of the COU, Livingstone Nkoyooyo, boasted about the cash-strapped Ugandan church rejecting $1 million from the United States: "We rejected the dollars because they were tainted with homosexuality."[27] The Family Life Network of Stephen Langa and Uganda Coalition for Moral Values (UCMV), a hitherto obscure group, organized the "Pass the Bill Now Campaign" to pressure government to debate and endorse the anti-homosexuality bill even if that placed Uganda on a collision path with the West. They appeared unconcerned about the risk of an economic collapse and social upheaval that would inevitably follow Western sanctions. Mr. Langa urged lawmakers to do "what is right even if it is not politically correct" and reminded them that their "first obligation and loyalty should be to the citizens of Uganda and our children who are our future."[28]

Pastor Ssempa lampooned and ridiculed President Barack Obama for his support of LGBT rights: "Obama, even if you do not give us money for medicine for our people, to hell with that money, we would rather die but die in dignity."[29] Playing off Obama's campaign slogan of "Change we can believe in," Pastor Ssempa admonished President Obama: "We wish to tell him that sodomy is not the change we want. Nor can we believe in it."[30] Indeed, it was commonplace for the Ugandan anti–LGBT bloc to show scorn towards President Obama for his support of LGBT rights.

Local radio talk-show hosts opened the lines to pro–Bahati bill Ugandans with their withering criticism of Obama's pro–LGBT stance while steering clear of any criticism of General Museveni. This led one commentator to remark that it was apparently okay for Ugandans to analyze the "performance of a far-away leader they do not vote for" while it was taboo to "discuss the performance of their own President on matters that affect them."[31] A local musician, Mr. Robert Kyagulanyi aka Bobi Wine, went on a tirade against the U.S. President, posting on his Facebook page: "So Obama comes to Africa with his wife and kids to promote homosexuality? … Oh what a shame. Obama you can be a fagot and a hypocrite, but plz keep off our children, our morality and our culture."[32] Bobi Wine has written songs with lyrics encouraging violence against homosexuals.

Faced with international disapproval and outcry, General Museveni sought to distance himself from the anti–LGBT crowd and Bahati's egregious anti-homosexuality bill. He dispatched his lieutenants to allay the angst of his Western allies. Uganda's foreign affairs minister, Sam Kutesa (he is also the father-in-law of General Muhoozi, General Museveni's son), claimed Bahati's bill was not a government-sponsored bill but rather the sole effort of one legislator, Mr. Bahati. Utterances by Mr. Bahati were therefore not representative of government policy. The minister asserted that Bahati's bill was unnecessary since the anti-sodomy laws that the country inherited from its British colonial masters were still in force. He seemed to suggest there was a need to strengthen the anti-sodomy laws to prevent "promoting homosexuality" and protect children.[33] This was yet another example of a high-ranking government official propagating falsehoods and creating fear among Ugandans by implying that homosexuals were sex predators and their Uganda agenda was to recruit minors into homosexuality. General Museveni was among those that believed in the recruitment myth, telling a group of Ugandan youth, "I hear European homosexuals are recruiting in Africa."[34]

Despite his strongman rhetoric against the LGBT community, General Museveni was not oblivious to the fact that signing Bahati's bill into law would tarnish the country's standing in the West, and perhaps draw pointed criticism of his authoritarian leadership and repressive government. In fact, as early as October 2009, immediately after Bahati had introduced his anti-homosexuality bill, General Museveni held a private meeting with the U.S. Assistant Secretary of State for African Affairs, Johnnie Carson, where he assured the U.S. diplomat that his government was not interested in a "war with homosexuals" and that the Bahati bill went "too far"—probably a reference to the bill's mandate of death for "aggravated homosexuality." He appeared to be advocating for inclusive-ness and assured the Americans he would veto the bill.[35] But the general continued to talk out both sides of his mouth, sending conflicting messages on his stance on Bahati's anti-homosexuality bill. Appearing on the BBC's current affairs program *Newsnight* in January 2010, Uganda's Permanent Representative to the United Nations, Dr. Ruhakana Rugunda, was pressed to explain his government's ambiguity on the anti-homosexuality bill. He said the "government has not taken a formal position on the matter."[36] In early January 2010, General Museveni openly acknowledged that the anti-homosexuality bill was hurting Uganda's image in the West. While addressing members of his ruling National Resistance Movement (NRM), he cautioned advocates of the bill to tread carefully since legislating against homosexuality was a sensitive foreign policy matter.[37] This statement to the NRM party was generally interpreted as the general's readiness to tor-pedo Bahati's bill and make concessions in face of withering pressure from Western countries. Many believed that General Museveni knew better than to alienate Western governments that provided the much-needed funds to prop up the country's economy and indeed his political fortune.

After General Museveni's acknowledgment of the bill's international notoriety, his cabinet met and agreed to form a committee that would fur-ther deliberate on the anti-homosexuality bill and advise government on the merits or demerits of the Bahati bill. By all accounts, the meeting was heated, pitting the liberal and pragmatic cabinet ministers who saw the bill as unnecessary and bad for the country on one hand and on the other the traditionalists and Christian conservatives supporting Bahati's harsh bill.[38] The cabinet committee finally issued their report in May 2010. The report noted that the authorship of the Bahati bill was unclear and further observed that it was riddled with "technical defects in form and content" and that the process of drafting the bill had not followed provisions of the Constitution, which meant that it was brought "illegally before Parlia-ment."[39] It appeared as though Bahati's bill was on its way to defeat without formal debate in Parliament, and that the country would move on beyond the distraction of the anti–LGBT legislation and rhetoric to tackle critical pressing national issues. However, in June 2010, General Museveni issued a forceful condemnation of homosexuality while disparaging the West. He complained that Europeans "are putting us under pressure because of homosexuality. They think we are against it because of our religious back-ground but even before religion was introduced in the country, we were against homosexuality and any form of sexual abuse."[40] General Museveni went on to prognosticate the demise of Western civilization, claiming,

"The church in Africa is very strong and has been at the fore in fighting homosexuality and moral decadence. We must look for modern ways of instilling discipline in society. The Europeans are finished and if we follow their western culture, we shall be headed for Sodom and Gomorrah."[41]

To seasoned Ugandan observers, it did not come as a surprise that despite reassurances to the Americans to veto Bahati's anti-homosexuality bill, General Museveni still spoke out against homosexuality although he had at one point appeared to reverse his hardline posture against LGBT people and had said homosexuals were free to live in accordance with their sexual orientation if they "did it quietly."[42] Why then was General Museveni continuing to berate and harass the LGBT community in 2010 after appearing to make concessions to his Western allies? LGBT hate-mongering was a potent populist political tool that the government used to distract Ugandans while pushing through unpopular pro–General Museveni policies. As much as the outcomes of the dubious presidential elections held under General Museveni's decades-long rule were never in doubt, thanks to massive vote-rigging and state-orchestrated violence and intimidation of the political opposition, the general never left anything to chance. With the 2011 presidential elections approaching it was unlikely that General Museveni would order Bahati to withdraw the anti-homosexuality bill. It was in his interest to keep the country energized and focused on the "evils" of homosexuality as a cynical weapon to deflect the populace from dwelling on the government's spectacular failures—widespread poverty and economic inequality, corruption and nepotism, militarization at the expense of democracy, political repression and the curtailing of basic human rights. Writing in Kenya's *Daily Nation*, Randall Smith noted that the "homosexuality debate in Uganda is simply a way to get the population to forget about whether they have enough food to eat, petrol for their cars and a truly representative government."[43]

General Museveni was re-elected with more than 68 percent of the vote in February 2011 in a presidential election that was widely believed to have been fraudulent. With that "win" the general's iron-fist rule was extended to a staggering 25 years in power, making him the longest-serving leader in East Africa. Meanwhile, Bahati's anti-homosexuality bill hibernated in committee limbo. It appeared the cabinet's select commit-tee's decision in May 2010 had derailed the egregious piece of draft leg-islation. Nonetheless, the bill, though lying dormant and neglected in Uganda's Parliament, served as a rallying cause for the anti–LGBT move-ment that never let up their assault. David Kato, an LGBT activist and a leading critic of Bahati's "Kill the Gays" bill was murdered in January 2011.

In the wake of Kato's death, Maria Burnett of Human Rights Watch noted that Bahati's bill has "already generated hatred before it has even been enacted and it should immediately be withdrawn by its author." She called upon General Museveni to "categorically reject the hate that lies behind this bill, and instead encourage tolerance of divergent views of sexuality and protect vulnerable minorities."[44] Kato's murder was widely condemned across the globe. And it brought renewed scrutiny to General Museveni's government's hostility towards sexual minorities. Foreign governments and major international institutions, such as the United Nations, made urgent pleas to the government to drop the bill and refrain from decriminalizing same-sex relationships. But Bahati was unimpressed; he too had been reelected in 2011 to Parliament and felt he had the mandate to pursue his anti-homosexuality agenda. Three months after Kato's murder, Bahati reaffirmed his commitment to reintroduce the anti-homosexuality bill with a focus on legislating against "promotion" of homosexuality and "behavior that is going to destroy the future of our children."[45] When in August 2011, General Museveni's cabinet said the anti-homosexuality bill was unnecessary and ought to be thrown out, Bahati retorted that the "future of this country's children will be determined by the peoples' representatives in Parliament" and not by the executive branch.[46] Indeed, Bahati was supported by several legislators who were adamant that the cabinet had no legal right to stop or suspend debate and voting on the bill. They accused the government of bowing to Western pressure, claiming Uganda was better off foregoing foreign financial aid. It was a price, these legislators argued, the country was ready to pay to protect its "traditional" values. Andrew Allen, a Ugandan legislator of British ancestry, representing one of the poorest constituencies in the country, delivered a bold message to the cabinet: "Whether they [cabinet] want or not, we are going to pass it [anti-homosexuality bill]. For government to come up and throw out such a Bill means we are living in a crazy world."[47] Mr. Andrew Allen did not bother to consider how passing a bill seeking to kill sexual minorities was proof that "we are living in a crazy world." In February 2012, Bahati reintroduced a revised anti-homosexuality bill, which excluded the provision to kill homosexuals.[48] The revised bill prescribed life imprisonment for those guilty of "aggravated homosexuality." The timing of the bill's reintroduction in Parliament was suspicious and smacked of a Machiavellian political maneuver by General Museveni, and much of it had to do with Uganda's oil reserves.

Accusations of gross corruption in Uganda's nascent oil industry began surfacing soon after the discovery of significant oil reserves in 2006 with several multinational oil concerns fighting it out for the rights to own and develop the vast oil fields. With a government bedeviled with corruption, it was a question of time before bribery scandals would emerge. Powerful government ministers with strong connections to General Museveni were soon named in multimillion dollar kickback schemes centered around secret oil exploration and development deals signed with foreign oil companies. Among those cited in the crooked deals and the massive bribery were Mr. Amama Mbabazi, the prime minister and a former agent of Idi Amin's much-dreaded secret service, and Mr. Sam Kutesa, Uganda's powerful and influential foreign affairs minister.[49] Mr. Kutesa publicly boasted of being worth a whopping $3 to $4 million in a country where 67 percent of the population are classified as poor or highly vulnerable to poverty.[50] In diplomatic cables released by WikiLeaks, an executive of a foreign oil firm appeared to implicate General Museveni in the kickback scheme. However, the general denied such accusations, calling them "contempt of the highest order" and he described the oil executive as an "idiot."[51]

Legislators, wary of oil's potential to be a curse rather than a windfall for many oil-producing sub–Saharan African countries, began speaking out against the repugnant fraud that had gripped Uganda's oil sector. They demanded a halt in the negotiation of oil contracts until government enacted legislation that provided for transparency and protected the "country from getting fleeced by oil dealers, and to also manage the oil for the benefit of the future generations."[52] Ugandan legislators, especially those belonging to General Museveni's ruling party, the NRM, are not given to challenging the general on policy matters that carry his imprimatur. That the legislators, even those belonging to the ruling NRM party, showed a rare unity in demanding clarity in the oil sector was tantamount to a revolt of the like that General Museveni had yet to experience in his decades-long autocratic rule. A youthful ruling party legislator, Ms. Cerinah Nebanda, summarized the mood among legislators best when she said, "If there is a rebellion, it is a rebellion against corruption. We cannot keep quiet when our people are suffering and all this [corruption] is happening when people [corrupt officials] are eating billions." Ms. Nebanda died in December 2012 under suspicious circumstances. Some of her colleagues in Parliament believed Uganda's notorious security agents had a hand in Ms. Nebanda's death.[53] However, the government strenuously denied any involvement, alleging she died of "multiple organ failure due to a combined effect of alcohol and drug toxicity."[54] The drugs in question were said to be heroin and cocaine.

In early February 2012, just before the re-introduction of Bahati's anti-homosexuality bill, the government gave in to the legislators' demands and introduced the Petroleum (Exploration, Production and Development) Bill, 2012. But the emboldened legislators were not impressed, seeing in the bill's clauses a deliberate lack of safeguards to mitigate the risk of corruption in the negotiating and endorsing of petroleum agreements with foreign companies. Of concern was a clause that granted the minister of energy the unilateral authority to make important decisions relating to the oil sector. The legislators understood more than anybody else that the minister of energy (or any minister for that matter) was at the beck and call of General Museveni, and for self-preservation would not go against the general's will. In effect, the bill was granting General Museveni sweeping powers to personally control Uganda's entire oil industry. Increasing the legislators' unease and the concern of ordinary Ugandans about the general's intent for the potential revenues from newly discovered oil was General Museveni's decision to assign the responsibility of protecting the oil fields to the Special Forces Command (SFC), an elite and ruthless Praetorian Guard headed by Museveni's son, General Kainerugaba Muhoozi. While the legislators were up in arms against clauses of the Petroleum Bill that they deemed objectionable and questionable, Mr. Museveni hurriedly summoned the speaker of Uganda's Parliament, Ms. Rebecca Kadaga. He admonished the speaker for not bringing to the floor *pending* bills from previous years. He ordered Parliament to first debate those bills and not focus on the Petroleum Bill, 2012. Immediately after making his intentions clear to Ms. Kadaga, General Museveni, without the knowledge of legislators and in total contempt of their demands for transparency, had his government's signature on a new oil production agreement with Tullow Oil, a London-based Anglo-Irish oil company. Before the legislators could raise their opposition, Bahati was dangling before them his anti-homosexuality bill, which was among the *pending* bills that General Museveni had referred to. By focusing legislators on homosexuality, a subject of fascination and a source of cheap political credits, the general successfully deflected "parliaments attention away from the contentious oil debate and then got his wish of having the [oil] agreements signed without major impediment."[55]

At the first reading of the re-introduced anti-homosexuality bill in February 2012, Ugandan legislators clapped and cheered Mr. Bahati with wild chants of "Our bill, our man."[56] The overriding sentiment was one in which legislators cared less about regulating the oil sector but more about criminalizing, and possibly killing, their fellow citizens. Kerry Kennedy, the daughter of Robert F. Kennedy and the president of the Robert F. Kennedy Center for Justice and Human Rights, was a vocal critic of the bill. On the bill's reintroduction in Uganda's Parliament in February 2012, she cautioned that it was a

> serious threat to the rights and freedoms of all Ugandans and is a clear violation of international law.... It creates an atmosphere of hate, intolerance, and fear. It criminalizes the actions of civil society organizations and individual citizens who work to defend the legal rights of their fellow Ugandans. And it puts the imprimatur of the law behind discrimination based on sexual orientation or gender identity. This is a blatant suppression of the rights of all Ugandans and an attempt to curtail the freedoms of speech and assembly of a vibrant civil society in Uganda.[57]

In March 2013, Kennedy led a delegation of U.S. human rights activists to Uganda to persuade the country to drop the contentious bill. She held meetings with General Museveni and his wife, Janet. During her meeting with General Museveni, Kennedy brought up the issue of the government's harassment of LGBT Ugandans, reminding the general that the anti-homosexuality bill before Parliament violated international human rights treaties to which Uganda was a signatory. General Museveni categorically dismissed suggestions of his government's persecution of the LGBT community saying that in Uganda "there were a few homosexuals. There was no persecution, no killings and no marginalization of these people but they were regarded as deviants. Sex among Africans including heterosexuals is confidential."[58]

Despite General Museveni's claims that his government did not persecute LGBT people, the contrary was true. For example, in 2012, the government had threatened to ban NGOs advocating for LGBT rights, including the Civil Society Coalition on Human Rights and Constitutional Law (CSCHRCL). The government claimed to have intercepted minutes of a CSCHRCL meeting, purportedly detailing strategies of promoting homosexuality. Father Lokodo, the minister of ethics and integrity, hailed the intercept of the minutes as a success and yet evidence of the global LGBT movement's hidden agenda to promote unacceptable sexual behavior: "We found that, on the pretext of humanitarian concerns, these organisations are being used to promote negative cultures. They are encouraging homosexuality as if it is the best form of sexual behavior."[59] In September 2012, David Cecil, a British playwright, staged a play, *The River and the Mountain,* in a Kampala theatre. The play centered on a gay factory owner. Cecil was promptly arrested for allegedly failing to obtain clearance to stage the play from Uganda's moral guardian—the Media Council. He spent four days in Uganda's notorious maximum security prison before being deported back to the U.K. Critics were quick to point out this was part of an ongoing regimen of repression and intimidation.[60]

Ugandan legislators supporting the anti-homosexuality bill were not prepared to show compassion or compromise. They wanted the bill passed and threw their weight behind efforts to vote for the bill, perhaps to curry favor with the president, especially coming off a contentious oil bill where their fealty to General Museveni could have been questioned. When Ms. Kennedy and her team met with members of Uganda's Parliament she got an earful.[61] One legislator, Alice Alaso, chided the Americans: "You [Westerners] have imposed on us enough of your bad practices, right from guns, and we shall not allow homosexuality in Uganda because the Bible forbids it." Another legislator, Safia Nalule, tinged her disapproval with sarcasm and mockery: "May I know whether you have seen anything good about this practice [homosexuality] that you can share with us?" Ms. Kennedy and her delegation returned to the U.S. without having secured any meaningful concessions to stop the Ugandans from passing the harsh anti-homosexuality bill. By December 2013, it was all but certain the legislators would vote to pass Bahati's bill. Mr. Buturo, no longer the minister of ethics and integrity but nonetheless a darling of the parliamentary Christian caucus and seen as a bulwark of traditional and Christian mores, beseeched his fellow legislators to pass the bill and send it to the president to sign into law. He warned that the country was under siege from pro–gay rights activists and the passage of the bill could not wait any longer: "A test of MPs' true commitment to protecting the people's interests will be assessed in their readiness to pass the bill without any further delay."[62] Ms. Rebecca Kadaga, the speaker of the Parliament of Uganda, had on several occasions indicated her commitment to supporting the passage of the Bahati bill.[63] At the October 2012 Inter-Parliamentary Union conference in Quebec, Ms. Rebecca Kadaga launched a scathing attack on Canada's foreign affairs minister, John Baird. Mr. Baird's crime was to condemn the anti-homosexuality bill that was before Uganda's Parliament: "If homosexuality is a value for the people of Canada they should not seek to force Uganda to embrace it. We are not a colony or a protectorate of Canada."[64] On her return to Uganda after the conference, speaker Kadaga received a heroine's welcome from the conservative anti–LGBT bloc. Prominent in the welcoming entourage at the country's international airport were Buturo and Pastor Ssempa.

Late Friday afternoon on December 20, 2013, Ugandan lawmakers overwhelmingly voted to approve Bahati's anti-homosexuality bill, 2009. There was a triumphant air in the house chamber as the bill's passage was celebrated. This was Bahati's crowning glory and he saw the bill's endorsement by his peers in Parliament as the "perfect Christmas gift we could give Ugandans."[65] The Archbishop of the COU, the Most Rev. Ntagali, remarked, "In Uganda, there are so many injustices.... I want to thank parliament for passing the Anti-Homosexuality Bill. I want the world to understand what we are saying."[66] The Church of Uganda describes itself as a "Jesus-loving, Bible-believing, Spirit-filled Anglican Church engaged in the mission of Jesus Christ in today's world."[67] Clearly, the archbishop of the COU did not see any inconsistency or contradiction between his support of the antigay bill that sought to criminalize gays, some of whom were undoubtedly members of his congregation, and the Church's mission of love and inclusiveness or the fact that passage of Bahati's bill piled another layer on the mountain of the many injustices he spoke about. Archbishop Ntagali had probably not bothered to listen to the message of love and compassion preached by his fellow Episcopalian Archbishop, Desmond Tutu, who has dedicated much of his life to building peace and fostering harmony:

> We are all—all of us—part of God's family. We all must be allowed to love each other with honor. Yet all over the world, lesbian, gay, bisexual, and transgender people are persecuted. We treat them as pariahs and push them outside our communities. We make them doubt that they too are children of God. This must be nearly the ultimate blasphemy. We blame them for what they are.... The Jesus I worship is not likely to collaborate with those who vilify and persecute an already oppressed minority.[68]

Uganda Parliament's passage of Bahati's anti-homosexuality bill, a cruel piece of legislation harking back to the dark ages, was a stark reminder of the flagrant disregard of civil rights, widespread abuse of human rights, and the general disdain for fundamental freedoms that have plagued and defined post-independence Uganda. By voting to pass Bahati's bill, the legislators were adding a new chapter to the country's checkered and blood-drenched history. Speaking to *Deutsche Welle*, a German broadcaster, the Ugandan LGBT activist Frank Mugisha called the bill's passage a "truly terrifying day for human rights in Uganda." He expressed fear for his own personal safety and life, "If this law is signed by President Museveni, I'd be thrown in jail for life and in all likelihood killed. We urgently need world leaders to call on President Museveni and demand he stops this bill of hate from becoming law."[69] Soon after Parliament's endorsement of Bahati's bill, the U.K. business tycoon Richard Branson, who was considering investing in Uganda, said he would shelve those plans. He also called on companies worldwide and tourists to boycott the country.[70] But would General Museveni veto the anti-homosexuality bill? Another presidential election was scheduled for February 2016. Speculation was rife the general would not step aside, but extend his rule to more than three decades. In the immediate aftermath of the legislators' vote on the anti-homosexuality bill and following widespread international criticism of Uganda's government, the general distanced himself from the Bahati bill. Tamale Mirundi, General Museveni's spokesperson, who had perfected the art of sycophantic comedy down to a science, laid the blame of passing Bahati's bill on opposition lawmakers. He claimed the opposition had passed the bill to shore up its support among Christians.[71] Meanwhile, General Museveni accused the speaker of Uganda's Parliament, Ms. Kadaga, for rallying "a small group of ... MPs [members of Parliament]" to pass the anti-homosexuality bill.[72]

Ms. Kennedy displayed her indefatigability as a human rights defender. She did not give up trying to persuade General Museveni not to sign the harsh Bahati bill. She sought Archbishop Desmond Tutu's intercession in setting up a meeting with General Museveni. Ms. Kennedy and her entourage were finally received by General Museveni on January 18, 2014. During the meeting, the general promised Archbishop Tutu and Ms. Kennedy he would reject the bill in its current draft and even called the legislation "fascist."[73] Soon after, General Museveni announced he would only assent to signing the bill if he received scientific evidence that homosexuality is an acquired behavior and not genetically determined.[74] To get his answer he appointed a Ministerial Scientific Committee on Homosexuality to study the matter and report back to him in early February 2014. The committee consisted of 11 scientific and medical experts, and included geneticists and psychiatrists. It is both curious and ironic General Museveni placed confidence in the opinion of Uganda's scientific and medical community to assist in a matter of policy. In the past, he had not hidden his disdain for Uganda's medical experts. For example, in 2003, he had the presidential jet fly his pregnant daughter at an estimated cost of $90,000 to deliver his granddaughter in a Germany hospital. He claimed this lavish extravagance was necessary because he distrusted the Ugandan medical community.[75]

The Ministerial Scientific Committee reviewed 16 publications appearing in the scientific literature between 1957 to 2012. Two weeks after General Museveni had announced his plans to constitute the committee, the team of experts was ready with the report "Scientific Statement on Homosexuality."[76] The report made several observations, including the fact that homosexuality "existed in Africa way before the coming of the white man. However, most African cultures controlled sexual practices, be they heterosexual or homosexual, and never allowed *exhibitionistic sexual behavior."* General Museveni and the anti–LGBT activists used the phrase "exhibitionistic sexual behavior" to refer to public display of sexuality or even public display of affection. Uganda's scientists and medical experts further noted the following: homosexuality could not be explained by a singular definitive gene; homosexuality is neither a disease nor an abnormality; homosexuals exist in every society and homosexuality can be influenced by environmental factors such as culture and religion. Their conclusion hardly supported the myth perpetuated by the anti–LGBT bloc that had argued homosexuality was solely a learned behavior imported from the West and not a biological orientation. However, General Museveni's interpretation of the scientific report was at odds with its findings. He claimed the scientists had unanimously concluded homosexuality was a learned behavior. At the end of February 2014, during a retreat of his ruling NRM lawmakers, General Museveni announced he would sign Bahati's "fascist" bill into law.[77] For the umpteenth time, the international community expressed outrage at General Museveni's intransigence and wanton disregard of fundamental human rights. President Barack Obama added his voice, yet again, in condemning the draft legislation. He warned General Museveni that signing the bill into law "will complicate our valued relationship with Uganda."[78] Uganda is an important U.S. ally in the War on Terror and receives considerable U.S. technical and security assistance. Whereas the U.S. does not have boots on the ground in Somalia to fight the Al-Shabaab, a jihadist militant group allied to al-Qaeda, Uganda provides the bulk of African troops fighting the Shabaab.

In response to Obama's warning, General Museveni wrote a contemptuous letter to the president of the United States in which he discouraged "the USA government from taking the line that passing this law will 'complicate our valued relationship.'"[79] He further admonished President Obama that "Countries and Societies should relate with each other on the basis of mutual respect and independence in decision making. 'Valued relationship' cannot be sustainably maintained by one Society being subservient to another society.... We do not want anybody to impose their views on us. This very debate was provoked by Western groups who come to our schools and try to recruit children into homosexuality."[80] A few days later, General Museveni sent another warning to President Obama, demanding the U.S. president desist from interfering in Uganda's internal affairs: "This is my home.... Go back to your home."[81] He also threatened to end Uganda's relationship with the U.S. and expressed a strong desire to cooperate more closely with the Russians because "they don't mix up their politics with other country's politics."[82] In 2013, Uganda was the recipient of more than $720 million in aid from the U.S.[83] Also, the U.S. is Uganda's largest bilateral donor.[84] The hubris of one of the world's longest serving authoritarian leaders tested the patience and resolve of the world's strongest democracy. Human Rights Watch appealed to the United States to demonstrate its "concern for Uganda's deteriorating human rights environment by temporarily recalling the U.S. ambassador."[85]

In early February 2014, when much of the world's attention was fixated on the Uganda Parliament's endorsement of Bahati's anti-homosexuality bill, General Museveni signed into law another morality legislation—the anti-pornography bill, 2011.[86] The bill was also referred to as the "miniskirt bill" because of its provision to outlaw the miniskirt. The "miniskirt bill" was purportedly drafted as a response to an "increase in pornographic material in the Ugandan mass media and the increase in nude dancing in the entertainment world" which warranted a need "to put in place a legal framework which can regulate such vices."[87] Also, importantly, the supporters of the anti-pornography bill had long argued that pornography was a gateway to homosexuality. The principal architect of the bill, Father Simon Lokodo, promised that his legislation would require the police to arrest any woman who wore anything above the knee or "dressed in something that irritates the mind and excites other people."[88] Ms. Stella Mukasa, a leading Ugandan lawyer and women rights activist, best summarized the law as a "rollback of women's personhood and autonomy as upheld by our constitutional guarantees on equality before and under the law, including laws that protect women from sexual and gender-based violence, intimate partner violence, and female genital mutilation, to mention a few."[89] But General Museveni could not be bothered to care. He gleefully signed this piece of repressive legislation that mostly targeted the urban Ugandan woman. There was an astonishing lack of international criticism to this assault on the urban woman. The West appeared content to let General Museveni have his way in what they perceived as a socially conservative society. It is this lack of forceful international condemnation of the miniskirt law that probably heightened General Museveni's hubris, which was all too familiar to Ugandans.

On February 24, 2014, General Museveni gathered local and international journalists at his official residence, the State House in Entebbe. The journalists watched as a nonchalant General Museveni appended his signature to Bahati's anti-homosexuality legislation. In the rambling press conference that followed, a dismissive, condescending and combative General Museveni fulminated against the evils of the West and the "disgusting" gay people.[90] He claimed it was the West's arrogance that had forced his hand to sign the anti-homosexuality bill.[91] In effect General Museveni was acknowledging that his endorsement of Bahati's bill was not because of his wily misrepresentation of the findings of the Ministerial Scientific Committee on Homosexuality. Many social commentators noted that the real reason behind General Museveni's morality laws was distraction of the public from the failings of his government and presenting the general as a popular, no-nonsense anti-imperialist African leader. This set him up nicely to mobilize support for a lifetime presidency. Joe Oloka Onyango, the human rights lawyer, remarked on how the anti-homosexuality and anti-pornography laws served to justify "discrimination against LGBTI people and against women. It also serves as a major point of distraction from more important issues of governance and democracy." And *The Star* noted that the Uganda morality laws were "designed solely to win votes from the evangelical churches for Museveni and the NRM [National Resistance Movement—General Museveni's political party] in the 2016 elections. They are shallow and oppressive pieces of legislation that close political space ... the new clothing rules are also anti-women. They are regulating women's clothing, not men's clothing. The assumption is that women need to be controlled by men."[92] All along, as Ugandan legislators debated and passed strict morality laws, General Museveni was the puppet master with ruling party functionaries like Buturo, Bahati and Father Lokodo dancing to his pull on the strings as he introduced reactionary and repressive moral legislations evocative of the Idi Amin era.

With the anti-homosexuality legislation endorsed as the law of the land, the anxiety and fear that gripped the Uganda LGBT community was profound. Frank Mugisha of Sexual Minorities Uganda resignedly tweeted, "I am officially illegal—President Museveni signs law to send me to jail."[93] The award-winning Kenyan author and gay activist, Binyanavanga Wainana, characterized the new anti-homosexuality Uganda law as unacceptable and retrogressive, observing that it was "a desperate act by a desperate dictator to find relevance in any way possible."[94] In the light of the new law, LGBT Ugandans treaded cautiously, retreating even further into the closet. They feared arrest or lynching at the hands of unruly mobs enforcing the anti-homosexuality law. Human Rights Watch and Amnesty International documented an uptick in incidences of discrimination, intimidation, harassment and abuse of LGBT Ugandans.[95] The rights organizations documented incidences of landlords evicting LGBT tenants, and employers dismissing LGBT workers. By late April 2014, more than 80 LGBT Ugandans had fled the country, seeking asylum in neighboring Kenya. As the LGBT community braced for an increase in intimidation, harassment and massive arrests, the Inter-Religious Council of Uganda that brings together Christians and Muslims organized a National Thanksgiving Service to congratulate General Museveni for signing Bahati's atrocious bill into law and vowing never to "approve the homosexuality vice."[96]

Meanwhile, there was the usual outcry and condemnation of General Museveni from international organizations and Western countries. Amnesty International called the anti-homosexuality law "deeply offensive" and an "affront to the human rights of all Ugandans."[97] No sooner was the ink dry on General Museveni's signature on the anti-homosexuality legislation than Uganda's major development partners upped their pressure on the country. European countries, including Uganda's most dedicated donors such as the Netherlands, Norway and Denmark, announced the freezing of millions of dollars in financial assistance.[98] The European Parliament urged member states to consider targeted sanctions, which could include imposing travel and visa bans for the key individuals responsible for drafting and adopting the anti-homosexuality law.[99] The United States said it would review its relationship with Uganda in light of the anti-homosexuality law that Secretary Kerry compared to Nazism and Apartheid.[100] The World Bank put on hold a $90 million loan to Uganda's Ministry of Health, funds that were earmarked to strengthen the health-care system. Following these major announcements withholding financial aid, the Uganda currency, the shilling, appeared to be headed for hard times, losing value against major currencies.[101] Uganda's trade with the international community was at risk. There were fears multinationals would boycott Ugandan products, especially agricultural produce. Uganda's economy is chiefly reliant on agriculture. In the meantime, the tourism sector showed dramatic decline. The number of foreign visitors to the country dropped by a staggering 50 percent.[102] It was evident the economy was taking a big hit, which the country could ill afford. Despite signs of a looming economic meltdown, General Museveni kept up his defiance. He claimed the country did not need financial aid from the West because Uganda is "one of the richest countries on earth."[103] If General Museveni had rephrased this statement to assert he ranked among the richest people on earth, then that would have been more credible. In 2008, some sources estimated his net worth at $1.7 billion, a figure his spokesperson could not confirm or deny as he retorted, "I am not his accountant."[104] In the meantime, General Museveni's ardent anti–LGBT cheerleaders urged him to stay the course and defy the West. Archbishop Ntagali of the COU counseled him to remain steadfast and not worry about losing foreign aid. Since it was widely anticipated Uganda's Western donors would cut funding for HIV prevention, treatment and care, Archbishop Ntagali proposed the formation of a special fund. The fund would rely on voluntary donations to keep HIV-infected Ugandans on life-saving anti-retroviral medicines. General Museveni liked the idea: "If our American friends are so careless and they want to cut off the aid so that 1.5 million people die [of AIDS], then we shall fund it [the HIV treatment] ourselves."[105]

As the U.S. publicly mulled the nature of punitive actions to impose on Uganda, General Museveni went on the offensive, attacking U.S. interests in Uganda. General Museveni had bullied Ugandans and the countries of the Greater Lakes region of central Africa for a long time. His repression of the political opposition and widespread human rights abuses coupled with military adventurism in neighboring countries, particularly in the Democratic Republic of the Congo where millions died, were barely condemned by the West. It appeared the West needed General Museveni more than he needed it, and he probably believed he was untouchable. In a high-stakes drama that unfolded on April 3, 2014, heavily armed Uganda police officers raided the offices of the U.S.–funded Makerere University Walter Reed Project (MUWRP) in the suburbs of Kampala and in the process arrested a project employee. A Uganda government spokesperson, Ofwono Opondo, alleged the MUWRP was engaged in "training youths for homosexuality," and the raid was part of the police's enforcement of the law.[106] Opondo accused MUWRP of acting like a brothel and facilitating money-exchange in return for illegal sexual liaison. On April 4, 2014, at 2:17 p.m., Opondo sent out a scurrilous tweet: "Top diplomat allegedly involved#paying one hundred thousand Ug [Uganda] shillings each masturbation."

The raid on MUWRP offices had all the hallmarks of being directed from higher government officials closer to power. Initially, the Uganda police denied knowledge of the raid. However, a few days later, the police issued a statement alleging they had infiltrated the MUWRP facility and collected evidence that showed the organization actively recruited and trained young men to engage in "unnatural sex" in exchange for money.[107] The MUWRP is a health clinic and medical research facility that was established in 2002. The project's mission is to "mitigate disease threats through quality research, health care and disease surveillance" in Uganda.[108] To that effect, MUWRP operated a program that provided HIV prevention and treatment services to thousands of Ugandans irrespective of their sexual orientation. The U.S. Department of State condemned the raid, characterizing it as an incident that "significantly heightens our concerns about respect for civil society and the rule of law in Uganda, and for the safety of LGBT individuals." MUWRP operations were temporally suspended.[109] In April 2014, the U.S. secretary of state John Kerry embarked on a tour of African countries. He visited Angola, Ethiopia, the Democratic Republic of the Congo, and South Sudan. Although Uganda is perceived as an important U.S. ally, particularly in the war against militant Islamic terrorism, Kerry's itinerary skipped Uganda. This was generally interpreted as a deliberate U.S. snub, and part of an evolving Western effort to isolate and punish General Museveni.[110]

In June 2014, the U.S. finally announced tangible punitive sanctions against General Museveni's regime.[111] The sanctions included a travel ban for certain Ugandan officials, especially those involved in human rights abuses against LGBT people. The list of Ugandans facing a U.S. travel ban was expanded to include persons "found responsible for significant public corruption." This latter list was significant, affecting many in General Museveni's inner circle, and potentially included many of his family members and close relatives. Further, the U.S. announced the discontinuation of funding to the Uganda police and suspended aid to some health programs. The U.S. had been planning to hold a military aviation exercise in Uganda. Those plans were shelved. Incredulously, a Uganda government spokesperson alleged the U.S. was imposing sanctions against Uganda as a political tactic to divert the U.S. public's attention from the wars in Syria and Iraq.[112] If the futility of engaging in a nasty direct conflict with the U.S. was not apparent to General Museveni, then this round of U.S. sanctions must have sent the general to reconsider his belligerence. General Museveni wanted to stay in the good books of the West; he needed that support to entrench his position as Uganda's authoritarian-in-chief. It was an open secret in Uganda that if the West, and particularly the U.S., withdrew its support, General Museveni's authoritarian regime would crumble in short order.

Despite the official Ugandan public rhetoric of defiance, it was apparent that General Museveni, who had grossly underestimated the resolve of his Western backers, was working on a behind-the-scenes détente. He had to deflect mounting international pressure and the looming economic meltdown because of Western sanctions. On July 7, 2014, Uganda's foreign affairs ministry issued a statement on the anti-homosexuality act, claiming the country's development partners had misconstrued the law. The anti-homosexuality legislation, the statement reassured, did not intend to "punish and discriminate against people of a 'homosexual orientation,'" and that "no activities of individuals, groups, companies or organizations will be affected by the Act. The intention of the Act is to stop promotion and exhibition of homosexual practice."[113] However, evidence of a retreat had begun around mid–March 2014. Then, the government had allowed a coalition of human rights activists, including indefatigable LGBT activists such as Dr. Paul Nsubuga Semugoma, Jacqueline Kasha Nabagesera, Julian Pepe Onziema, and Frank Mugisha to challenge the anti-homosexuality law in the Constitutional Court. The activists contended the Bahati law was draconian and a flagrant abuse of basic human rights and should therefore be nullified. Further, the petitioners argued Parliament had passed the Bahati bill in December 2013 without the requisite quorum, and hence the law could not pass legal muster.[114] On August 1, 2014, five judges of the Constitutional Court unanimously ruled to nullify the anti-homosexuality law on grounds that Parliament did not have the necessary quorum when it passed the bill.[115] LGBT advocates had registered a landmark victory albeit the Constitutional Court's nullification of the anti-homosexuality law was based on procedural grounds and not because the legislation was an infringement of LGBT rights. This, therefore, opened the door for reintroducing the bill and ensuring it passed with a full parliamentary quorum. Indeed, Bahati promised to continue the campaign against the LGBT community: "The court case ruling is no victory at all, the morals of the people of Uganda will prevail."[116] But perhaps most importantly, there were no howls of protests in the streets of Ugandan cities because the judges had nullified the anti-homosexuality legislation. People could not care less. This goes to further illustrate that before General Museveni opened the first vicious salvo against the Ugandan LGBT community in September 1999, the country had no history of harassment or attacks directed against sexual minorities.

After the Constitutional Court's ruling, General Museveni distanced himself from a bill that he had signed into law under the full glare of the world's media. He claimed he was not aware Parliament had passed the bill in December 2013 without the necessary quorum: "When the bills come to me, I assent to them.... I don't look at how they are passed."[117] General Museveni chastised the legislators for their unfamiliarity with parliamentary etiquette, blaming them for bringing him a procedurally flawed bill. It is significant that Uganda's Constitutional Court struck down the anti-homosexuality law three days before the start of the first U.S.–Africa Summit in Washington, D.C., which was held August 4–6, 2014. The summit focused on trade and investment between Africa and the U.S.

Nearly 50 African leaders were invited. The U.S. pointedly did not invite the leaders of four African countries with a human rights record as odious as General Museveni's—Eritrea, Central African Republic, Sudan and Zimbabwe. General Museveni's invitation to the summit was extended in June 2014.[118] Rights activists, citing General Museveni's anti–LGBT legislation, called on the Obama administration to rescind the general's invitation to the summit.[119] There is no doubt the U.S. conducted aggressive backroom discussions with General Museveni, leaving him under no illusion the Obama administration would widen its punishing sanctions and possibly marginalize the Uganda dictator, including rescinding the invitation to the historic August 2014 U.S.–Africa summit. General Museveni had incentive to comply or else run the risk of losing his main Western backers. The targeted Western sanctions were hurting the country's economy. This had the potential of creating significant social and political unrest, which could challenge General Museveni's decades-long rule. Further, because of Uganda's adoption of egregious anti-homosexuality laws, the general's reputation in the West had grossly diminished and he was no longer the "darling" benign autocrat. The West was speaking out on General Museveni's human rights record. The Kampala regime feared this new scrutiny could potentially lead to revisiting past human rights abuses in the Democratic Republic of the Congo, or even the widespread atrocities in northern and eastern Uganda. To contain the emerging Western consensus of disapproval, General Museveni hired the services of a U.S. public relations firm to help salvage his tarnished image and defend his repressive regime.[120] On his return from the U.S.–Africa Summit in Washington, D.C., General Museveni said he had "no problem with two adults consenting to doing their things privately, but I have a problem with those who are luring our young people."[121] It was a remarkable turnaround for a man that had defied the international community and only months earlier had signed into law one of the world's cruelest anti-homosexuality legislation.

In the immediate aftermath of the Constitutional Court's ruling, which struck down the Bahati law, the most vocal critics of the LGBT community like Pastor Ssempa and Buturo indicated they would appeal the court's judgment or force a referendum and have Ugandans decide on criminalizing homosexuality. Meanwhile, other legislators continued to explore avenues to reintroduce the legislation. Mr. Latif Ssebagala jumped to the fore, spearheading efforts for the bill's reintroduction. He alleged he had the backing of most lawmakers and Parliament would approve the new anti-homosexuality bill in December 2014.[122] The new bill, which explicitly avoided mention of the word "homosexuality," proposed life behind bars for persons engaging in "unnatural sexual practices," defined as intercourse between same-sex or transgender persons, anal sex among heterosexual couples, and bestiality. In voicing support for the new anti-homosexuality bill, Uganda lawmaker Ms. Nabilah Naggayi Sempala said, "We are going to reassert our cultural values, not only on men sleeping with fellow men, but the unnatural processes of sex. Anal sex is not a cultural thing for Uganda nor is it an African culture."[123] She therefore advocated for a provision in the new bill that would "protect women against anal sex in the precincts of their marital homes."[124] In fact Ms. Sempala had previously showed support to the LGBT community, and her turnaround was a surprise to human rights activists. However, she later appeared to regret supporting the revival of the anti-homosexuality bill, emphasizing she was not homophobic and that sexual minorities and other marginalized segments of Uganda's society were "citizens" whose fundamental human rights must be respected and protected.[125]

But Museveni's views on homosexuality had evolved and changed; he struck a conciliatory and accommodating tone. He told Ugandans the Constitutional Court had spoken, and it was about time to move beyond homosexuality and focus the country on growing the economy for the people's benefit.[126] Once General Museveni had made his change of heart clear, the political opportunists who had pushed the anti-homosexuality legislation on his behalf were unlikely to defy his will as much as they agitated for the reintroduction of the bill. The religious clergy did not let up in their crusade of demonizing LGBT people either. Their continuing rhetoric ensures matters of sexual orientation and gender identity remain on the national agenda.[127] Even some in the political opposition borrowed from General Museveni's populist playbook by stoking anti–LGBT sentiments. Mr. Abed Bwanika, who was among several people running for president in the 2016 elections, declared on the campaign trail that "Uganda is no area for homosexuality." He alleged that LGBT people were possessed by demons and his party had "specialists to chase out demons."[128] Mr. Bwanika fared badly. General Museveni "won" a controversial fifth term in office with over 60 percent of the vote.

Since the Constitutional Court's repeal of the Bahati anti-homosexuality act in August 2014, reports of persecutions and arrests of LGBT Ugandans are few and far between. The LGBT community has certainly welcomed this development but are nonetheless cautious. Significantly, LGBT organizations can operate in the country without risking closure from moralizing government officials. The community has successfully organized high-profile events without police harassment. Gay pride parades in 2014 and 2015 were not dispersed by police. In fact, in an unprecedented show of accommodation, the police provided security to the marchers. These are small victories. Nonetheless, they are important milestones, which represent a glimmer of hope for every LGBT Ugandan. Dr. Martin Luther King, Jr., taught that the "arc of the moral universe is long, but it bends towards justice." One day, Ugandans will be able to choose who they love and how they dress without having to fear death, imprisonment or harassment from their government.

Chapter Notes

Chapter I

1. Henry Ochieng. "President Tells Off Homosexuals." *Monitor.* July 22, 1998.
2. Yasiin Mugerwa. "How Events Unfolded at the 1986 Swearing In." *Daily Monitor.* January 26, 2016.
3. BBC *HardTalk*, February 2012, 24.
4. Solomon Arinaitwe. "NRM Historicals Split on 'Muhoozi Project.'" *Daily Monitor.* May 18, 2013.
5. Nathan Etengu. "Bishop Okille Attacks Homosexuals in Church." *New Vision.* April 28, 1998.
6. Nathan Etengu. "Bishop Okille Attacks Homosexuals in Church." *New Vision.* April 28, 1998.
7. Editorial. "No!" *New Vision.* April 29, 1998.
8. Jim Mugunga. "Press Attacks Compaore Before Museveni." *Monitor.* May 4, 1998.
9. Henry Ochieng. "President Tells Off Homosexuals." *Monitor.* July 22, 1998.
10. Karyeija Kagambirwe. "Nkoyooyo Raps West Over Gays." *New Vision.* June 4, 1998.
11. Anonymous. "Museveni Backs Clinton." *New Vision.* October 22, 1998.
12. Anonymous. "Arrest Homos, Says Museveni." *New Vision.* September 28, 1999.
13. Enock Kakande. "Nkoyooyo Supports Museveni on Gays." *New Vision.* November 13, 1999.
14. U.S. Department of State. October 15, 1999. http://1997–2001.state.gov/www/briefings/statements/1999/ps991015a.html.
15. James Magode Ikuya. "Government Can Never Embrace Homosexuals." *Monitor.* November 3, 1999.
16. Katende Kisuule Magala. "Homos Create Lobby Group." *Monitor.* November 5, 1999.
17. Katende Kisuule Magala. "MPs for Big Homosexual Debate Today." *Monitor.* November 28, 1999.
18. Fred Ouma. "Vice Rate Worries Buturo." *New Vision.* April 9, 2004.
19. Anonymous. "Matembe Names Kampala Homo Pubs." *New Vision.* April 26, 2002.
20. Anonymous. "Matembe Names Kampala Homo Pubs." *New Vision.* April 26, 2002.
21. Samuel Wossita. "Internet Cafes Blamed for Homosexuality." *Monitor.* April 23, 2002.
22. Jude Etyang and Jude Katende. "No Debate on Gays, Says Orombi." *New Vision.* March 4, 2005.
23. Anonymous. "Prostitutes Reported to Kabaka." *New Vision.* August 10, 2002.
24. Apollo Mubiru. "Makerere University Homos Worry Nsibambi." *New Vision.* February 8, 2005.
25. Emma Masumbuko. "Makerere Toughens on Homosexuality." *Monitor.* April 18, 2005.
26. F. Ahimbisibwe. "Students Warned on Homosexuality." *New Vision.* February 4, 2005.
27. Anonymous. "NGO to Petition Parliament on Homosexuality in Schools." *New Vision.* March 25, 2009.
28. John Senyonyi. "Homosexuality Unhealthy." *New Vision.* March 11, 2003.
29. Carol Natukunda and Richard Kirembeka. "Homos Storm Schools." *New Vision.* May 19, 2005.
30. Mohamed Ssengooba. "White Homos Beasts, Says Minister." *Monitor.* November 11, 1999.
31. Editorial. "Gay Strategy for Uganda." *New Vision.* May 6, 2006.
32. James Wasula. "Africans Must Join Hands and Fight Homosexuality." *New Vision.* June 13, 2005.
33. David Bahati. "The Anti-Homosexuality Bill, 2009." *Uganda Gazette.* September 25, 2009.
34. David Bahati. "I Insist, Mwenda Is Wrong on Gays." *The Independent.* December 1, 2009.
35. Mireya Navarro. "2 Decades On, Miami

Endorses Gay Rights." *New York Times.* December 2, 1998.

36. Manning Marable. "Fascism Is Growing." *Tuskegee News.* June 23, 1977.

37. *The Rachel Maddow Show.* December 8, 2010.

38. Harriet Anena. "How Many People Did Amin Really Kill?" *Daily Monitor.* September 28, 2012.

39. Timothy Kalyegira. "Where Are Nagenda's 600 Victims of Idi Amin?" *Daily Monitor.* April 6, 2007.

40. P. Lloyd. "The Dangers of Moral Certainty." *Philosophy Now*, 1996, Vol. 15, pp. 23–25.

41. alterglobalization. "Ugandan Minister of Ethics and Integrity Says Men Raping Girls Is Natural." https://www.youtube.com/watch?v=YguoemEGN1k.

42. Ian Burrell. "Stephen Fry Says the 'Frothing' Homophobia of Ugandan Politician Led Him to Try to Kill Himself." *The Independent.* February 8, 2016.

43. Josh Kron. "Resentment Toward the West Bolsters Uganda's New Anti-Gay Bill." *New York Times.* February 28, 2012.

44. Jeff Sharlet. "Straight Man's Burden." *Harper's.* September 2010.

45. Anonymous. "Lokodo Vows to Arrest Prostitutes and Their Clients." *Monitor.* March 6, 2015.

46. Josephine Maseruka and Susan Ninsiima. "Pornography Traffickers Face Jail." *New Vision.* January 29, 2009.

47. Moses Mulondo. "I Am Going to Wipe Out Pornography." *New Vision.* August 28, 2010.

48. Joan Mugenzi. "Porno Destroyed My Family." *New Vision.* June 18, 2002.

49. Perez Rumanzi. "Indecent Rape Victims to Blame, Says Youth Minister." *Daily Monitor.* September 24, 2013.

50. Moses Walubiri. "Anti-Pornography Bill Not About Miniskirts—Minister." *New Vision.* April 10, 2013.

51. Cyprian Musoke and Joyce Namutebi. "Marriage Bill Tabled in House." *New Vision.* December 22, 2009.

52. Sylvia Tamale. "Law Reform and Women's Rights in Uganda." *East African Journal of Peace and Human Rights.* Volume 1 (1993).

53. Parliament of Uganda. "Bill No. 19. the Marriage and Divorce Bill." 2009.

54. Sheila Naturinda. "Museveni Supports Marriage Bill." *Daily Monitor.* March 16, 2013.

55. David Tash Lumu and Sadab Kitatta Kaaya. "Marriage Bill: How Museveni Killed It." *The Observer.* April 10, 2013.

56. Mercy Nalugo. "Museveni Writes to MPs on Marriage Bill." *Daily Monitor.* March 22, 2013.

57. David Tash Lumu and Sadab Kitatta

Kaaya. "Marriage Bill: How Museveni Killed It." *The Observer.* April 10, 2013.

Chapter II

1. Sylvia Nannyonga-Tamusuza. "Female-Men, Male-Women, and Others: Constructing and Negotiating Gender Among the Baganda of Uganda." *Journal of Eastern African Studies.* Vol. 3, 2 (2009), pp. 367–380.

2. Radio Netherlands Worldwide, May 21, 2014.

3. Milton Olupot. "Avoid Gay Sex, Janet Tells Youth." *New Vision.* January 12, 2000.

4. James Nichols. "Janet Museveni, Ugandan First Lady, Claims Lack of Gay Cows Invalidates Same-Sex Attraction." *The Huffington Post.* March 20, 2014.

5. Stephen Otage. "Man of God Backs Government Against Gays." *Daily Monitor.* December 6, 2009.

6. Emmanuel Gyezaho. "Museveni Warns Against Homosexuality." *Daily Monitor.* November 16, 2009.

7. Henry Ochieng. "Museveni Still Tough on Homosexuals." *Monitor.* November 24, 1999.

8. Anonymous. "President Museveni's Full Speech at Signing of Anti-Homosexuality Bill." *Daily Monitor.* February 24, 2014.

9. Yoweri K. Museveni. "Museveni to Kadaga, MPs on Homosexuality Bill—What Sort of Parliament Is This?" *The Observer.* February 16, 2014.

10. Rudi C. Bleys. *The Geography of Perversion: Male-to-Male Sexual Behavior Outside the West and the Ethnographic Imagination, 1750–1918.* New York: NYU Press, 1996.

11. Ian Katusiime and Joan Akello. "Standing Firm on Anti-Gay Law." *The Independent.* March 6, 2014.

12. The Ministerial Scientific Committee on Homosexuality. "Scientific Statement from the Ministry of Health on Homosexuality." *Pambazuka.* February 28, 2014.

13. Moses Mulondo. "Eight Denounce Homosexuality." *New Vision.* March 25, 2009.

14. Josh Kron. "Pulling Out All the Stops to Push an Antigay Bill." *New York Times.* April 13, 2011.

15. Josh Kron. "Pulling Out All the Stops to Push an Antigay Bill." *New York Times.* April 13, 2011.

16. Martin Ssempa. "Sodomites, Prostitutes Should Not Be Equated to Teachers and Doctors." *Daily Monitor.* February 23, 2012.

17. Solomon Male. http://solomonmale.blogspot.com.

18. Stephen O. Murray. *Homosexualities.* Chicago: The University of Chicago Press, 2000.

19. D. Lewis. "Representing African Sexu-

alities." In Sylvia Tamale, ed., *African Sexualities: A Reader.* 2011.

20. Sylvia Tamale. "Out of the Closet: Unveiling Sexuality Discourses in Uganda." *Feminist Africa.* 2003, 2.

21. M. Epprecht. "'Bisexuality' and the Politics of Normal in African Ethnography." *Anthropologica.* 2006, Vol. 48, pp. 187–201.

22. *The World Debate.* BBC, March 12, 2011.

23. Aernout Zevenbergen. *Spots of a Leopard: On Being a Man.* Cape Town: Laughing Leopard Productions, 2009.

24. James Magode Ikuya. "Government Can Never Embrace Homosexuals." *Monitor.* November 3, 1999.

25. Aernout Zevenbergen. *Spots of a Leopard: On Being a Man.* Cape Town: Laughing Leopard Productions, 2009.

26. A. Barfoot. "Women, Homosexuality, and the Bible." http://philippians-1-20.us/alison.htm.

27. Political Research Associates. http://www.politicalresearch.org/profiles-on-the-right-alison-barfoot/#sthash.tAcKzxuX.dpbs.

28. Aernout Zevenbergen. *Spots of a Leopard: On Being a Man.* Cape Town: Laughing Leopard Productions, 2009.

29. J.F. Cunningham. *Uganda and Its Peoples; Notes on the Protectorate of Uganda, Especially the Anthropology and Ethnology of Its Indigenous Races.* London: Hutchinson & Company, 1905.

30. J.H. Driberg. *The Lango: A Nilotic Tribe of Uganda.* London: T. Fisher Unwin, 1923.

31. J.C.D. Lawrance. *The Iteso: Fifty Years of Change in a Nilo-Hamitic Tribe of Uganda.* Oxford: Oxford University Press, 1957.

32. Sylvia Nannyonga-Tamusuza. *Baakisimba: Gender in the Music and Dance of the Baganda People of Uganda.* London: Routledge, 2005.

33. M. Mushanga "The Nkole of Southwestern Uganda." In A. Molnos, ed., *Cultural Sources Materials for Population Planning in East Africa: Beliefs and Practices.* Nairobi: East African Publishing House, 1973.

34. Stephen O. Murray and Will Roscoe, eds.. *Boy-Wives and Female Husbands: Studies of African Homosexualities.* New York: Palgrave Macmillan, 1998.

35. Interview with General Museveni. CNN, April 18, 2012.

36. Interview with General Museveni. *Hard-Talk.* London: BBC, February 24, 2012.

37. Henry M. Stanley. *Through the Dark Continent.* New York: Harper & Brothers, 1878.

38. Stephen Kyeyune. *Shaping the Society: Christianity and Culture. Special Reference to the African Culture of Baganda, Volume II.* AuthorHouse. 2012.

39. David Robinson and Douglas Smith.

Sources of the African Past. Lincoln: iUniverse, 1999.

40. Sylvia Nannyonga-Tamusuza. *Baakisimba: Gender in the Music and Dance of the Baganda People of Uganda.* London: Routledge, 2005.

41. Chris Mondloch. "Bacha Bazi: An Afghan Tragedy." *Foreign Policy,* October 28, 2013.

42. Najibullah Quaraishi. "Uncovering the World of 'Bacha Bazi.'" PBS, 2010.

43. Chris Mondloch. "Bacha Bazi: An Afghan Tragedy." *Foreign Policy,* October 28, 2013.

44. Sylvia Nannyonga-Tamusuza. *Baakisimba: Gender in the Music and Dance of the Baganda People of Uganda.* London: Routledge, 2005.

45. John F. Faupel. *African Holocaust: The Story of the Uganda Martyrs.* Nairobi: Paulines Publications Africa, 2007.

46. Ham Mukasa. *Uganda's Katikiro in England; Being the Official Account of His Visit to the Coronation of His Majesty King Edward VII.* London: Hutchinson, 1904.

47. John F. Faupel. *African Holocaust: The Story of the Uganda Martyrs.* Nairobi: Paulines Publications Africa, 2007.

48. K. Hamilton. *The Flames of Namugongo: Postcolonial, Queer, and Theological Reflections on the Narrative of the 1886 Ugandan Martyrdom.* Cincinnati: Union Institute and University, 2007.

49. Aisha Ahmad. "70 Muslims Martyred for Calling Kabaka a Kafir." *New Vision.* May 31, 2007.

50. Gillian Nantume. "The Roots of Islam in Buganda." *Daily Monitor.* May 11, 2015.

51. J. Ndyabahika. "Islam and Christianity in Uganda: Conflict, Dialogue, and Search for Partnership." In P.M. Dikirr, R. Ostergard Jr., M. Toler, P. Macharia and A.A. Mazrui, eds., *Africa's Islamic Experience: History, Culture, and Politics.* New Delhi: Sterling Publishers, 2009.

52. Henry M. Stanley. *Through the Dark Continent.* New York: Harper & Brothers, 1878.

53. Henry M. Stanley. *Through the Dark Continent.* New York: Harper & Brothers, 1878.

54. D.A. Low. *The Mind of Buganda: Documents of the Modern History of an African Kingdom.* Berkeley: University of California Press, 1971.

55. Mawere Munyaradzi. *Divining the Future of Africa. Healing the Wounds, Restoring Dignity and Fostering Development.* Bamenda: Langaa RPCIG, 2014.

56. Marinus Rooijackers. "The Beginning of the White Fathers' Mission in Southern Uganda and the Organization of the Catechumenate 1879–1914." *Society of Missionaries of Africa*: Issue 9 of History series, 2008.

57. Rodney Muhumuza. "Sodomy, the Un-

told Story in Boarding Schools." *Daily Monitor.* June 21, 2008.

58. Semakula Kiwanuka. *A History of Buganda: From the Foundation of the Kingdom to 1900.* Teaneck: Holmes & Meier, 1972.

59. Megan Vaughan. *Curing Their Ills: Colonial Power and African Illness.* Palo Alto: Stanford University Press, 1991.

60. Albert R. Cook. "Syphilis in Uganda." *The Lancet,* 1908, Vol. 172, p. 1771.

61. H.W. Weatherhead. "Progress and Difficulties in Uganda." *Church Missionary Review.* 1907, Vol. 58, pp. 705–712.

62. J.D. Mullins and H. Mukasa. *The Wonderful Story of Uganda, to Which Is Added the Story of Ham Mukasa, Told by Himself.* London: Church Missionary Society, 1904.

63. J.D. Mullins and H. Mukasa. *The Wonderful Story of Uganda, to Which Is Added the Story of Ham Mukasa, Told by Himself.* London: Church Missionary Society, 1904.

64. M. Epprecht. "The Making of 'African Sexuality': Early Sources, Current Debates." *History Compass.* 2010, Vol. 8, pp. 768–779.

65. Stephen O. Murray and Will Roscoe, eds. *Boy-Wives and Female Husbands: Studies of African Homosexualities.* New York: Palgrave Macmillan, 1998.

66. Stephen O. Murray and Will Roscoe, eds. *Boy-Wives and Female Husbands: Studies of African Homosexualities.* New York: Palgrave Macmillan, 1998.

67. Robert Bwire. *Bugs in Armor: A Story of Malaria and Soldiering.* Lincoln: Writers Club Press, 2000.

68. J.P. Rushton. *Race, Evolution, and Behavior: A Life History Perspective.* New Brunswick: Transaction Publishers, 1997.

69. J.P. Rushton. *Race, Evolution, and Behavior: A Life History Perspective.* New Brunswick: Transaction Publishers, 1997.

70. Wayne Dynes. "Homosexuality in Sub-Saharan Africa: An Unnecessary Controversy." *Gay Books Bulletin* 9 (Spring-Summer 1983): 20–21, 27.

71. George Sale, George Psalmanazar, Archibald Bower, John Campbell, George Shelvocke and John Swinton. *An Universal History, from the Earliest Account of Time, Volume 35.* London: T. Osborne, 1760.

72. William Smith. *A New Voyage to Guinea.* London: John Nourse, 1745.

73. Jeffrey J. Kripal. *Roads of Excess, Palaces of Wisdom: Eroticism and Reflexivity in the Study of Mysticism.* Chicago: University of Chicago Press, 2001.

74. Denis Altman. "Globalization and the International Gay/Lesbian Movement." In Steven Seidman and Diane Richardson, eds., *Handbook of Lesbian and Gay Studies.* London: Sage, 2002.

Chapter III

1. Anonymous. "Exclusive—General Amin Talks to DRUM." *DRUM.* March 1973.

2. Ali A. Mazrui and Etin Anwar. *The Politics of Gender and the Culture of Sexuality: Western, Islamic and African Perspectives.* Lanham, MD: University Press of America, 2014.

3. Eugene Kalisa. "Miniskirt Ban: Some Things in Uganda Politics Never Change." *Daily Monitor.* February 24, 2014.

4. Immy Wamimbi. "Dress Decently—President: Minis Banned—So Are Hot Pants and V-Split Maxis." *Uganda Argus.* May 29, 1972.

5. Anonymous. "Jinja Girl in Court on 'Mini Dress' Charge." *Uganda Argus.* June 12, 1972.

6. Rebecca Katumba and Betty Nagadya. "Mini Girls Molested by Men." *Uganda Argus.* May 31, 1972.

7. Wayne Bennett. *Uganda Argus* Clippings Collection, 1970–1972. MacOdrum Library, Carleton University, Archives and Research Collections. https://arc.library.carleton.ca/exhibits/uganda-collection/view-within-uganda-argus-newspaper.

8. Anonymous. "Women's Trousers Banned in Offices." *Voice of Uganda.* January 15, 1973.

9. Anonymous. "Women's Trousers Banned in Offices." *Voice of Uganda.* January 15, 1973.

10. Anonymous. "Decree Bans Women's Wigs and Trousers." *Voice of Uganda.* February 5, 1974.

11. Anonymous. "Decree Bans Women's Wigs and Trousers." *Voice of Uganda.* February 5, 1974.

12. Anonymous. "Decree Bans Women's Wigs and Trousers." *Voice of Uganda.* February 5, 1974.

13. Anonymous. "Documents Depict Amin's Paranoid Secret Service." *The Cornell Daily Sun.* April 23, 1979.

14. Anonymous. "Feature: The Anti-Man Cometh." *Transition,* 1975, Vol. 48.

15. Anonymous. "President Amin Bans Use of Skin Make-Up." *Voice of Uganda.* May 6, 1975.

16. Anonymous. "Now Women Can Wear Trousers Again." *Voice of Uganda.* November 23, 1974.

17. Ali A. Mazrui. "The Black Woman and the Problem of Gender: An African Perspective." *Research in African Literatures.* 1993, Vol. 24, 1.

18. Immy Wamimbi. "Dress Decently—President: Minis Banned—So Are Hot Pants and V-Split Maxis." *Uganda Argus.* May 29, 1972.

19. Desiree Lewis. "Against the Grain: Black Women and Sexuality." *African Feminism.* 2005, Vol. 2, pp 11–24.

20. Anonymous. "Challenge Men in All Fields." *Voice of Uganda.* September 13, 1978.

21. Willy Mukasa. "City Slums to Look Anew." *Voice of Uganda.* February 5, 1975.

22. Anonymous. "Governor Bars Drinking at Mulago." *Voice of Uganda.* December 16, 1976.

23. Wazarwahi Bwengye. "Present Prostitution Laws Are Unsatisfactory." *Voice of Uganda.* November 11, 1976.

24. Rebecca Katumba. "Ban on Shabby Hair Hailed by Ugandans." Wayne Bennett. *Uganda Argus* Clippings Collection, 1970–1972. MacOdrum Library, Carleton University, Archives and Research Collections. https://arc.library. carleton.ca/exhibits/uganda-collection/view-within-uganda-argus-newspaper.

25. Wanume Kibedi. "The Story Continues: Kibedi's Open Letter to Amin." *Transition.* 1975, 49.

26. Rebecca Katumba. "Ban on Shabby Hair Hailed by Ugandans." *Uganda Argus.* Wayne Bennett. *Uganda Argus* Clippings Collection, 1970–1972. MacOdrum Library, Carleton University, Archives and Research Collections. https://arc.library.carleton.ca/exhibits/uganda -collection/view-within-uganda-argus-news-paper.

27. Alicia C. Decker. *In Idi Amin's Shadow: Women, Gender, and Militarism in Uganda.* Athens: Ohio University Press, 2014.

28. Wanume Kibedi. "The Story Continues: Kibedi's Open Letter to Amin." *Transition.* 1975, 49.

29. Anonymous. "General Amin Has One Wife and Others Are Out!" *Voice of Uganda.* March 26, 1974.

30. Louise Pirouet. "Religion in Uganda Under Amin." *Journal of Religion in Africa.* 1980, Vol. 11.

31. George Roberts. "The British Government and Uganda Under Idi Amin, November 1972 to April 1979." http://www.academia.edu/ 2317564/the_British_government_and_Uga nda_under_Idi_Amin_November_1972_to_ April_1979.

32. Jack Anderson. "Food for Politics." *The Courier.* December 5, 1974.

33. Anonymous. "Idi Amin Discusses Social Views Over Uganda Airwaves." *Jet.* June 5, 1975.

34. Anonymous. "Rest of British Firms Will Be Taken Over." *Voice of Uganda.* May 23, 1973.

35. Loyal N. Gould and James Leo Garrett, Jr. "Amin's Uganda: Troubled Land of Religious Persecution." *Journal of Church and State.* 1977, Vol. 19, 3.

36. Colin Legum. "Behind the Clown's Mask." *Transition,* no. 75/76, 1976.

37. B.L. Jacobs. "The Autumn of Our Dis-content: The Uganda Scene (Continued)." *Africa Today.* 1974, Vol. 21, 1.

38. Colin Legum. "Behind the Clown's Mask." *Transition,* no 75/76, 1976.

39. Alicia C. Decker. *In Idi Amin's Shadow: Women, Gender, and Militarism in Uganda.* Athens: Ohio University Press, 2014.

40. Anonymous. "Uganda Under Military Rule." *Africa Today.* Vol.20, 1973.

41. Wayne Bennett. *Uganda Argus* Clippings Collection, 1970–1972. MacOdrum Library, Carleton University, Archives and Research Collections. https://arc.library.carleton. ca/exhibits/uganda-collection/view-within-uganda-argus-newspaper. [Cited: June 8, 2015.]

42. Anonymous. "Vendors Tried Over Porn." *New Vision.* March 27, 2001.

43. Anonymous. "Raped by Demons." *New Vision.* November 6, 2012.

44. Geoffrey Kamali. "Pornography Exported to Uganda." *New Vision.* March 27, 2002.

45. Samuel Wossita. "Internet Cafes Blamed for Homosexuality." *Monitor.* April 23, 2002.

46. Scott Lively. *Witness to Revival in Africa: A Report of the Ministry of Scott and Anne Lively in Uganda, Kenya and Egypt, June 12–25, 2002.* Citrus Heights: Abiding Truth Ministries, 2002.

47. Joan Mugenzi. "Porno Destroyed My Family." *New Vision.* June 18, 2002.

48. Joan Mugenzi. "Porno Destroyed My Family." *New Vision.* June 18, 2002.

49. Ganzi Muhanguzi. "Pornography Causing Crime—Research." *New Vision.* November 14, 2008.

50. Henry H. Ssali. "Nkoyoyo Leads Demo Against *Red Pepper." Monitor.* May 13, 2003.

51. Anonymous. "Nude Dancers Sentenced." *New Vision.* February 25, 2004.

52. Elias Biryabarema. "MPs Told to Ban Tabloid." *Monitor.* February 24, 2004.

53. Barbara Among. "Makerere Students in Protest." *Daily Nation.* March 15, 2005.

54. Anonymous. "MUK Students Hold AIDS Demo." *Monitor.* March 16, 2004.

55. Sarah Kiyingi. "Presentation, Consideration and Adoption of the Report of the Select Committee on Pornography." Parliament of the Republic of Uganda. Kampala: 2005.

56. Anonymous. "Govt to Pass Law on Sexual Abstinence." *New Vision.* September 20, 2004.

57. Moses Mulondo. "I Am Going to Wipe Out Pornography." *New Vision.* August 28, 2010.

58. Francis Kagolo. "Irked Ethics Minister Tells Media to Reduce on Sex Talk." *New Vision.* July 19, 2012.

59. Charles Mukiibi, Chris Ocowun and Milton Olupot. "Gulu Chief Bans Mini-Skirts." *New Vision.* June 10, 2009.

60. Charles Mukiibi, Chris Ocowun and

Milton Olupot. "Gulu Chief Bans Mini-Skirts." *New Vision*. June 10, 2009.

61. Anonymous. "Uganda Pastor Screens Gay Porn in Church." *Daily Nation*. February 17, 2010.

62. Darren Foster, Jim Fraenkel and Alex Simmons, prods. "Missionaries of Hate." Current TV, 2010.

63. Flavia Nakagwa. "Amakula Homosexual Movies Blocked." *New Vision*. May 9, 2008.

64. Parliament of the Republic of Uganda. "Parliament Passes Anti-Pornography Law." http://www.parliament.go.ug/new/index.php/about-parliament/parliamentary-news/325-parliament-passes-anti-pornography-law.

65. Perez Rumanzi. "Indecent Rape Victims to Blame, Says Youth Minister." *Daily Monitor*. September 24, 2013.

66. Cullen Murphy. *God's Jury: The Inquisition and the Making of the Modern World*. Boston: Mariner Books, 2013.

67. Parliament of the Republic of Uganda. "Parliament Passes Anti-Pornography Law." http://www.parliament.go.ug/new/index.php/about-parliament/parliamentary-news/325-parliament-passes-anti-pornography-law.

68. Anonymous. "Lokodo Tries to Arrest MP Wearing Miniskirt." *The Observer*. April 20, 2015.

69. Umaru Kashaka. "If I Catch You in a Lodge at Lunchtime...." *New Vision*. July 5, 2015.

70. Al Mahdi Ssenkabirwa. "Dp's Nambooze Arrested." *Monitor*. November 2, 2009.

71. Yazid Yolisigira. "Mob Undresses 10 People Over Indecent Exposure." *Daily Monitor*. February 26, 2014.

72. Uganda Women's Network. https://www.facebook.com/media/set/?set=a.734830479874247.1073741834.213096348714332&type=3.

73. Yudaya Nangonzi. "Lokodo Anti-Porn Push Breaking the Law." *The Observer*. November 26, 2014.

74. Jemimah Kansiime. https://www.youtube.com/watch?v=c4h0hnqCxxc.

75. Edward Anyoli. "Candida Jailed for Falsely Accusing Soldiers of Shaving Her." *New Vision*. February 18, 2011.

76. Sadab Kitatta Kaaya. "How FDC Woman Was Undressed." *The Observer*. October 14, 2015.

77. NTV. https://www.youtube.com/watch?v=AFFD18dgH6w.

78. Anonymous. "FDC's Fatuma Undressed Herself—Police." *The Observer*. October 12, 2015.

79. Job Bwire. "Who Undressed Fatuma? Police Block FDC Women Activists Marching to Parliament." *Daily Monitor*. October 14, 2015.

80. Anonymous. "FDC's Fatuma Undressed Herself—Police." *The Observer*. October 12, 2015.

81. Grace Natabaalo. "Buturo to Name Sex Workers and Their Clients." *Daily Monitor*. September 19, 2008.

Chapter IV

1. Paul Nsubuga Semugoma. http://gayuganda.blogspot.com/2011/03/religion.html.

2. Sarah Elspeth Coughtry. "Patriarchy and the Trap of Masculinity: A Post-Colonial Analysis of Violence Against Sexual Minorities in Uganda." Theses, Dissertations, and Projects. Smith College School for Social Work, Northampton, MA, 2011.

3. Sylvia Tamale. "A Human Rights Impact Assessment of the Ugandan Anti-Homosexuality Bill 2009." *Equal Rights Review*, 2009, Vol. 4, pp. 49–57.

4. Stephen O. Murray and Will Roscoe, eds. *Boy-Wives and Female Husbands: Studies of African Homosexualities*. New York: Palgrave Macmillan, 1998.

5. John "Longjones" Abdallah Wambere. https://www.youtube.com/watch?v=mqYZ01d8J54.

6. Hassan Badru Zziwa. "Chris Mubiru—Likeable, Generous but Moral Disgrace." *The Observer*. December 16, 2012.

7. Rodney Muhumuza. "Country's Toothless Battle on Gays." *Daily Monitor*. October 30, 2009.

8. Stephen Wandera. "Ugandan Family Disown Son Studying in UK for Being Gay." *Daily Monitor*. September 8, 2014.

9. Katherine Roubos. "Rally Denounces Homosexuality." *Monitor*. August 22, 2007.

10. Herbert Ssempogo, Jeff Lule, Matthias Mazinga. "Father Musaala Named Homosexual." *New Vision*. March 31, 2009.

11. Jeffrey Gettleman. "Americans' Role Seen in Uganda Anti-Gay Push." *New York Times*. January 3, 2010.

12. Editorial. "Gay Strategy for Uganda." *New Vision*. May 6, 2006.

13. Southern Poverty Law Center. https://www.splcenter.org/fighting-hate/extremist-files/individual/scott-lively.

14. Patrick Onyango. "Gay Body Targets MPs, Journalists." *Monitor*. August 28, 2003.

15. Bettina R. Scholz. *The Cosmopolitan Potential of Exclusive Associations: Criteria for Assessing the Advancement of Cosmopolitan Norms*. Lanham: Lexington Books, 2015.

16. Irene Monroe. "The Anglican Communion's Fall Guy." http://www.irenemonroe.com/2007/06/08/the-anglican-communions-fall-guy/

17. Stephen Noll. "The Anglican Commun-

ion in Crisis." Global South Anglican Online. January 23, 2006.

18. Anglican Consultative Council. http://www.anglicancommunion.org/media/127746/1978.pdf.

19. Anglican Communion. "Resolution 64. Human Rights for Those of Homosexual Orientation." Lambeth Conference, 1988.

20. Miranda K. Hassett. *Anglican Communion in Crisis: How Episcopal Dissidents and Their African Allies Are Reshaping Anglicanism.* Princeton: Princeton University Press, 2007.

21. Anglican Communion. "Resolution 26. Church and Polygamy." Lambeth Conference, 1988.

22. Albert Ogle. "4 Missteps That Let AIDS Continue to Spread." http://76crimes.com/2013/06/04/4-missteps-that-let-aids-continue-to-spread/.

23. Louie Crew Clay. *Letters from Samaria: The Prose & Poetry of Louie Crew Clay.* New York: Morehouse Publishing, 2015.

24. D. Serwadda, R.D. Mugerwa, N.K. Sewankambo et al. "Slim Disease: A New Disease in Uganda and Its Association with HTLV–III Infection." *Lancet,* Vol. 2. October 19, 1985.

25. Ann Wlazelek. "Ignorance of AIDS Is Killing Ugandans." *The Morning Call.* May 25, 1993.

26. Colin Stewart, Albert Ogle, Eric O. Lembembe, Miles Tanhira, Andy Kopsa, Rac-hel Adams and Clare Byarugaba. *From Wrongs to Gay Rights: Cruelty and Change for LGBT People in an Uncertain World.* Laguna Niguel: P.C. Haddiwiggle Publishing, 2013.

27. J.P. Thoonen. *Black Martyrs.* London: Sheed & Ward, 1941.

28. Rahul Rao. "The Locations of Homophobia." *London Review of International Law,* Vol. 2. 2014.

29. Arthur Baguma. "My Grandpa Survived Martyrdom—Nkoyooyo." *New Vision.* June 4, 2004.

30. Karyeija Kagambirwe. "Nkoyooyo Raps West Over Gays." *New Vision.* June 4, 1998.

31. Anglican Communion. "Resolution I.10: Human Sexuality." Lambeth Conference, 1998.

32. James Thrall. "Conference Takes Conservative Stance on Human Sexuality." *The Lambeth Daily.* August 6, 1998.

33. George F. Woodliff III. "Rediscovering Christian Orthodoxy in Episcopal Anglicanism." http://www.standfirminfaith.com/media/RediscoveringOrthodoxy.pdf.

34. Samuel Wossita. "Gays Are Rebels, Archbishop Nkoyoyo Says." *Monitor.* November 13, 2003.

35. www.churchofuganda.org/articles/237.

36. Larry B. Stammer. "Ugandan Cleric Backs Breakaway Parishes." *Los Angeles Times.* August 24, 2004.

37. Geoffrey M. Araali. "Orombi Cautions Flock Against Gays." *Daily Monitor.* November 20, 2012.

38. Raymond Baguma and Vicky Wandawa. "Rt. Rev Stanley Ntagali Is New COU Archbishop." *New Vision.* June 22, 2012.

39. Ephraim Kasozi. "Ntagali Enthroned as Museveni Preaches Against Homosexuality." *Daily Monitor.* December 17, 2012.

40. Edward Ssekika. "Gay Law—Uganda Plans New AIDS Fund." *The Observer.* April 1, 2014.

41. Rahul Rao. "The Locations of Homophobia." *London Review of International Law,* Vol. 2. 2014.

42. Kevin Ward. "Same-Sex Relations in Africa and the Debate on Homosexuality in East African Anglicanism." *Anglican Theological Review.* 2002, Vol. 84, 1, pp. 81–111.

43. Gloria Haguma. "Even in Retirement He Stands Tall." *Sunday Monitor.* November 18, 2012.

44. Norman Katende. "Church Speaks Out on Kabaka's Son." *New Vision.* January 25, 2012.

45. http://www.newvision.co.ug/mobile/Detail.aspx?NewsID=628579&CatID=1.

46. Uganda Human Rights Commission. *Child Sacrifice in Uganda and Its Human Rights Implication.* Kampala: Uganda Human Rights Commission, 2015.

47. Zadock Amayisa. "Ntagali Dismisses Orombi Claims of Demon Attacks." *Sunday Monitor.* January 11, 2015.

48. Timothy Bukumunhe. "Who Are the Richest People in Uganda?" *New Vision.* April 7, 2007.

49. Paul Gifford. *African Christianity: Its Public Role.* Bloomington: Indiana University Press, 1998.

50. Eriasa Mukiibi Sserunjogi, Henry Lubega and Gillian Nantume. "100 Most Influential Ugandans—Part VI." *Daily Monitor.* August 30, 2015.

51. Anonymous. "Bishops Attack Judges on Adultery Ruling." *Daily Monitor.* April 8, 2007.

52. Will O'Bryan. "In Harm's Way." *Metro Weekly.* November 23, 2011.

53. http://gayuganda.blogspot.com/2009/02/official-invitation.html.

54. Karooro Okurut. "Kampala Can Truly Become City of God." *New Vision.* December 10, 2007.

55. Gerard Bareebe, Kristof Titeca. "Personalisation of Power Under the Museveni Regime in Uganda." In Filip Reyntjens, Stef Vandeginste and Marijke Verpoorten, eds., *L'Afrique des Grands Lacs. Annuaire 2011–2012.* Paris: L'Harmattan, 2013.

56. Janet Kataaha Museveni. *My Life's Journey.* Kampala: Fountain Publishers, 2010.

57. Tabu Butagira. "Wikileaks: Why Musev-

eni Made Wife Minister." *Africa Review*. September 9, 2011.

58. Alex B. Atuhaire and Angelo Izama. "Politicians, Religious Leaders, Musicians Top List of Most Influential 100 Ugandans." *Daily Monitor*. September 29, 2007.

59. Anonymous. "How Bahati, Anite Became Ministers." *The Insider*. March 1, 2015.

60. Jeff Sharlet. "Straight Man's Burden." *Harper's*. September 2010.

61. Nancy Goldstein. "No Prayers for David Kato." *The Nation*. February 4, 2011.

62. Paul Gifford. *African Christianity: Its Public Role*. Bloomington: Indiana University Press, 1998.

63. Alex B. Atuhaire and Angelo Izama. "Politicians, Religious Leaders, Musicians Top List of Most Influential 100 Ugandans." *Daily Monitor*. September 29, 2007.

64. Ivan R. Mugisha. "First Ladies Host Prayer Breakfast." *New Times*. June 18, 2012.

65. Milton Olupot. "Avoid Gay Sex, Janet Tells Youth." *New Vision*. January 12, 2000.

66. James Nichols. "Janet Museveni, Ugandan First Lady, Claims Lack of Gay Cows Invalidates Same-Sex Attraction." *Huffington Post*. March 20, 2014.

67. Wamboga-Mugirya. "Gays' Hide-Outs Found." *Monitor*. October 4, 1999.

68. Alfred Wasike. "Youth Rap Gays." *New Vision*. January 17, 2000.

69. Janet Museveni. "First Lady Challenges Parliamentarians to Build a Better Uganda." http://janetmuseveni.org/ruhaama/better_uganda.php.

70. Isaac Imaka. "Janet Behind Gays Bill." *Daily Monitor*. September 11, 2011.

71. Fawzia Sheikh. "Uganda Bans Vagina Monologues." Worldpress.org. May 14, 2005.

72. F. Ahimbisibwe and Grace Wafula. "MP Matembe Backs Vagina Monologues." *New Vision*. February 19, 2005.

73. Janet Museveni. "First Lady Challenges Parliamentarians to Build a Better Uganda." http://janetmuseveni.org/ruhaama/better_uganda.php.

74. Andrew Bagala. "Mufti Wants Gays Abandoned on Island in Lake Victoria." *Monitor*. October 15, 2007.

75. Anonymous. "Mufti Shaban Mubajje Denied U.S. Visa." *Saturday Vision*. September 27, 2014.

76. John Tugume. "Bishops Want Shelved Anti-Gay Bill Dusted." *Daily Monitor*. June 10, 2012.

77. Moses Talemwa. "Archbishop Lwanga Lists 2013's Worst Sins." *The Observer*. December 29, 2013.

78. Julius Ocungi. "Do Not Harm Homosexuals, Archbishop Odama Appeals." *Daily Monitor*. August 18, 2014.

79. Rachel Donadio. "On Gay Priests, Pope Francis Asks, 'Who Am I to Judge?'" *New York Times*. July 29, 2013.

80. Vocativ. "A Secret, Illegal Gay Wedding in Uganda." https://www.youtube.com/watch?v=uRhxbNoLMJg.

81. NBS TV. "Morning Breeze Homosexuality Debate." https://www.youtube.com/watch?v=LKP-PUAI96U.

82. Stephen Wandera. "Muslim Cleric Blames Drought on Moral Decay." *Daily Monitor*. March 17, 2015.

83. Yoweri Museveni. "Why I Support Mabira Forest Give-Away to Mehta Group." *New Vision*. April 19, 2007.

84. Richard M. Kavuma. "Plan to Sacrifice Forest for Sugar Puts Economy Before Ecosphere in Uganda." *The Guardian*. August 22, 2011.

85. *Voice of America*. "Ugandan Environmentalists Protest Plan to Lease Forest Reserve to Developers." November 1, 2009.

86. Yoweri Kaguta Museveni. *Sowing the Mustard Seed: The Struggle for Freedom and Democracy in Uganda*. London: Macmillan Education, 1997.

87. Emmanuel Ainebyoona and Albert Tumwine. "Emulate Catholic Church, Museveni Tells Anglicans." *Daily Monitor*. June 4, 2015.

88. Richard Downie. "Religion and the State in Uganda: Co-Option and Compromise." In Richard Downie and Jennifer G. Cooke, *Religious Authority and the State in Africa*. Washington, D.C.: CSIS/Rowman & Littlefield, 2015.

89. Francis Kagoro. "Museveni Tips Christians on Income Generation." *New Vision*. May 4, 2014.

90. Alfred Tumushabe. "President Commends Born-Again Civil Servants." *Daily Monitor*. September 3, 2014.

91. Anonymous. "Arinaitwe: God's Faithful Who Nearly Killed Dr Besigye." *The Observer*. April 30, 2011.

Chapter V

1. Julius Mucunguzi. "Museveni Softens Stand on Homos." *Monitor*. November 17, 1999.

2. Faustin Mugabe. "Why Were There No Prayers at Museveni Swearing In?" *Daily Monitor*. February 8, 2015.

3. xposeuganda. "Museveni and Child Soldiers." https://www.youtube.com/watch?v=upITVcXw_Gk.

4. Y.K. Museveni. *What Is Africa's Problem?* Minneapolis: University of Minnesota Press, 2000.

5. Anonymous. "Wandegeya Homos Marry." *Sunday Vision*. September 12, 1999.

6. Anonymous. "Arrest Homos, Says Museveni." *New Vision*. September 28, 1999.

7. Anonymous. "Arrest Homos, Says Museveni." *New Vision.* September 28, 1999.

8. Mohamed Ssengooba. "White Homos Beasts, Says Minister." *Monitor.* November 11, 1999.

9. Daniel K. Kalinaki. "Kategaya Was a Good Man Who Blew the Chance to Become Great." *New Vision.* March 7, 2013.

10. Charles Onyango-Obbo. "Are Homo's NRM's New Political Ladder? Yes." *Monitor.* November 7, 1999.

11. Julius Mucunguzi. "Museveni, Police Homo Probe Out 'Story Was Made Up.'" *Monitor.* October 5, 1999.

12. James Magode Ikuya. "Movt Can Never Embrace Homos." *Monitor.* November 4, 1999.

13. J.S. La Fonatine. *The Gisu of Uganda.* London: International African Institute, 1959.

14. James Magode Ikuya. "Movt Can Never Embrace Homos." *Monitor.* November 4, 1999.

15. Felix Bryx. *Voodoo Eros: Ethnological Studies in the Sex Life of the African Aborigines.* New York: United Guild, 1964.

16. Wamboga-Mugirya. "Gays' Hide-Outs Found." *Monitor.* October 4, 1999.

17. Anonymous. "CMI or JATT: UPDF Keeps Torture Tradition Going." *The Independent.* April 22, 2009.

18. Amnesty International. *Crimes of Hate, Conspiracy of Silence: Torture and Ill-Treatment Based on Sexual Identity.* London: Amnesty International Publications, 2001.

19. Julius Mucunguzi. "Museveni Softens Stand on Homos." *Monitor.* November 17, 1999.

20. Julius Mucunguzi. "Uganda Has No Homosexuals, Says Museveni." *Monitor.* March 6, 2002.

21. Cissy Makumb and Julius Ocungi. "I Was Beaten, Sodomised by Soldiers—Namokora Massacre Survivor." *Sunday Monitor.* August 24, 2014.

22. Siraje Lubwama. "Museveni Promised Kandida He'd Punish Torture Updfs." *Monitor.* August 16, 1999.

23. Amnesty International. *Uganda: Human Rights Violations by the National Resistance Army.* New York: Amnesty International, 1991.

24. Chris Obore. "The Untold Story of the 1989 Mukura Massacre." *Monitor.* January 21, 2007.

25. Tom Cooper. *Great Lakes Conflagration: Second Congo War, 1998–2003.* Solihull: Helion and Company, 2013.

26. Benjamin Coghlan, Pascal Ngoy, Flavien Mulumba et al. "Mortality in the Democratic Republic of Congo: An Ongoing Crisis." International Rescue Committee, 2007.

27. Panel of Experts on the Democratic Republic of the Congo. "Final Report of the Panel of Experts on the Illegal Exploitation of Natural Resources and Other Forms of Wealth of the Democratic Republic of the Congo." New York: United Nations, 2002. S/2002/1146.

28. Richard Wanambwa. "Close Allies Now Accuse Museveni of Poor Leadership." *Monitor.* July 9, 2008.

29. Linda Goretti Nansanga. "Journalism Ethics and the Emerging New Media Culture of Radio Talk Shows and Public Debates (Ekimeeza) in Uganda." *Journalism*, 2008, Vol. 9, pp. 646–663.

30. Steven Candia. "Ekimeeza Panelist Summoned." *New Vision.* December 3, 2004.

31. Henry Mukasa. "Museveni Defends Uganda in Malta." *New Vision.* November 26, 2005.

32. Yoweri Museveni. "Activism at the Hill." In Karim F. Hirji, *Cheche: Reminiscences of a Radical Magazine.* Dar es Salaam: Mkuki na Nyota, 2010.

33. Andrew Ivaska. *Cultured States: Youth, Gender, and Modern Style in 1960s Dar es Salaam.* Durham: Duke University Press, 2011.

34. Ronald Aminzade. *Race, Nation, and Citizenship in Postcolonial Africa: The Case of Tanzania.* New York: Cambridge University Press, 2013.

35. Andrew Ivaska. *Cultured States: Youth, Gender, and Modern Style in 1960s Dar es Salaam.* Durham: Duke University Press, 2011.

36. Karim F. Hirji. *Cheche: Reminiscences of a Radical Magazine.* Dar es Salaam: Mkuki Na Nyota Publishers, 2010.

37. Priya Lal. *African Socialism in Postcolonial Tanzania.* New York: Cambridge University Press, 2015.

38. Andrew Ivaska. *Cultured States: Youth, Gender, and Modern Style in 1960s Dar es Salaam.* Durham and London: Duke University Press, 2011.

39. Priya Lal. "Militants, Mothers, and the National Family: Ujamaa, Gender, and Rural Development in Postcolonial Tanzania." *Journal of African History*, 2010, Vol. 51, pp. 1–20.

40. J. Oloka-Onyango. "'New-Breed' Leadership, Conflict, and Reconstruction in the Great Lakes Region of Africa: A Sociopolitical Biography of Uganda's Yoweri Kaguta Museveni." *Africa Today*, 2004, Vol. 50, pp. 29–52.

41. J. Oloka-Onyango. "'New-Breed' Leadership, Conflict, and Reconstruction in the Great Lakes Region of Africa: A Sociopolitical Biography of Uganda's Yoweri Kaguta Museveni." *Africa Today*, 2004, Vol. 50, pp. 29–52.

42. Henry Ochieng. "Museveni Gets HIV/AIDS Award." *Monitor.* March 4, 2002.

43. Hamis Kaheru and Juliet Nankinga. "Museveni Restates Besigye Has AIDS." *New Vision.* March 28, 2001.

44. Julius Mucunguzi. "Museveni Possible Nobel Candidate." *New Vision.* May 29, 2004.

45. Joyce Namutebi and Henry Mukasa. "MPs Warn Aid Donors on Gay Lobby." *New Vision*. November 7, 2003.

46. Richard Mutumba. "Gae Fans Shock Minister." *New Vision*. September 11, 2003.

47. H. Mukasa. "Government Battles Nude Dancers." *New Vision*. November 5, 2003.

48. Izama Angelo. "Uganda's Media Has Less Freedom." *Monitor*. October 24, 2003.

49. Editorial. "Dr. Buturo Comes with a New Hope." *Monitor*. May 27, 2003.

50. John Kazoora. "Nsaba Buturo Should Be the Last Person to Talk About the NRA." *Daily Monitor*. March 28, 2012.

51. Anonymous. "Nagenda, Museveni Secrets Revealed, How Wikileaks Caused Fallout." *The Observer*. September 11, 2011.

52. Sam Akaki. "Buturo Blackmailing British Government." *Monitor*. March 8, 2005.

53. Barbara Among and Abbey Mutumba-Lule. "Third Term: Minister Says Museveni Must Stand in 2006." *The East African*. November 22, 2004.

54. Ebenezer Bifubyeka. "Movt God-Sent, Says Nsaba Buturo." *New Vision*. July 14, 2004.

55. Hussein Bogere and Charles Mwanguhya Mpagi. "Media Not Patriotic, Says Govt." *Monitor*. May 20, 2005.

56. Fred Ouma. "Buturo Wary of Media Freedom." *New Vision*. May 5, 2004.

57. Nsaba Buturo. "Only Anger Against Evil Will Bring Back Morality." *New Vision*. August 16, 2009.

58. James Nsaba Buturo. "Anti-God Secularists Want to Dictate National Agenda." *New Vision*. June 1, 2009.

59. Henry Mukasa. "MPs Grill Buturo Over Pornography." *New Vision*. September 2, 2004.

60. Jude Etyang. "Reject Kisanja Bribe—Muntu." *New Vision*. October 31, 2004.

61. Anne Mugisha. "Foreigners Funding Opposition." *New Vision*. March 12, 2004.

62. Anne Mugisha. "Buturo Blasts Envoy Over Gays." *New Vision*. October 22, 2004.

63. Emmanuel Mulondo and Richard Mutumba. "Homosexual Rights Divide Cabinet." *Monitor*. July 8, 2005.

64. Julius Mucunguzi. "Uganda Has No Homosexuals, Says Museveni." *Monitor*. March 6, 2002.

65. Jeff Sharlet. "Straight Man's Burden." *Harper's*. September 2010.

66. David Bahati. "The President's Nation Address Raises Hope." *Monitor*. July 11, 2006.

67. Andrew Bagala. "Christians Advised to Develop Reading Culture." *Monitor*. October 17, 2007.

68. Robert Muhereza. "Kabale in Prayer Week for Peace in North." *Monitor*. September 6, 2006.

69. David Bahati. "I Insist, Mwenda Is Wrong on Gays." *The Independent*. December 1, 2009.

70. Emmanuel Gyezaho. "Museveni Warns Against Homosexuality." *Monitor*. November 16, 2009.

71. Sylvia Tamale. "Out of the Closet: Unveiling Sexuality Discourses in Uganda." In Takyiwaa Manuh and Catherine M. Cole. *Africa After Gender?* Bloomington: Indiana University Press, 2007.

72. Mohamed Ssengooba. "White Homos Beasts, Says Minister." *Monitor*. November 11, 1999.

73. Isaac Imaka. "Wikileaks: Janet Behind Gays Bill." *Sunday Monitor*. September 11, 2011.

74. Anonymous. "Govt to Pass Law on Sexual Abstinence." *New Vision*. September 20, 2004.

75. Peter Gill. *Body Count: How They Turned AIDS into a Catastrophe*. London: Profile Books, 2010.

76. Grace Matsiko. "First Lady Calls for Census of Virgins." *Daily Monitor*. December 2, 2004.

77. Max Blumenthal. "Rick Warren's Africa Problem." *The Daily Beast*. January 7, 2009.

78. Helen Epstein. "God and the Fight Against AIDS." *New York Review of Books*. April 28, 2005.

79. Yasiin Mugerwa. "MPs Have Nine Days to Return Shs20m 'Bribe.'" *Daily Monitor*. January 27, 2011.

80. Tabu Butagira. "Leaked Cable—Why Museveni Made Wife Minister in Shuffle." *The Citizen*. September 9, 2011.

81. Gerard Bareebe and Kristof Titeca. "Personalisation of Power Under the Museveni Regime in Uganda." In Filip Reyntjens, Stef Vandeginste, and Marijke Verpoorten, eds., *L'Afrique des Grands Lacs. Annuaire 2011–2012*. Paris: L'Harmattan, 2013.

Chapter VI

1. Kasha Jacqueline Nabagesera. "Improving Conditions of LGBTI in Uganda." TedX. Sao Paulo: April 2014.

2. Stephen Charles Kaduuli. "Perceptions of LGBT in Uganda and Africa." http://ssrn.com/abstract=1510822.

3. Anonymous. "Homosexuality and the Law." https://sebaspace.wordpress.com/2009/01/31/homosexuality-and-the-law/.

4. Sylvia Tamale. "Out of the Closet: Unveiling Sexuality Discourses in Uganda." *Feminist Africa*. 2003, 2.

5. Mirriam Achieng. "Sexual Orientation and the Law: A Case Study of Homosexuals in Kampala District." http://hdl.handle.net/10570/3215.

6. Anonymous. "School Girl Commits Suicide." *Red Pepper*. December 12, 2003.

7. Alfred Wasike. "Kampala Homosexuals Speak Out." *New Vision*. August 16, 2007.

8. Anonymous. "Museveni Doesn't Mind Quiet Gays." *New Vision*. November 16, 1999.

9. Yoweri K. Museveni. "Anti-Gay Bill—Museveni Responds to Obama." *The Observer*. February 21, 2014.

10. Richard Ssebaggala. "Straight Talk on the Gay Question in Uganda." *Transition*. 2011, 106, pp. 44–57.

11. Joachim Buwembo. "The Evidence Stripping Brenda Didn't Cover Up." *The East African*. November 11, 1998.

12. Anonymous. "Man Defends Port Bell 'Woman.'" *New Vision*. October 30, 1998.

13. Anonymous. "Man Defends Port Bell 'Woman.'" *New Vision*. October 30, 1998.

14. Paul Kiwuuwa. "Homosexual Admits Recruiting Students." *New Vision*. March 23, 2009.

15. Human Rights Watch. "Protect Sexual Rights Activists: Ensure Due Process for All Citizens." Washington, D.C.: 2008.

16. Denis Jjuuko. "Counselors Disregard Inborn Homosexuality." *New Vision*. August 30, 2002.

17. Sebudde Lule. "We're There in Kampala in Numbers!" *New Vision*. June 2, 2001.

18. Charles Mwanguhya Mpagi. "Gays Threaten to Form Party." *Monitor*. October 6, 2003.

19. Denis Jjuuko. "Counselors Disregard Inborn Homosexuality." *New Vision*. August 30, 2002.

20. Denis Jjuuko. "Amanda, the Man Who Heads Kampala's Latest Lewd Dancers." *New Vision*. April 24, 2003.

21. Peter G. Mwesige. "Flying Moral Red Flag Over the Bare Bottoms." *Monitor*. April 24, 2003.

22. Denis Jjuuko. "Amanda, the Man Who Heads Kampala's Latest Lewd Dancers." *New Vision*. April 24, 2003.

23. Uganda, NTV. "Life on the Shores of Lake Albert: Cross-Dressing Shaban Lives a Quiet Life as Hairdresser." https://www.youtube.com/watch?v=SUXRkKd4YT4.

24. Radio Netherlands Worldwide. "Kasha's Fight Against Homophobia in Uganda." November 2, 2011.

25. Wamboga-Mugirya. "Gays' Hide-Outs Found." *Monitor*. October 4, 1999.

26. Robert Kabushenga. "Homosexuals? Don't Waste Energy, Nature Will Deal with Them." *New Vision*. October 3, 1999.

27. Julius Mucunguzi and Katamba G. Mohammed. "Out of Congo, Probe Defence—Byanyima." *Monitor*. October 2, 1999.

28. Anonymous. "Gay Doctor Flees Uganda." *New Vision*. November 7, 1999.

29. Julius Mucunguzi. "Mazrui Attacks Museveni Over Homo Arrests." *Monitor*. October 6, 1999.

30. Andrew Mwenda. "Stop Gay-Bashing Already!" *Monitor*. October 10, 1999.

31. Philippa Croome. "Will the Gay Bill Face Tougher Battles?" *Daily Monitor*. May 22, 2011.

32. Andrew Mwenda. "Don't Kill in God's Name." *The Independent*. December 11, 2009.

33. Charles Onyango-Obbo. "In Africa, Gays Are Easy Targets for Macho Leaders." *The East African*. October 12, 1999.

34. Tina Turyagyenda. "Ssenyonjo Earns Sh30,000 a Month." *New Vision*. May 27, 2001.

35. Mercy Nalugo. "Ssenyonjo Is a Rebel—Nkoyooyo." *Daily Monitor*. March 18, 2006.

36. Ndawula Kalema. "Ssenyonjo's Fight for Gays." *New Vision*. May 6, 2001.

37. Charles Ariko. "MUK Don Fights for Gay Rights." *New Vision*. February 5, 2003.

38. Charles Ariko. "MUK Don Fights for Gay Rights." *New Vision*. February 5, 2003.

39. Sylvia Tamale. "Out of the Closet: Unveiling Sexuality Discourses in Uganda." *Feminist Africa*. 2003, 2.

40. Sylvia Tamale. "Out of the Closet: Unveiling Sexuality Discourses in Uganda." *Feminist Africa*. 2003, 2.

41. Sylvia Tamale. "A Human Rights Impact Assessment of the Ugandan Anti-Homosexuality Bill 2009." *The Equal Rights Review*. 2009, Vol. 4, pp. 49–57.

42. Christine Abia. "Living Dangerously: Gays and Lesbians in Uganda." *Deutsche Welle*. August 10, 2013.

43. Richard Lusimbo. "Q & A with Ugandan LGBTI Activist Richard Lusimbo." http://benetech.org/2014/03/25/q-a-with-ugandan-lgbti-activist-richard-lusimbo/.

44. Radio Netherlands Worldwide. "Kasha's Fight Against Homophobia in Uganda." November 2, 2011.

45. Juliet Victor Mukasa. "Uganda—Juliet Victor Mukasa." *Front Line Defenders*. https://www.frontlinedefenders.org/node/387.

46. Richard Ssebaggala. "Straight Talk on the Gay Question in Uganda." *Transition*. 2011, 106, pp. 44–57.

47. Sexual Minorities Uganda. https://sexualminoritiesuganda.com/.

48. Charles Mpagi Mwanguhya and Hussein Bogere. "Police Told to Probe MUK Gays." *Monitor*. October 31, 2004.

49. Rosebell Kagumire. "FM Station Penalised Over Gays." *Monitor*. October 3, 2004.

50. Moses Mulondo and Wendy Glauser. "Gay Activist Vows to Sue LCI for Raiding Her Home." *Daily Monitor*. July 28, 2005.

51. Moses Mulondo and Wendy Glauser. "Gay Activist Vows to Sue LCI for Raiding Her Home." *Daily Monitor*. July 28, 2005.

52. Hillary Nsambu. "Govt to Pay Suspected

Lesbians Sh13 Million." *New Vision.* January 7, 2009.

53. Alfred Wasike. "Kampala Homosexuals Speak Out." *New Vision.* August 16, 2007.

54. Ephraim Kasozi. "Churches Plan Demo Against Homos." *Daily Monitor.* August 21, 2007.

55. Katherine Roubos. "Rally Denounces Homosexuality." *Daily Monitor.* August 22, 2007.

56. Lisa M. Krieger. "Stanford Student Under Fire in Uganda for Covering Gay Issues." *San Jose Mercury News.* September 3, 2007.

57. Al-Mahdi Ssenkabirwa and Ephraim Kasozi. "Tabliqs Plan Squad to Fight Gays." *Daily Monitor.* August 28, 2007.

58. Moses Sserwanga. "Kichwamba Death Toll Rises Up to 80." *New Vision.* June 10, 1998.

59. Anonymous. "Gay Shock!" *Red Pepper.* August 8, 2006.

60. Anonymous. "Kampala's Notorious Lesbians Outed." *Red Pepper.* September 8, 2006.

61. Edris Kisambira. "Saleh to Declare Wealth." *New Vision.* June 19, 2001.

62. Anonymous. "100 Pictures of Uganda's Top Homos Leak." *Rolling Stone.* October 2, 2010.

63. Malika Zouhali-Worrall and Katherine Fairfax Wright. "Call Me Kuchu." 2012.

64. Anonymous. "More Homos' Faces Exposed." *Rolling Stone.* November 3, 2010.

65. Anthony Wesaka. "High Court Judge Opts to Retire Early." *Daily Monitor.* September 9, 2014.

66. Kevin Kelley. "Rights Groups—It's a Blow to Progress of Democracy." *The East African.* December 7, 2009.

67. Joseph Oloka-Onyango. "We Are More than Just Our Bodies: HIV/AIDS and the Human Rights Complexities Affecting Young Women Who Have Sex with Women in Uganda." Kampala: Makerere University. Human Rights and Peace Centre, 2012. Vol. HURIPEC working paper; no. 36.

68. The White House. "Statement by the President on the Killing of David Kato." Washington, D.C.: January 27, 2011. https://www.whitehouse.gov/the-press-office/2011/01/27/statement-president-killing-david-kato.

69. U.S. Department of State. "Murder of Ugandan LGBT Activist David Kato." Washington, D.C.: January 27, 2011. http://m.state.gov/md155520.htm.

70. Malika Zouhali-Worrall and Katherine Fairfax Wright. "Call Me Kuchu." 2012.

71. Malika Zouhali-Worrall and Katherine Fairfax Wright. "Call Me Kuchu." 2012.

72. Martin Ssebuyira. "Ethics Minister Shuts Down Gay Rights Conference." *Daily Monitor.* February 14, 2012.

73. Patience Akumu. "Ethics Minister Storms, Closes Gay Meeting." *The Observer.* February 15, 2012.

74. Amnesty International. "Government Raid on LGBT-Rights Workshop." 2012.

75. Daniel Kalinaki. "Those Who Go After Gays and Sex Workers Will One Day Go After Teachers and Doctors." *Daily Monitor.* February 16, 2012.

76. Laurie Goodstein. "Ugandan Gay Rights Group Sues U.S. Evangelist." *New York Times.* March 14, 2012.

77. David Smith. "Ugandan Group Sues Anti-Gay Pastor in U.S." *The Guardian.* March 15, 2012.

78. The Rafto Organization. http://www.rafto.no/the-rafto-prize/sexual-minorities-uganda.

Chapter VII

1. Martin Ssebuyira and Risdel Kasasira. "I'll Work with Russians, Museveni Tells Obama." *Sunday Monitor.* February 23, 2014.

2. *The Rachel Maddow Show.* December 8, 2010.

3. Jocelyn Edwards. "Bahati—The Unlikely Gay Basher." *The Independent.* January 13, 2010.

4. Jocelyn Edwards. "Bahati—The Unlikely Gay Basher." *The Independent.* January 13, 2010.

5. Yasiin Mugerwa. "450,000 Sign to Kill Anti-Gay Bill." *Daily Monitor.* March 2, 2010.

6. The Civil Society Coalition on Human Rights and Constitutional Law. "Embrace Diversity; End Discrimination in Uganda." Kampala: 2009.

7. Solome Nakaweesi-Kimbugwe and Frank Mugisha. "Bahati's Bill—A Convenient Distraction for Country's Government." *Pambazuka News.* October 16, 2009.

8. Opiyo Oloya. "The Homosexual Struggle Is a Human Rights Issue: Perspective of a Ugandan in Canada." *New Vision.* July 3, 2007.

9. Muniini K. Mulera. "I Say, Let Gays Do Their Thing." *Daily Monitor.* February 16, 2003.

10. Rodney Muhumuza. "Uganda Hits Back Over Gay Criticism." *Daily Monitor.* November 30, 2009.

11. Rodney Muhumuza. "New Uganda Anti-Gay Law Irks Sweden." *The Citizen.* December 4, 2009.

12. Norman Miwambo. "100 British MPs Sign Motion Against Anti-Gay Bill." *The Independent.* April 13, 2010.

13. Rodney Muhumuza. "Bahati Faces UK Travel Ban Over Bill." *Daily Monitor.* April 21, 2010.

14. Laura Rozen. "Bipartisan Senate Resolution Condemns Uganda Anti-Gay Legislation." *Politico.* February 4, 2010.

15. European Union. "European Parliament Resolution on Uganda: Anti-Homosexual Draft Legislation." 2009.

16. United Nations. Panel discussion on

"Opposing Grave Human Rights Violations on the Basis of Sexual Orientation and Gender Identity." New York: 2009.

17. United Nations. "Opposing Grave Human Rights Violations on the Basis of Sexual Orientation and Gender Identity." New York: 2009.

18. Anonymous. "Holy See Reiterates Opposition to Violation of Homosexual Persons' Human Rights." *Catholic News Agency.* December 14, 2009.

19. George Pitcher. "Dr Rowan Williams: Taking a Break from Canterbury Travails." *The Telegraph.* December 12, 2009.

20. Peter Kenny. "World Church Leader Concerned About Anti-Homosexual Bill." *Ecumenical News International.* December 22, 2009.

21. Mark S. Sisk. "The 'Anti-Homosexuality Laws' Proposed in Uganda: A Statement from The Rt. Rev. Mark S. Sisk." New York: 2009. http://www.episcopalcafe.com/bishop_sisk_on_the_ugandan_bill/.

22. Desmond Tutu. "To Ugandan MPs: God Does Not Discriminate Among Our Family." *Daily Monitor.* December 12, 2012.

23. Anonymous. "Uganda Under Military Rule." *Africa Today.* 1973, Vol. 20, 2, pp. 11–31.

24. Angelo Izama, Ismail Musa Ladu. "Get Off Our Backs, Donors Told." *Daily Monitor.* January 17, 2010.

25. Anonymous. "Uganda: Homophobe Extremists and Homosexual Scapegoats." *The Guardian.* December 24, 2009. http://www.theguardian.com/world/us-embassy-cables-documents/241596.

26. Wilber Muhwezi. "Nation Shouldn't Bow to Donors Over Gays." *The Observer.* December 22, 2011.

27. Sam Muwanguzi. "Anglican Church Rejects Gay Cash." *New Vision.* June 17, 2006.

28. Anonymous. "Parents Launch Bid to Pass Shelved Gays Bill." *Daily Monitor.* September 5, 2011.

29. Pauline Kairu, Dalton Wanyera. "Hundreds Attend Jinja Anti-Homosexuality Rally." *Daily Monitor.* February 17, 2010.

30. Fredrick Nzwili. "Church Leader Blasts Obama for Comment on Anti-Gay Bill." *Ecumenical News International.* February 5, 2010.

31. Daniel Kalinaki. "Don't Criticise Obama—Question Museveni." *Daily Monitor.* January 21, 2010.

32. Melanie Nathan. "Ugandan Musician Calls President Obama a Faggot." https://oblogdeeoblogda.me/2013/07/01/ugandan-musician-calls-president-obama-a-faggot/

33. Steven Candia. "Government Defends Need to Legislate on Homosexuality." *New Vision.* December 21, 2009.

34. Emmanuel Gyezaho. "Museveni Warns Against Homosexuality." *Daily Monitor.* November 16, 2009.

35. Flavia Nalubega and Stephen Wandera. "Museveni Will Block Anti-Gay Bill—Reports." *Daily Monitor.* December 23, 2009.

36. Norman Miwambo. "Rugunda in Latch Over Anti-Gay Bill." *The Independent.* January 12, 2010.

37. Milton Olupot and Cyprian Musoke. "Museveni Warns NRM on Homosexuality Bill." *New Vision.* January 12, 2010.

38. Barbara Among. "Cabinet Debates Homosexuality Draft Law." *New Vision.* January 20, 2010.

39. Rodney Muhumuza. "Cabinet Committee Rejects Bahati Bill." *Daily Monitor.* May 8, 2010.

40. Ephraim Kasozi and Patience Ahimbisibwe. "Opposed to Homosexuality—Museveni." *Daily Monitor.* June 4, 2010.

41. Ephraim Kasozi and Patience Ahimbisibwe. "Opposed to Homosexuality—Museveni." *Daily Monitor.* June 4, 2010.

42. Julius Mucunguzi. "Museveni Softens Stand on Homos." *Monitor.* November 17, 1999.

43. Randall Smith. "Museveni Wants to Shift Public Attention." *Daily Nation.* April 29, 2011.

44. Human Rights Watch. "Promptly Investigate Killing of Prominent LGBT Activist." Washington, D.C.: Human Rights Watch, 2011.

45. Anonymous. "MP to Persevere with Anti-Homosexuality Bill." *IRIN.* May 17, 2011.

46. Sheila Naturinda. "Cabinet Drops Bahati's Gay Bill." *Daily Monitor.* August 22, 2011.

47. Isaac Imaka. "Blocking Gays Bill Is Moral Corruption—MPs." *Daily Monitor.* August 23, 2011.

48. Joyce Namutebi. "Bill to Outlaw Homosexuality Re-Tabled." *New Vision.* February 8, 2012.

49. Yasiin Mugerwa. "Oil Bubble Bursts." *Daily Monitor.* October 11, 2011.

50. Innocent Anguyo. "67% of Ugandans Vulnerable to Poverty." *New Vision.* March 19, 2013.

51. Tabu Butagira. "Museveni: I've Never Received Oil Bribes." *Daily Monitor.* October 13, 2011.

52. Isaac Imaka. "Ministry to Expedite Tabling of Oil Laws." *Daily Monitor.* October 15, 2011.

53. Helen Epstein. "Murder in Uganda." *New York Review of Books.* April 3, 2014.

54. Eriasa Mukiibi Sserunjogi. "Fresh Questions Over Nebanda Death." *Sunday Monitor.* December 28, 2014.

55. Edris Kiggundu and Emma Mutaizibwa. "Oil Agreements—How Museveni Tricked MPs." *The Observer.* February 10, 2012.

56. Joyce Namutebi. "Bill to Outlaw Homosexuality in Uganda Re-Tabled." *New Vision.* February 8, 2012.

57. Kerry Kennedy. "Ugandan Parliament Acts to Legalize Hate Against the LGBTI Community." *The Huffington Post*. February 9, 2012.

58. Anonymous. "President Museveni Speaks Out on Homosexuality." *New Vision*. March 19, 2013.

59. Anonymous. "NGOs' Gay Plans Leak, Government Furious." *The Observer*. June 27, 2012.

60. Patience Akumu. "British Artiste Promoting Homosexuality in Uganda." *The Observer*. September 18, 2012.

61. David Tash Lumu and Deo Walusimbi. "U.S. Pro-Gay Delegation Leaves Empty-Handed." *The Observer*. March 31, 2013.

62. Yudaya Nangonzi. "Buturo Rallies MPs on Bahati Gay Bill." *The Observer*. December 4, 2013.

63. Henry Sekanjako. "Clerics to Continue Commenting on Politics." *New Vision*. May 2, 2012.

64. Yasiin Mugerwa. "Kadaga, Canadian Minister in Gay Row." *Daily Monitor*. October 25, 2012.

65. Sadab Kitatta Kaaya and Sulaiman Kakaire. "Anti-Gay Bill—How MPs Outfoxed NRM, Donors." *The Observer*. December 22, 2013.

66. Anonymous. "Anti-Gays Bill, Repentance Top Xmas Sermons." *Daily Monitor*. December 27, 2013.

67. Church of Uganda. http://churchofuganda.org/.

68. Desmond Mpilo Tutu. *God Is Not a Christian: And Other Provocations*. New York: HarperCollins, 2011.

69. Anonymous. "Sterner Homosexual Law Clears Parliament in Uganda." *Deutsche Welle*. December 20, 2013.

70. Felix Osike. "UK Billionaire to Visit." *New Vision*. June 8, 2005.

71. Sadab Kitatta Kaaya. "Anti-Gay Law—Museveni at Crossroads." *The Observer*. January 2, 2014.

72. Yasiin Mugerwa. "Museveni Blocks Anti-Homosexuality Bill." *Daily Monitor*. January 17, 2014.

73. Ismail Musa Ladu. "U.S. Group, Bishop Tutu 'Compel' Museveni Not to Sign Anti-Gay Bill." *Daily Monitor*. January 21, 2014.

74. Sadab Kitatta Kaaya. "Museveni Sets Terms for Signing Gay Bill." *The Independent*. January 26, 2014.

75. Yoweri Kaguta Museveni. "I Paid for Natasha's Bills in Germany—Museveni." *Monitor*. October 5, 2003.

76. Ministerial Scientific Committee on Homosexuality. "Scientific Statement on Homosexuality." Entebbe: Ministry of Health, Uganda, 2014.

77. Yoweri Museveni. "Making Sense of Museveni's Decision to Sign the Anti-Homosexual Bill." *The Independent*. February 16, 2014.

78. The White House. "Statement by the President on the Anti-Homosexuality Bill in Uganda." Washington, D.C.: February 16, 2014. https://www.whitehouse.gov/the-press-office/2014/02/16/statement-president-anti-homosexuality-bill-uganda.

79. Yoweri K Museveni. "Anti-Gay Bill—Museveni Responds to Obama." *The Observer*. February 21, 2014.

80. Yoweri K Museveni. "Anti-Gay Bill—Museveni Responds to Obama." *The Observer*. February 21, 2014.

81. Martin Ssebuyira and Risdel Kasasira. "I'll Work with Russians, Museveni Tells Obama." *Sunday Monitor*. February 23, 2014.

82. Martin Ssebuyira and Risdel Kasasira. "I'll Work with Russians, Museveni Tells Obama." *Sunday Monitor*. February 23, 2014.

83. Joseph Were. "Museveni Anti-Gay Misstep." *The Independent*. July 6, 2014.

84. U.S. Department of State. "U.S. Relations with Uganda." Washington, D.C. http://www.state.gov/r/pa/ei/bgn/2963.htm.

85. Human Rights Watch. "Anti-Homosexuality Law Will Come at a Serious Cost." https://www.hrw.org/news/2014/02/19/uganda-anti-homosexuality-law-will-come-serious-cost.

86. Francis Kagolo and Priscillar Alinda. "Uganda Bans Miniskirts, Pornography." *New Vision*. February 18, 2014.

87. Sarah Namulondo. "Anti-Pornography Bill." *The Independent*. April 20, 2013.

88. Francis Kagolo and Priscillar Alinda. "Uganda Bans Miniskirts, Pornography." *New Vision*. February 18, 2014.

89. Joe Oloka Onyango. "Laws on Public Order, Gays and 'Miniskirts' Are Birds of a Feather." *The Observer*. April 6, 2014.

90. Anonymous. "Gays Are Disgusting, Museveni Tells CNN." *The Observer*. February 28, 2014.

91. Joseph Kimbowa. "After Signing, Museveni Says Anti-Gay Bill Was Necessitated by 'Arrogant Groups.'" *The Observer*. February 24, 2014.

92. Anonymous. "New Ugandan Dress Code Is Anti-Women." *The Star*. February 21, 2014.

93. Joseph Kimbowa. "After Signing, Museveni Says Anti-Gay Bill Was Necessitated by 'Arrogant Groups.'" *The Observer*. February 24, 2014.

94. Nduta Waweru. "Binyavanga Blasts M7 Over Anti-Gay Law." *The Star*. February 25, 2014.

95. Human Rights Watch (Washington, D.C.). "Anti-Homosexuality Act's Heavy Toll—

Discriminatory Law Prompts Arrests, Attacks, Evictions, Flight." Washington, D.C. 2014. https://www.hrw.org/news/2014/05/14/uganda-anti-homosexuality-acts-heavy-toll.

96. The State House of Uganda. "Ugandans Hold Colourful National Thanksgiving Sevice to Celebrate Signing of Anti-Homosexuality Bill." http://www.statehouse.go.ug/media/news/2014/03/31/ugandans-hold-colourful-national-thanksgiving-sevice-celebrate-signing-anti-ho.

97. Amnesty International. "President Museveni Signs Anti-Homosexuality Bill." London: 2014.

98. Jill Mahoney. "Uganda's Anti-Gay Law Causes Significant Cuts to Foreign Aid." *The Globe and Mail.* February 26, 2014.

99. European Parliament. "Launching Consultations to Suspend Uganda and Nigeria from the Cotonou Agreement in View of Recent Legislation Further Criminalising Homosexuality." 2014. http://www.europarl.europa.eu/sides/getDoc.do?type=TA&reference=P7-TA-2014-0254&language=EN&ring=P7-RC-2014-0251.

100. Anonymous. "Kerry Compares Ugandan Anti-Gay Law to Nazism, Apartheid." *Voice of America.* February 26, 2014.

101. Jeff Mbanga. "Same-Sex Talk Will Not Ruin Uganda's Economy." *The Observer.* March 6, 2014.

102. Anonymous. "Kicking Out the Anti-Gay Act." *The Independent.* August 10, 2014.

103. Anonymous. "Museveni Calls Promoters of Homosexuality 'Criminals.'" *The Star.* March 31, 2014.

104. Moses Mulondo. "Clarify Riches, FDC Tells Museveni." *New Vision.* October 20, 2008.

105. Edward Ssekika. "Gay Law—Uganda Plans New AIDS Fund." *The Observer.* April 1, 2014.

106. Associated Press. "Police Raid U.S.-Financed Health Project." *New York Times.* April 5, 2014.

107. Stephen Kafeero and Agatha Ayebazibwe. "Makerere Project Recruited Gays—Police." *Daily Monitor.* April 9, 2014.

108. Makerere University Walter Reed Project. http://www.muwrp.org/.

109. U.S. Department of State. "Raid on the Makerere University Walter Reed Project by Ugandan Authorities." http://www.state.gov/r/pa/prs/ps/2014/04/224431.htm.

110. Joseph Were. "Kerry Maintains Museveni's International Isolation." *The Independent.* May 11, 2014.

111. Peter Baker. "Anti-Gay Law Draws Sanctions." *New York Times.* June 19, 2014.

112. Tabu Butagira. "U.S. Punishes Uganda for Anti-Gay Law: Withdraws Support to Police, UPDF and Health." *Daily Monitor.* June 20, 2014.

113. Ministry of Foreign Affairs, The Republic of Uganda. "Statement by the Government of Uganda on the Anti-Homosexuality Act, 2014." Kampala: 2014.

114. Derrick Kiyonga. "10 Challenge Anti-Homosexuality Law." *The Observer.* March 12, 2014.

115. Joan Akello. "Judges Jettison the Anti Gay Law." *The Independent.* August 1, 2014.

116. Job Bwire. "Government to Petition Court Over Anti-Gay Law Ruling." *Daily Monitor.* August 1, 2014.

117. Derrick Kiyonga and Siraje Lubwama. "Museveni Behind Gay Law Victory?" *The Independent.* August 3, 2014.

118. Charles Etukuri. "Obama Invites Museveni for African Leader's Summit." *New Vision.* June 10, 2014.

119. Milton Allimadi. "U.S.–Africa Summit: President Obama Should Dis-Invite Uganda Dictator Gen. Museveni." *Huffington Post.* July 29, 2014.

120. Edris Kiggundu. "Museveni Hires U.S. Firm for PR." *The Observer.* August 13, 2014.

121. Sulaiman Kakaire and Sadab Kitatta Kaaya. "Museveni Okays 'Private' Gays." *The Observer.* August 13, 2014.

122. Isaac Imaka. "Uganda MPs Seek to Pass Anti-Gay Bill as 'Christmas Gift.'" *The East African.* December 5, 2014.

123. Edris Kiggundu. "MP Nabilah Caught in U.S. Homosexuality Rights U-Turn." *The Observer.* September 24, 2014.

124. Nabilah Naggayi Sempala. "Hon. Nabilah Naggayi Sempala on Gay Rights and the AHA." *The Independent.* September 25, 2014.

125. Nabilah Naggayi Sempala. "Hon. Nabilah Naggayi Sempala on Gay Rights and the AHA." *The Independent.* September 25, 2014.

126. Yoweri Kaguta Museveni. "The Way Forward on Homosexuality." *The Independent.* October 6, 2014.

127. Robert Muhereza. "Shun Politicians Who Support Homosexuality—Archbishop Ntagali to Voters." *Daily Monitor.* December 21, 2015.

128. Paul Tajuba. "Bwanika Vows to Rehabilitate Homosexuals." *Daily Monitor.* November 5, 2015.

Bibliography

Books and Other Works

Achieng, Mirriam. "Sexual Orientation and the Law: A Case Study of Homosexuals in Kampala District." http://hdl.handle.net/10570/3215.

Altman, Denis. "Globalization and the International Gay/Lesbian Movement." In Steven Seidman and Diane Richardson, eds. *Handbook of Lesbian and Gay Studies.* London: Sage, 2002.

Aminzade, Ronald. *Race, Nation, and Citizenship in Postcolonial Africa: The Case of Tanzania.* New York: Cambridge University Press, 2013.

Amnesty International. *Crimes of Hate, Conspiracy of Silence: Torture and Ill-Treatment Based on Sexual Identity.* London: Amnesty International Publications, 2001.

Amnesty International. "Government Raid on LGBT-Rights Workshop." 2012.

Amnesty International. "President Museveni Signs Anti-Homosexuality Bill." London: 2014.

Amnesty International. "Uganda: Human Rights Violations by the National Resistance Army." New York: Amnesty International, 1991.

Anglican Communion. "Resolution 26. Church and Polygamy." Lambeth Conference, 1988.

Anglican Communion. "Resolution 64. Human Rights for Those of Homosexual Orientation." Lambeth Conference, 1988.

Anglican Communion. "Resolution I.10: Human Sexuality." Lambeth Conference, 1998.

Bareebe, Gerard, and Kristof Titeca. "Personalisation of Power Under the Museveni Regime in Uganda." In Filip Reyntjens, Stef Vandeginste, and Marijke Verpoorten, eds. *L'Afrique des Grands Lacs, Annuaire 2011–2012.* Paris: L'Harmattan, 2013.

Barfoot, A. "Women, Homosexuality, and the Bible." http://philippians-1-20.us/alison.htm.

Bleys, Rudi C. *The Geography of Perversion: Male-to-Male Sexual Behavior Outside the West and the Ethnographic Imagination, 1750–1918.* New York: NYU Press, 1996.

Bryx, Felix. *Voodoo Eros: Ethnological Studies in the Sex Life of the African Aborigines.* New York: United Guild, 1964.

Bwire, Robert. *Bugs in Armor: A Story of Malaria and Soldiering.* Lincoln: Writers Club Press, 2000.

The Civil Society Coalition on Human Rights and Constitutional Law. "Embrace Diversity; End Discrimination in Uganda." Kampala: 2009.

Clay, Louie Crew. *Letters from Samaria: The Prose & Poetry of Louie Crew Clay.* New York: Morehouse Publishing, 2015.

Coghlan, Benjamin, Pascal Ngoy, Flavien Mulumba, et al. "Mortality in the Democratic Republic of Congo: An Ongoing Crisis." International Rescue Committee, 2007.

Cooper, Tom. *Great Lakes Conflagration: Second Congo War, 1998–2003.* Solihull: Helion and Company, 2013.

Coughtry, Sarah Elspeth. "Patriarchy and the Trap of Masculinity: A Post-Colonial Analysis of Violence Against Sexual Minorities in Uganda." Theses, Dissertations, and Projects. Smith College School for Social Work, Northampton, MA, 2011.

Cunningham, J.F. *Uganda and Its Peoples; Notes on the Protectorate of Uganda, Especially the Anthropology and Ethnology of Its Indigenous Races*. London: Hutchinson & Company, 1905.

Decker, Alicia C. *In Idi Amin's Shadow: Women, Gender, and Militarism in Uganda*. Athens: Ohio University Press, 2014.

Downie, Richard. "Religion and the State in Uganda: Co-Option and Compromise." In Richard Downie and Jennifer G. Cooke, *Religious Authority and the State in Africa*. Washington, D.C.: CSIS/Rowman & Littlefield, 2015.

Driberg, J.H. *The Lango: A Nilotic Tribe of Uganda*. London: T. Fisher Unwin, 1923.

European Parliament. "Launching Consultations to Suspend Uganda and Nigeria from the Cotonou Agreement in View of Recent Legislation Further Criminalising Homosexuality." 2014. http://www.europarl.europa.eu/sides/getDoc.do?type=TA&reference=P7-TA-2014-0254&language=EN&ring=P7-RC-2014-0251.

European Union. "European Parliament Resolution on Uganda: Anti-Homosexual Draft Legislation." 2009.

Faupel, John F. *African Holocaust: The Story of the Uganda Martyrs*. Nairobi: Paulines Publications Africa, 2007.

Gifford, Paul. *African Christianity: Its Public Role*. Bloomington: Indiana University Press, 1998.

Gill, Peter. *Body Count: How They Turned AIDS into a Catastrophe*. London: Profile Books, 2010.

Hamilton, K. *The Flames of Namugongo: Postcolonial, Queer, and Theological Reflections on the Narrative of the 1886 Ugandan Martyrdom*. Cincinnati: Union Institute and University, 2007.

Hassett, Miranda K. *Anglican Communion in Crisis: How Episcopal Dissidents and Their African Allies Are Reshaping Anglicanism*. Princeton: Princeton University Press, 2007.

Hirji, Karim F. *Cheche: Reminiscences of a Radical Magazine*. Dar es Salaam: Mkuki Na Nyota Publishers, 2010.

Human Rights Watch. "Anti-Homosexuality Act's Heavy Toll—Discriminatory Law Prompts Arrests, Attacks, Evictions, Flight." Washington, D.C., 2014. https://www.hrw.org/news/2014/05/14/Uganda-Anti-Homosexuality-Acts-Heavy-Toll.

Human Rights Watch. "Anti-Homosexuality Law Will Come at a Serious Cost." https://www.hrw.org/news/2014/02/19/uganda-anti-homosexuality-law-will-come-serious-cost.

Human Rights Watch. "Promptly Investigate Killing of Prominent LGBT Activist." Washington, D.C.: Human Rights Watch, 2011.

Human Rights Watch. "Protect Sexual Rights Activists: Ensure Due Process for All Citizens." Washington, D.C., 2008.

Ivaska, Andrew. *Cultured States: Youth, Gender, and Modern Style in 1960s Dar es Salaam*. Durham: Duke University Press, 2011.

Kaduuli, Stephen Charles. "Perceptions of LGBT in Uganda and Africa." http://ssrn.com/abstract=1510822.

Kibedi, Wanume. "The Story Continues: Kibedi's Open Letter to Amin." *Transition* (1975), 49.

Kiwanuka, Semakula. *A History of Buganda: From the Foundation of the Kingdom to 1900*. Teaneck: Holmes & Meier, 1972.

Kiyingi, Sarah. "Presentation, Consideration and Adoption of the Report of the Select Committee on Pornography." Parliament of the Republic of Uganda. Kampala: 2005.

Kripal, Jeffrey J. *Roads of Excess, Palaces of Wisdom: Eroticism and Reflexivity in the Study of Mysticism*. Chicago: University of Chicago Press, 2001.

Kyeyune, Stephen. *Shaping the Society: Christianity and Culture. Special Reference to the African Culture of Baganda, Volume II*. AuthorHouse, 2012.

La Fontaine, J.S. *The Gisu of Uganda.* London: International African Institute, 1959.

Lal, Priya. *African Socialism in Postcolonial Tanzania.* New York: Cambridge University Press, 2015.

Lawrance, J.C.D. *The Iteso: Fifty Years of Change in a Nilo-Hamitic Tribe of Uganda.* Oxford: Oxford University Press, 1957.

Lewis, D. "Representing African Sexualities." In Sylvia Tamale, ed., *African Sexualities: A Reader.* 2011.

Lively, Scott. "Witness to Revival in Africa: A Report of the Ministry of Scott and Anne Lively in Uganda, Kenya and Egypt, June 12–25, 2002." Citrus Heights: Abiding Truth Ministries, 2002.

Low, D.A. *The Mind of Buganda: Documents of the Modern History of an African Kingdom.* Berkeley: University of California Press, 1971.

Mazrui, Ali A., and Etin Anwar. *The Politics of Gender and the Culture of Sexuality: Western, Islamic and African Perspectives.* Lanham, MD: University Press of America, 2014.

Ministerial Scientific Committee on Homosexuality. "Scientific Statement on Homosexuality." Entebbe: Ministry of Health, Uganda, 2014.

Mukasa, Ham. *Uganda's Katikiro in England; Being the Official Account of His Visit to the Coronation of His Majesty King Edward VII.* London: Hutchinson, 1904.

Mullins, J.D., and H. Mukasa. *The Wonderful Story of Uganda, to Which Is Added the Story of Ham Mukasa, Told by Himself.* London: Church Missionary Society, 1904.

Munyaradzi, Mawere. *Divining the Future of Africa. Healing the Wounds, Restoring Dignity and Fostering Development.* Bamenda: Langaa RPCIG, 2014.

Murphy, Cullen. *God's Jury: The Inquisition and the Making of the Modern World.* Boston: Mariner Books, 2013.

Murray, Stephen O. *Homosexualities.* Chicago: The University of Chicago Press, 2000.

Murray, Stephen O., and Will Roscoe, eds. *Boy-Wives and Female Husbands: Studies of African Homosexualities.* New York: Palgrave Macmillan, 1998.

Museveni, Janet Kataaha. *My Life's Journey.* Kampala: Fountain Publishers, 2010.

Museveni, Y.K. *What Is Africa's Problem?* Minneapolis: University of Minnesota Press, 2000.

Museveni, Yoweri. "Activism at the Hill." In Karim F. Hirji, ed., *Cheche: Reminiscences of a Radical Magazine.* Dar es Salaam: Mkuki na Nyota, 2010.

Museveni, Yoweri Kaguta. *Sowing the Mustard Seed: The Struggle for Freedom and Democracy in Uganda.* London: Macmillan Education, 1997.

Mushanga, M. "The Nkole of Southwestern Uganda." In A. Molnos, ed., *Cultural Sources Materials for Population Planning in East Africa: Beliefs and Practices.* Nairobi: East African Publishing House, 1973.

Nannyonga-Tamusuza, Sylvia. *Baakisimba: Gender in the Music and Dance of the Baganda People of Uganda.* London: Routledge, 2005.

Ndyabahika, J. "Islam and Christianity in Uganda: Conflict, Dialogue, and Search for Partnership." In [ed.] P.M. Dikirr, R. Ostergard Jr, M. Toler, P. Macharia, and A.A. Mazrui, eds., *Africa's Islamic Experience: History, Culture, and Politics.* New Delhi: Sterling Publishers, 2009.

Noll, Stephen. "The Anglican Communion in Crisis." Global South Anglican Online. January 23, 2006.

Oloka-Onyango, Joseph. "We Are More Than Just Our Bodies: HIV/AIDS and the Human Rights Complexities Affecting Young Women Who Have Sex with Women in Uganda." Kampala: Makerere University. Human Rights and Peace Centre, 2012. Vol. HURIPEC working paper; no. 36.

Panel of Experts on the Democratic Republic of the Congo. "Final Report of the Panel of Experts on the Illegal Exploitation of Natural Resources and Other Forms of Wealth of the Democratic Republic of the Congo." New York: United Nations, 2002. S/2002/1146.

Parliament of Uganda. "Bill No. 19. the Marriage and Divorce Bill." 2009.

Roberts, George. "The British Government and Uganda under Idi Amin, November 1972 to April 1979." http://www.academia.edu/2317564/The_British_government_and_Uganda_under_Idi_Amin_November_1972_to_April_1979.

Robinson, David, and Douglas Smith. *Sources of the African Past.* Lincoln: iUniverse, 1999.

Rushton, J.P. *Race, Evolution, and Behavior: A Life History Perspective.* New Brunswick: Transaction Publishers, 1997.

Sale, George, George Psalmanazar, Archibald Bower, John Campbell, George Shelvocke, and John Swinton. *An Universal History, from the Earliest Account of Time, Volume 35.* London: T. Osborne, 1760.

Scholz, Bettina R. *The Cosmopolitan Potential of Exclusive Associations: Criteria for Assessing the Advancement of Cosmopolitan Norms.* Lanham: Lexington Books, 2015.

Sisk, Mark S. "The 'Anti-Homosexuality Laws' Proposed in Uganda: A Statement from the Rt. Rev. Mark S. Sisk." New York: 2009. http://www.episcopalcafe.com/bishop_sisk_on_the_ugandan_bill/.

Smith, William. *A New Voyage to Guinea.* London: John Nourse, 1745.

Stanley, Henry M. *Through the Dark Continent.* New York: Harper & Brothers, 1878.

Stewart, Colin, Albert Ogle, Eric O. Lembembe, Miles Tanhira, Andy Kopsa, Rachel Adams, and Clare Byarugaba. *From Wrongs to Gay Rights: Cruelty and Change for LGBT People in an Uncertain World.* Laguna Niguel: P.C. Haddiwiggle Publishing, 2013.

Tamale, Sylvia. "Out of the Closet: Unveiling Sexuality Discourses in Uganda." In Takyiwaa Manuh and Catherine M. Cole, *Africa After Gender?* Bloomington: Indiana University Press, 2007.

Thoonen, J.P. *Black Martyrs.* London: Sheed & Ward, 1941.

Thrall, James. "Conference Takes Conservative Stance on Human Sexuality." *The Lambeth Daily,* August 6, 1998.

Tutu, Desmond Mpilo. *God Is Not a Christian: And Other Provocations.* HarperCollins Publishers, New York. 2011.

Uganda Human Rights Commission. "Child Sacrifice in Uganda and Its Human Rights Implication." Kampala: Uganda Human Rights Commission, 2015.

United Nations. "Opposing Grave Human Rights Violations on the Basis of Sexual Orientation and Gender Identity." New York, 2009.

United Nations. "Opposing Grave Human Rights Violations on the Basis of Sexual Orientation and Gender Identity." Panel discussion, New York, 2009.

U.S. Department of State. "Murder of Ugandan LGBT Activist David Kato." Washington, D.C.: January 27, 2011. http://m.state.gov/md155520.htm.

U.S. Department of State. "Raid on the Makerere University Walter Reed Project by Ugandan Authorities." http://www.state.gov/r/pa/prs/ps/2014/04/224431.htm.

U.S. Department of State. "U.S. Relations with Uganda." Washington, D.C., http://www.state.gov/r/pa/ei/bgn/2963.htm.

Vaughan, Megan. *Curing Their Ills: Colonial Power and African Illness.* Palo Alto: Stanford University Press, 1991.

The White House. "Statement by the President on the Anti-Homosexuality Bill in Uganda." Washington, D.C.: February 16, 2014. https://www.whitehouse.gov/the-press-office/2014/02/16/statement-president-anti-homosexuality-bill-uganda.

The White House. "Statement by the President on the Killing of David Kato." Washington, D.C.: January 27, 2011. https://www.whitehouse.gov/the-press-office/2011/01/27/statement-president-killing-david-kato.

Woodliff, George F., III. "Rediscovering Christian Orthodoxy in Episcopal Anglicanism." http://www.standfirminfaith.com/media/RediscoveringOrthodoxy.pdf.

Zevenbergen, Aernout. *Spots of a Leopard: On Being a Man.* Cape Town: Laughing Leopard Productions, 2009.

Newspapers and Periodicals

Africa Review, 2011.
Africa Today, 1973, 1974, 2004.
African Feminism, 2005.
Anglican Theological Review, 2002.
Anthropologica, 2006.
The Church Missionary Review, 1907.
The Citizen (Dar es Salaam), 2009, 2011.
Cornell Daily Sun, 1979.
The Courier, 1974.
The Daily Beast, 2009.
Daily Monitor (Kampala), 2005–2016.
Daily Nation (Nairobi), 2005, 2010–2011.
DRUM, 1973.
The East African, 1998–1999, 2004, 2009, 2014.
East African Journal of Peace and Human Rights, 1993.
Ecumenical News International, 2009, 2010.
The Equal Rights Review, 2009.
Foreign Policy Magazine, 2013.
Gay Books Bulletin, 1983.
The Globe and Mail, 2014.
The Guardian, 2009, 2011, 2012.
Harper's, 2010.
History Compass, 2010.
Huffington Post, 2012, 2014.
The Independent (Kampala), 2009–2010, 2013–2014, 2016.
The Insider (Kampala), 2015.
IRIN, 2011.
Jet, 1975.
Journal of African History, 2010.
Journal of Church and State, 1977.

Journal of Eastern African Studies, 2009.
Journal of Religion in Africa, 1980.
Journalism, 2008.
Lancet, 1908, 1985.
London Review of International Law, 2014.
Los Angeles Times, 2004.
Metro Weekly, 2011.
Monitor (Kampala), 1998–2005.
The Morning Call, 1993.
The Nation (New York), 2011.
New Times (Kigali), June 18, 2012.
New Vision (Kampala), 1998–2016.
New York Review of Books, 2005, 2014.
The New York Times, 1998, 2010–2014.
The Observer (Kampala), 2011–2015.
Pambazuka News, 2009.
Philosophy Now, 1996.
Politico, 2010.
Red Pepper (Kampala), 2003, 2006.
Research in African Literatures, 1993.
Rolling Stone (Kampala), 2010.
San Jose Mercury News, 2007.
Society of Missionaries of Africa (History series), 2008.
The Star (Nairobi), 2014.
Sunday Monitor (Kampala), 1999–2015.
The Telegraph, 2009.
Transition, 1975, 1976, 2011.
Tuskegee News, 1977.
Uganda Argus, 1972.
Uganda Gazette, 2009.
Voice of Uganda, 1973–1976, 1978.

Index

www.ingramcontent.com/pod-product-compliance
Lightning Source LLC
Chambersburg PA
CBHW031135270326
41929CB00011B/1629